First Edition Collectible

*Genuine Autographed Manuscript*

------------------------

# Thinking of You

Gift Card

Date:

To:

From:

Message:

# LOVERTIME

Romance, Literature, Fiction

**LOVERTIME**
Copyright @2021 by Amanda Ardens. All rights reserved.

**Contact Information**
Author website: www.AmandaArdens.com
Fan Mail: info@amandaardens.com

ISBN: 978-1-885872-59-3 (paperback)
PCN: 2021915515

**Publisher**
Published in the United States by
Palm Beach Book Publisher, Florida
Phone: 917-767-5843

**Global Distribution**
INGRAM Global Distribution: 615-793-5000
Baker and Taylor: 800-775-1800

**Book Title and Book Designer**
Creative Genius Sharon Esther Lampert
www.sharonestherlampert.com

**Editor**
Karl Bardosh


Manufactured in the United States of America

**FIRST EDITION**

*A Romance Novel*

# LOVERTIME

*Amanda Ardens*

*Volume 1*

## *Dedication*

### To My Dear Olgi Granny

"There through the veil of fantasies we did
not hope for on the edges of unspoken prayers.
There on the border of losing our minds,
we met: you & me."

Zs K.

Legal Disclaimer for a Work of Fiction

This is a work of fiction. Unless otherwise indicated, all the names, characters, businesses, places, events and incidents in this book are either the product of the author's imagination or used in a fictitious manner. Any resemblance to actual persons, living or dead, or actual events is purely coincidental. The opinions expressed are those of the characters and should not be confused with the author's.

What Do Books Do?
## BOOKS ARE POWERFUL!
Books **Educate**!
Books **Enlighten**!
Books **Empower**!
Books **Entertain**!
Books **Emancipate**!
Books Are **Eternal**!
Books Drive **Exploration**!
Books Spark **Evolution**!
Books Ignite **Revolution**!

Sharon Esther Lampert

Palm Beach Book Publisher
Full Service Book Publisher

# Contents

1. Being Lost   1

2. Fragments of the Past   27

3. Trust Me   135

4. Hope   213

5. Butterfly   259

6. Falling   311

# Being Lost

Finally it happened. I let him go. Two weeks ago, we officially divorced. I never imagined I will say this, but I'm grateful to fate it happened like this.

I believe. We were together for ten years, we went through everything, that can happen in a relationship and marriage.

Wild desire, highs and lows, then a painfully suffocating still water.

And now I am sitting here ashore all alone and am praying for the cleansing power of the water that shall wash the suffering out of my heart and erase the memories that forced me to dive into the chilly water. I am cold.

My tears are rolling down on my face. I feel empty. I let the soft waves console me, let them permeate every cell of my body. I am floating and grieving myself, him, us and the wasted years.

-Ann! Ann! Where are you?

And all of a sudden, I wake from my melancholic thoughts and see Peter standing on the meadow in front of the cabin, he did not notice me yet in the water.

I quickly jump out, pick up a towel and run to him through the wet grass. My heart is racing, while I'm looking at him.

-Hi, I did not expect you this early. I guess your work ended earlier in the office. It's so great to see you at last!

He looks at me with his beautiful brown eyes and I see his love for me, love I haven't seen in a man's eyes for a long time.

-I hurried to see you, wanted to be with you as soon as I could.

He gives a quick kiss on my cheek, embraces me so I don't feel the cold till we get to the house. I drop my towel to an old faded brown sofa and I see he is staring at me.

What can he see in me? My wet black swimsuit adheres to my body, my wet hair sticks to my back and my eyes are red from crying. He steps closer to me and I can sense the magnetic pull between us that almost hurts.

He studies me, never saw me in bathing suit, in reality he only saw me in my uniform at work. Does he notice my stretch marks from bearing a child, that makes me look like a little piglet? Is he looking at those?

They are everywhere, but the birth of my son is worth every sacrifice. I am not a model type. Wide hips, round butt, small breasts, creole skin, my hair is dirty blonde, brown eyes, my face is pretty—at least that's what they say. I am 29 years old yet I look 20, guess my genetics can be blamed for that. He holds my face.

-Ann, you're beautiful!

He sees that I am looking at my tummy, but before I could say a word, he kisses me feverishly and slowly. He starts to caress my back, my arms, the outline of my hip, but I push him away.

My God, I am really pushing him away? What do I want then? Here is this fantastic man, who wants me, but I'm not ready to be his yet. I was someone else's for too long, it was too long that I tried to find myself.

-What's wrong? Don't you want it?

## Being Lost

-Forgive me but I need time, I just got divorced. I am so grateful to you for arranging to come here and rest and grateful for all your help. Thank god, my Mom is able to watch Ben, so I could come to see you, but please be patient with me, give me time...

He covers my mouth with his hands, shuts me up and throws a light kiss on my lips.

-It's ok, I promise not to force anything, only ask you to stay and let's enjoy this weekend together. I want to be with you... you don't have to sleep with me if you don't want yet. I will wait for you, as I did up to now.

He opens the fridge gets two sodas, gives me one with a smile and sits on the sofa.

-No worries, go take a shower, I can see you're shivering, I will find a good movie in the meantime.

-Thanks, I will be quick, then we can cuddle under the sheets. It will be so great to relax.

I feel his eyes on me, as I hurry up on the stairs in the cabin's bathroom. Finally, alone for a few minutes, I need time to compose myself before I go down again. I get out of the bathing suit and step into the shower.

I enjoy as the hot water runs through my skin. I look into the mirror after the quick shower. My god? I look terribly worn out. Will he still want me? My eyes are puffy, my hair... all over the place. This is me right now. A wreck. I can't make myself look now any better, so I quickly put my hair into a ponytail, throw a little mascara and that's it. I will not force to look more beautiful, I jump into a body-hugging sweat pants and a long t-shirt, this should work.

-You were so quick, I already found a cool action movie for us.

-Wow, that's super!

He pulls me close under the soft green cover.

-At least I won't be cold.

I'm looking at him and I can see he still wants me. He looks really great, I find him very sexy, yet my mind stops me. His brown hair is disheveled, he breaths loud, his two-day old scruff makes him look even sexier. He leans close and sniffs my neck.

I am not wearing perfume, I hope my body smells nice, although my husband always found it sexy. All of a sudden, I feel his smell, a mix of a sophisticated and pleasant perfume and his body. They say we pick our partners based on the body odor, this is how attraction and chemistry work, and we are a great match. He sits up and starts the movie. Clearly, he tries to be fair and not be pushy as he promised. I am trying to concentrate on the film, but he slowly and sensually massages my feet and I start to levitate between being awake and dreaming.

I stretch, still am a bit dopy, I don't really remember what planet I am on, all of a sudden, his gorgeous face is right in front of me, he's holding a tray with coffee and fresh pastry.

-Good morning. Did we pass out on the sofa?

-Yes. We slept together here, cuddling all night, you already fell asleep at the top of the film, but I didn't have the heart to wake you up, instead I stayed here with you. I brought breakfast from outside, while you were sleeping.

-Thank you. I can imagine how I look just waking up. I quickly fix my hair, sit up and smile at him, make him feel that I am grateful for his thoughtfulness. It's been a long time when I got breakfast in bed from a guy, usually I gobble up my breakfast on the way to work or prepare it for the week for the entire family on the weekend.

# Being Lost

From now on I will only do it for my son, since Gabriel will not be with us anymore. I stuff myself with the cookies, this time I'm not too ladylike, since yesterday I almost had nothing to eat all day, then I drink my coffee quickly, too.

-Did you already get breakfast?

-I ate downtown while you were asleep. I change quickly into something comfortable and we can go for a hike into the forest, if you feel like it.

-That's a great idea, at least I can see the neighborhood, I clear my head in the fresh air and until I get tired. That's what I need now. I will hurry and change, too.

I jump into my pants, T-shirt, sweater and boots and I spray myself with mosquito repellant. Let's play safe. I brush my teeth and I'm ready to go. Hiking together in the forest will be so romantic. I did not have real fun for months. Is Ben doing ok with my Mom? I will call them, when we get back from the forest, he is probably waking up just now, then he will eat, then play. He will be all right with them, they love him so much. I feel a bit guilty leaving him there alone, but I felt I would suffocate, I felt I had to escape a little, he shouldn't sense on me this lethargy, the pain, the stress.

I need to pull myself together before I get back home on Sunday, I need to be the mommy to him he used to know. Why is Peter so sweet with me? What does he want from me? I feel that he wants me, but he may just want to have sex with me and throw me away when he gets bored with me? Why would he want me, a divorced woman with a 5-year-old boy... shattered and distressed.

-Are you ready? I see you got lost in your thoughts. Shall we get going?

-Oh, sure, sorry, let's go!

He reaches for my hand, we start walking holding hands. He looks so handsome in his sweat suit, he exudes masculinity that secretly disarms me for months now. We walk without saying a word, slowly, the beautiful forest encompasses us, we sink into our own separate little worlds. I hear the birds' chirping, I see the lizards running in the grass, also the small beetles that are running for safety from under our feet. We are walking for a half hour when I notice a purple butterfly on one of the flowers. I lean closer to admire it. It is me...

Peter stops behind me and just watches me as I am admiring the butterfly. All of a sudden, I feel an arm on my waist, he pulls me close and kisses me. This kiss is different from the one yesterday. I feel, he wants to let me know, he is here for me. He slowly reaches under my T-shirt, starts to stroke my back, then he reaches my tummy and his hand wonders further up. He reaches my breast, that fits into his palm, he starts to stroke it- than he moves closer to me and I can feel his huge erection on my stomach. He pinches one of my nipples, and I hear myself sighing. It's impossible that he can turn me on just like this. He continues kissing me, I become feistier, I take his manhood into my hand to feel his size. My stomach is in my throat and I hear his sighing. We are touching each other, discovering each other's bodies. It feels amazing, we start to lose control, but I can't go further with him yet. So I start to talk choosing to break the silence and the magic.

-Khm... Let's go on, long road is ahead of us. I can't lose my head.

-Ohhh... As you wish. Forgive me but I could not hold back, I had to touch you. I wanted to you so bad.

-Me too but... doesn't matter, forget about it.

-Good, come and let's climb this hill and let's rest on the top a bit.

# Being Lost

He is not forcing to talk about what just happened, so I keep quiet, too. He is holding my hand, we are walking and I feel that liberating power of nature. I get lost looking at the stones, the little creek that runs next to us, the humming bees, like a bird who just escaped. I calm down. We are arriving to the top of the hill, and sit down next to each other. I look around and I see the giant valley. I think I could live here instead of the concrete jungle. Only nature, calmness and peace around me.

-I always loved to hike around here. I was a little boy when my grandparents bought this charming cottage. I spent the summers here almost every year, till I got 14 years of age. My grandfather taught me a lot of different things. Cutting wood, hunting, the love of nature. Since they passed, I rarely come here, maximum once a year, but I made an exception for you, I knew this place will help you to calm down. In the past few months I watch as you sink deeper and deeper into your own world, trying to hide the problems you're struggling with. I often saw you looking out the window of your office, crying. I feel awful seeing you like this, but I hope the announcement of your divorce will ease your suffering.

-Thank you. You can't even imagine how much I need this, especially knowing that I could have come here on Friday morning alone, and I enjoy it with you too. It makes me so happy that we can get to know each other outside of the office, too. Let's go back to the house, I'm hungry, I will make some pasta, or we can order pizza in. Then we can continue our conversation sipping some wine

-I'm hungry too, let's order pizza, so you can relax. This weekend is strictly about relaxing.

We are walking down the hill through the forest back to the cottage, except we only sense each other, the outside world doesn't seem to exist. We keep looking at each other, between us vibrate all the unspoken things and the magnetic attraction. I feel butterflies in my stomach, I feel like I'd felt right before my first date in highschool. I feel he feels the same, although he is 33 years old, still it seems unfamiliar for him to meet someone new, too. So far what I know about him is that he got all the gals, he did not date too long, women loved him and kept going after him. Let's be honest, he always had more attractive girlfriends than me, without a kid, and he had lots of one-night stands. And he is still here next to me. I don't even know what I want from him. A relationship? An affair? Or should I be alone? Almost sensing my thoughts he squeezes my hand, raises it to his lips and kisses it.

-Finally, we are here, beautiful. I'll call the pizza place, I know a great one around here, it's where I always order from when I'm here. What pizza you want?"

-The Hawaiian, I love that one. Call them, I'll undress in the meantime."

-Allright, just close the door when you're changing, don't tempt me!

I quickly undress and sit down on my bed, call my Mom, want to talk with Ben. Maybe he still is not taking his nap.

-Hi Mom. How are you doing? Ben?

-Hi sweetie! Everything is fine, we ate, drank, played games as we always do. I just wanted him to start his nap. And how are you doing?

-Everything is fine, I've been able to relax a bit. Can I talk to my little prince now?

-Sure.

# Being Lost

-Hey sweetie! How are you? Mom is missing you very much! Did you eat enough? What did you play with Grandma?

-Hi Mom! I ate a lot, we played Lego, I was drawing, we played cards, stuff like that.

-I'm so happy to hear, I love you very much, please wear your hat, when you go out to the yard as the sun is very strong, and always listen to Grandma, remember! I'll hurry home tomorrow.

-Ok, Mom, love you.

-Take good care of yourself! Love you!

-Me too. Bye!

I'll put down the phone and I feel like the worst mother in the world for not being with Ben. I know he is in good hands but still. I was selfish to come here to take a break, when I could be playing Lego with him, I would read him his favorite tale before bed and I could cuddle up with him. I feel it's better for me to pull myself together, chase my thoughts away before coming back to my reality, full of doubts and questions.

-The pizza is here, beautiful, come down!

Dear God, I'm up here already for 50 minutes? I jump into jeans and a comfy white top and am running down to Peter.

-Oh. It smells divine. I get a plate and glasses for wine.

-Don't worry, I already prepared the table while you were up there.

-I'm hungry, so let's eat.

We eat our pizzas. Peter devours 4 slices, of course, he's a man. I chew slowly on my 2 slices. He pours red wine into my glass and he's staring at me as I'm sipping slowly from this divine nectar.

-This wine is to die for.

-I was hoping you love red, I saw you drinking that at the office party last Christmas.

-You are a fantastic observer, indeed I went to a lot of winetasting with Gabriel.

I loved our outings then. A transient shadow crosses my face. I hope Peter didn't notice. After every winetasting event with Gabriel we made love like crazy and enjoyed every moment with each other, at that time Ben was not born yet. I was free, carefree and bohemian. We pampered each other for hours, and being tipsy, we fall asleep and this went on and on all weekend. Peter pours into my glass again and puts his hand onto my thigh. He holds my face with his right hand and he is staring at me. I can see in his eyes, he is fighting the urge to kiss me, his desire is simmering. I place my hand on his hand and try to tell him with my eyes, I would want him just be gentle approaching me, don't rush, I want to move forward slowly. This is all new to me, a new man beside me, whom I find attractive but who makes me feel guarded, although I am afraid of myself even more. I don't want to be mesmerized by a man, again—and fall into a trap again.

-Listen, Ann, when you look at me like this, I can't stop myself wanting to kiss you, touching you. I'm trying to hold back, but it's torture.

-I'm sorry, guess better not to look at each other. Ok, I'm kidding, I'm fighting the urge too, believe me, but... I know, you told me.

-Tell me about yourself.

-What do you want to know?

-Let's start with... what is your favorite color?

-Are you kidding?

-Of course. So. Why do you come here so seldom, this is an amazing place, fresh air, and it's still close to town.

# Being Lost

-Since I lost my grandparents, I don't like to come here, everything reminds me of them. I come once a year to check if everything is allright. I'm weeding, cut grass, do this and that and then I am running back to the city."

-Did you ever consider renting it so someone else would keep it in order?

-Never, they put this property on my name when they were alive, I don't want anyone to remodel it, wear it down, stuff like that.

-I truly thank you.

-Don't keep thanking me, it's enough, to be honest I was a bit selfish bringing you here.

-Who would have thought so?

As I say this I'm reaching for my slice of pizza and I don't notice knocking off my wine glass with my elbow, the wine pours all over the table. I'm running for the paper towel and start to clean up. Something is strange as I feel my top is wet, too. I look down and notice it got covered with wine spots as I was leaning over the table. Gee, I'm so sloppy, behaving like a drunk teenager, it's good I don't say silly things in my girlish embarrassment. Peter cleans the table, brings everything to the kitchen, and I see him smiling. He comes closer.

-You have take this off before you catch a cold. You use every opportunity to tempt me. Right?

-No, I'm not.

-Shhh...

He is gazing at me, like a leopard hunting down the innocent gazelle chewing on fresh grass. He is the hunter, I'm the hunted. He takes my waist, grabs the edge of the T-shirt, pulls it over my head, meanwhile keeps looking into my eyes. He drops it on the floor and waits, he wants me to make the next move, I can respect that. I'm pretty clear on that he needs a lot of discipline to not to push me against the wall and start to make love.

My heart beats wildly, I know I have to do something. I want him, of course, I am not immune to an attractive man like him. Then he grabs me. I start to enjoy this game, this flirtation, playing with self-control, who can endure longer to hold back, the sexual tension burning us. I don't want to be an easy prey, to let myself be caught so easy. I start losing my mind over my hesitation, I also want him to take me right now, actually that's all I want right now, but he has to wait. He sees my struggle, so he wisely steps back and sits down on the sofa. He is a great strategist. He feels if he doesn't come on to me now, he will not lose me, so he won't pressure me to do something I'm not ready for. The good hunter can wait and hunts the prey down slowly, seizing the right moment when the prey is not watching out and vulnerable.

-Peter, I'm sorry. I going to leave!

I start pacing up and down in the living room meanwhile trying to pull my thoughts together, how should I explain to him my feelings.

-Let's not torture each other. I tried, but I'm not ready yet. I want you, I'm sure you can tell, but I still don't know what I want. I don't want my physical desire overide my common sense. If I slept with you now I would regret it later. I'm not an easy case, on top of everything I'm not alone, I have a son.

-Ann, I understand all of this. As I said yesterday, I can wait, but I'm still a man and every cell of my body wants you, I want you to be mine, completely. I have a hard time not to keep trying. I am crazy for you, and this will never change, not today, not tomorrow, not ever. You drive me crazy!

-Why?

-Why what?

# Being Lost

-Why do you want me? You don't even know me really. You know nothing about me!

I stop the pacing and sit beside him.

-I want to get to know you. That's why I offered to come here. I started with the company half a year ago, and since I saw you first, I could only see you. I did not dare to start anything with you cause I knew you were married so I kept the distance, but it was difficult. I followed you from a distance, I was hoping you notice me and feel something can develop between us. I did not want to ruin the possibilities. I was waiting for the right situation and moment to approach you. I saw you getting disheartened, you smiled less and less, you did not chat with the colleagues that much. It was tough to watch you suffer. A few weeks ago. I learned from Monique that you got divorced. I got the idea that I can help you and get closer to you at the same time. I am hoping you accept my offer, don't get scared, don't feel that you're pressured to return any favor. Please, don't leave!

    This is too much for me. As he's slowly talking to me, my tears start to roll down on my face. I don't even clearly know why, maybe because he said he has only seen me since he saw me first time, or maybe the tension just escalated in me that has been building up in the past few weeks. Up to now I had to be strong for my son and my duties. But I don't want to hold back now. He embraces me. I can feel the temperature of his body, his enticing smell, I can feel his strong hands stroking my back as we are slowly rocking together. This is what I was missing in the past few weeks, the embrace of a man that calms me down, makes me feel safe again. Roughly 15 minutes later I run out of tears, I slowly unfold from his embrace. If I didn't scare him away with my crying, than he can stand anything. I know, man usually can't handle a crying woman.

-Thanks for comforting me and asking me to stay. I want to get to know you too. If you promise not to force me to do anything for the rest of the night. I will stay.

-My boyscout word to that!

That makes us smile both. The tension disappeared.

-Let's start at the beginning, Tell me about your childhood. How was Peter as a little boy?

-Cute and small.

-Nah, for real? Where did you grow up? Schools? Family background?

-I grew up in a small city, in the suburbs, in a big house. My father is a gynecologist, my mother is a podiatrist. From my childhood they wanted me to become a doctor, too, like them, to continue the family tradition, but I resisted. I have no siblings, so I enjoyed all the family's attention. They overprotected me, I was raised in a bubble. So after finishing high school I wanted to be free and a little spoiled, so I came to the big city university. And as you know I became a lawyer.

He stands up, walks out to the kitchen and brings the wine and glasses. Smiles at me and pours for us.
I guess I can drink some more, it will relax me.

-Why exactly a lawyer?

-Because I enjoyed the challenges and complicated cases.

-And you, beautiful? Where did you grow up? Your parents? Schools?

-I grew up in a big city housing project. I completed high school there, then I got my diploma in PR at the university. My father is a policeman and my mother is a kindergarten teacher, and I was 12 years old when they divorced. My mom got married again, my father lives alone since. I don't have any siblings. Just like you, I

# Being Lost

was showered with attention, too, both parents wanted to make up for the damages of their divorce caused me.

-So, you stayed with your Mom or Dad after divorce?

-With my Mom. It was difficult after divorce for a few years, but when I became 18 she met George and they decided to get married.

Our glasses got empty, I poured again. Thank God I did not spill this time.

-Your eyes are so gorgeous, even now, as they are immersed in pain. I lose myself in them.

-Thanks. The eyes are the window for the soul.

-What's your hobby?

-I love hiking, hunting and love to read. Only I have very little time for these things. And you?

-Me too. Love to read, since early childhood I devour books. They were my escape from reality. I love to hike as well, and I adapt to any hobby what Ben likes, too.

So, we can share some quality time together. For instance, painting rocks, or collect stones from the beach. We already have a huge collection of beautiful stones.

-You are very young and Ben is already 5 years old. How long were you together with your husband?

-I know I look younger... Sometimes, at the playground they think he is my little brother. He is the best thing ever happened to me, by the way we stayed together 10 years.

-First love?

-Yes, this was the first true love, although I had a boyfriend before him.

-Where did you meet him?

-In a club, where we went to chill out with my girlfriends. He came on to me, and I let him.

-Can you tell more about it?
-No. It's not really interesting story. It's your turn!
-My longest-term relationship was 2 years, before and after I only had short affairs, one-nightstands, lots of them.
-So, you didn't find the one you could imagine your future with?
-Now I...

His phone starts to ring on the coffee table, he reaches for it and I notice he becomes flustered for a moment.

-Sorry, I have to take this one.
-Sure, take it.

He hurries to the balcony and I don't hear what is he talking about, but I can see on his body language that he's tense. I'll go to the kitchen, take the strawberry and chocolate ice cream out from the freezer. I'm after something sweet, so after putting out two servings of ice cream into white saucers, I pour an extra amount of chocolate sauce on it. Hm...I simply have to taste it, I put a spoonful into my mouth. And some more. I lick the spoon to enjoy the last drops of the dripping chocolate sauce, and for that I have to use my tongue over the entire length of the spoon.

-Do this again.

This caught me unguarded, I jump up in surprise dropping the spoon on the floor. I pick it up.

-You scared me. I will not put on an erotic solo number with the spoon for you. This should be enough!
-Will I get some too?

With malicious smile on his face, he takes a saucer with the ice cream from the counter. I sit back onto the sofa and we both have a ball devouring the sweets.

-So, what are your dreams and desires?
-You.

# Being Lost

-And outside of this?

-Outside of this is you, you and you. What about you beautiful?

-Great question. I have many. I would love to feel complete again, feel happy, inner peace, safety, I would love a vacation by the beach, new shoes and...

-I see, it's truly long list.

-All right, nah, I just got started.

-And the end wanted to be a kiss?

-No, instead a...

I can't finish the sentence, because he is already kissing me, ruffles my hair, and his tongue circles mine, I take in his intoxicating smell, his desire. Our desire. He stops and gives me a sharp little bite in my lower lip, than he starts to suck the place he bit me. My god!

He keeps kissing me with more and more passion, my neck first, than throws small kisses on my shoulder. He is not rushing. I also kiss his neck by the bottom of his ear, I take his earlobe into my mouth, I lick it a bit than I keep traveling down with my kisses and start to suck next to that throbbing blood vessel nice and slow. He starts to sigh. Turns his head away and takes off his grey T-shirt. For a moment I get lost looking at his gorgeously sculpted upper body. I take my top off too, except the bra. I hesitate for a moment. If I go on now there will be no stopping. Do I want that? He leans closer and closer and unties it. Ok. This is the end of me. I have goose bumps. He gently touches one of my nipples, strokes it, while takes the other one in his mouth and sucks it, tastes it, licks it like the sweetest thing in the world. My pussy is pulsing, it's on fire. He pulls my pants down to my knees along with the black lace panties. He strokes both of my thighs. He wets his finger and sticks it up, although it was not necessary, because I already was swimming in my squirt. I sigh out loud, while he comes in and out with his finger without stopping. He pulls out and adds another finger going in. I'm gasping for air, he takes my nipple into his gorgeous lips again, keeping the rhythm. I'm trembling from orgasm. He pulls his finger out, than places it into his mouth licking my cum.

-You taste amazing, and when you were coming that was the most erotic sight in the world. I want to see it again.

He bends down and places a kiss on my stomach. I want more already, too and I pull his pants down. My God he looks so attractive. Only the black boxer stayed on him, he seems perfectly ready. I stroke it a few times, then I keep my hands on it. He can't hold back much longer, his body is full of expansive energy, and waits for me to play with him. I would pull his boxer down, but I just don't do it. What was I thinking? I have to stop myself and him too. If we go on, we are done.

-Beautiful, this is your night, I want to serve your pleasure. If you wanted thousand times after one another.

I hold his shoulder and start stroking him.
-You know what else I want?
My voice is more than a sigh.
-What?
-I would love to swim in the middle of the night naked. Let's go together to swim, that may cool us down.

He doesn't understand what happened with me all of a sudden. I jump up and run out the door without waiting for an answer. It's colder than I thought, therefore I speed up my steps and I am already by the water. I sink into it slowly. I enjoy the cold that cools my

# Being Lost

heated body down. I start to swim. After a few rounds I start to warm up. In the middle of the lake, I stop to rest and look up. The sky is clear and I can see lots of stars shining. It reminds me of infinity, the transience of humanity, the vulnerability of my soul. I lay on the top of the water, kick with my legs, start to swim and keep watching the brightness of the stars. No one could paint more beautiful sight than this. It calms me down. In a little bit I hear Peter coming into the water and I hear him swimming toward me. It takes a few minutes for him to reach me and swim close to me.

-I know you thought I won't come.

-It's good that you decided to come so you can see this beauty around us.

-I see this, in the past half a year.

We orbit around each other in the water, like two beetles that got mesmerized and dizzy by the lamplight in the dark night. They know they would be burning if they fly close yet can't resist.

-What are you thinking when you're looking at the stars?

-Desires, dreams. I always think of the people through thousands of years who made their wishes looking at them.

-Let's wish for something together, maybe it will come true.

We swim back idly, time has stopped. We step onto the shore, we walk back to the cottage holding hands. It is so idyllic, almost too beautiful. We step into the house, sit down on the sofa. We are naked, I started to feel cold.

-What would you like to do now?

-I feel I'm tired, I will take a shower and would love to sleep.

I can't tell him, that I don't want to be tempted again, I don't want my desires dictate what my body is doing. If I stay down here with him, we can't hold ourselves back. Nothing changes that. So better this way. My previous experiences taught me not to make rash decisions that I might regret later. We are grownups, we need to be able to sort out what is what. I would love to have a clear head and feelings before I surrender myself to my passion.

-Are you sure?
-Yes.
-There is nothing I can do to change your mind?
-No. I will take a shower and then I will sleep. Have nice dreams.
I can see sadness in his eyes seeing me going up.
-All right, beautiful. You too, dream about me.

I'm in my room and I feel emptiness, pain, loneliness, doubts. It torments my heart, squeezes, suffocates. I start to gasp for air... I see how he squirms on his body, like a snake as he coils around his victim before his grand dinner. He shakes his red hair all around and screams—more! I freeze. My throat is paralyzed, no word is coming out and I can see the coldest pair of blue eyes in the world that is staring at me ... My extremities are hurting, I fight my tears, he wants to break out of my body before pulls me down to the deep. It started... My panic attack came back, although I thought I was strong enough to fight it so it won't find me again. I was wrong. I couldn't hide. It found me. It won. I pull myself in fetal pose, breathing deeply. I'm sweating. I'm waiting. I would love to scream. I am strong! I rule my body! It will pass! I won't die! Everything is allright! I start to count in my head. 1-2-3-4-5... It doesn't help. Then finally the bittersweet relief is coming, I can hear myself from outside as I'm crying out loud. I feel nothing anymore. Someone lifts me up from the floor, puts me down onto the bed and embraces me. I'm in his arms. Everything goes dark.

## Being Lost

My head is throbbing. I open my eyes and I see Peter sleeping next to me. How amazing. He probably heard my attack last night and came up to comfort me. Why did he sneak out this time? I tiptoe out to the bathroom, I didn't want to wake him. I quickly take a shower, brush my teeth, let my hair down. I put just a little bit of make up on my face. I put on a nice pink floral dress that fits my body perfectly.

-Good morning! You are beautiful this morning.

-You, too! And thanks.

-Don't thank me, facts are facts. I came to take a shower.

He drops his boxer and promenades in front of me naked to the shower. He is not embarrassed at all. He is a proud male. His body is drop-dead gorgeous. He is very proportionate. His legs are muscular, chiseled upper body, perfect butt. He knows I am staring at him. I choose to go down to the kitchen and prepare some breakfast. I take a pill for headache turn on the radio and listen to my favorite number that's on. I start to dance. I put the drip-coffee cup on the stove and I make omelet, 5 eggs with onions and bacon. I pour the coffee into cups, I prepare milk and sugar and sweetener on the side. I don't know how Peter is having his coffee. To the omelet I add tomatoes, pepper, cucumber. I set the table and am waiting for Peter. He is walking down the stairs, freshly shaved, wearing white T-shirt and jeans. Even in simple clothes like this he looks great. He is surprised to see I prepared breakfast.

-I'm very hungry, it means a lot to me that you made breakfast.

-Then, bon appétit.

Both of us started to eat the omelet. We finished it quickly, it was yummy.

-How do you take coffee? Let me serve you.

-Black, one sugar. Thanks. You with 2 sugars and little milk-right?

-Yes, but how did you know?

-It's my intuition. How would you feel about going to picnic after breakfast?

-Great idea.

I quickly clean up after breakfast, wash the dishes. Peter packs the fruits into a picnic-basket, he puts in sodas and chocolate, too.

-I could get used to do this with you every Sunday.

I don't answer, doesn't make sense. I'm putting on my shoes and he is ready to go too.

-Shall we?

-Yes.

The sun is shining bright, the birds are chirping. The meadow is close by, so we get there quickly. Beautiful flowers are blooming in the grass of the forest, as far as we can see. There are a few trees offering shade. We sit down under the biggest one. Peter lays down our green blanket, I sit down and he sits in front of me. The grass is fresh green, the sun didn't burn it yet and the smell of the flowers is intoxicating. I tear off a few beauties and start to weave a wreath. When I was a child my Mom taught me how to do that. When we went hiking, we always weaved wreath for each other and pretended we were flower fairies. I'm proceeding slowly with the weaving because some of the stalks are not long enough so I need to grab new ones. So, it takes a long time to finish. The flowers making up the wreath are yellow, white and lilac. I admire it for a moment, then I put it in my hair.

-I am the flower fairy.

I'm smiling at Peter, I see he doesn't understand why.

## Being Lost

-With my Mom we always weaved wreaths for each other when we hiked and we pretended to be fairies.

-Would you like a magic stick into your hand? Oh- a pole.

-Please...

-I was not thinking that, bad is the one who is thinking bad.

I'm blushing. He stands up and walks further away. Have no idea what he's doing. He's searching for something. He is walking up and down and checking the ground. Then hurries back to me, so happy like a little boy. In his hand a nice stick.

-I found it.

-You brought this for me?

-Yes. This will be your own magic stick. Weave flowers around it and bring it home to Ben, so you can play together the fairy game with him. I'll give it to you with two conditions. One: the flowers should stay in your hair. Two: a kiss.

-The fairies are not making contact with mortals.

-So, I have to convince a fairy to make an exception.

-Only, if you catch it.

I start to run, before he realizes I am in the middle of the meadow. I turn back, he is running after me. I'm running faster, bolt out straight forward. He's in better shape than me, he starts catching up. All of a sudden, he is right behind me, I fall on my knees as he tries to catch me. Only thing he achieves that we fall on each other. We are laughing like little kids.

-There you are! You cannot run from me, I'll catch you anyways.

He has playful light in his eyes. He leans on top of me, gets ready to kiss me.

I look into his eyes, grab his shoulder, and push him a bit. He loses his balance, he wasn't prepared and he falls on his butt. I use the opportunity and start to run back to our tree. I am laughing. I run very fast, he starts to follow.

-You can't catch me!
-We'll see!

He speeds his steps, but I reach the blanket earlier than him since I was so much ahead.

-I won!
-Right, cause I let you! Why are you flirting like this all the time?
-Just because.
-You drive me crazy to the point where I can't hold back. That's what you want?

I smile at him and take some grapes from the basket.

-What do you want me to get for you?
-Chocolate.

I start to devour the grapes, he starts eating his chocolate. He feeds me the next little cube. Next is the strawberry. The two flavors are great after each other. Hmm... Orgy of flavors. He keeps feeding me for minutes. We lay on the blanket and face each other.

-Since when you have been having them?
-What?
-The panic attacks?
-Why would you think this was not the first time?
-Cause, I had the feeling when I heard you. I couldn't decide what to do. I tried to figure out which one is better for you if I go and help or if I don't see you like that. But then I couldn't hold back, I had to help, so I went up.
-Listen, this is a sensitive topic for me.

## Being Lost

   -I would love to know, so I'm able to help.
   -All right. I have problems with it when I'm under stress or sometimes when I'm relaxed. It started roughly a year ago. Sometimes doesn't come out for months, then suddenly comes again. You know, I have to sort it out in myself.
   -What happened?
   -Many things. I can handle it. I'm strong.
   -You didn't seem to be.
   -Possible, but I don't want you to think about this. I told you, I'm not in my best shape these days. I need to think my life through, figure out which way to go forward.
   -What is what you really want?
   -I would love to build up my own world again. To find my place and feel good all alone. I don't want Ben to have any shortcomings in his life. I don't want him to suffer any damage. I still need to sort out a lot of complicated issues. In the court agreement we mutually decided with Gabriel that Ben can spend every other weekend with him and weekdays, too, if he wishes to see him. We shall see how this will work out.
   -And with me?
   -I don't know. I don't plan ahead.
   Why is he inspecting me so thoroughly? I start to feel uncomfortable. I would love to just run away again.
   -And you, what are your plans?
   -I would love to be a part of your life, if you let me.
   -This is not... I'm not... I feel this is not the right time...
   -So, you decide alone, and you leave me out? It doesn't count what I want?

-Of course, it counts, but we still barely know each other. Maybe you should choose a less complicated women.

-I already made my choice, you can't scare me away.

-That's what you think!

He takes my hand and holds it tight. I look down, I know if I lookup I lose him. But he lifts my head up and looks into my eyes. I look to the side.

-Listen, just give me a chance. I would want to prove to you, you can count on me at every level and I want you with everything! Please let me!

-I can't. I would love to go home now. Let's leave now, please.

I get up from the blanket, and pat down my dress. I need to start going back, he can't see my tears that started to roll down. I start to run again and don't stop till I get to the cabin. I hurry up to the first floor. I grab my red suitcase, pack all my stuff, even take the toiletry from the bathroom. I check if anything is missing than I take a piece of paper out of my bag. I go down to the kitchen with my suitcase. I put the slip of paper on the kitchen counter, but I end up writing just a little.

-Thanks for everything, but I need more time... Ann.

I take the car keys from my bag, I hurry outside. I throw my luggage into my small red beauty of a car then I get in and start the car. I look out the window, I say goodbye to him in my head. I see Peter coming back from the meadow, the picnic basket and the blanket in his hand. He seems to be sad, but fortunately he lets me leave.

## The Fragments of the Past

I check myself in the rearview mirror, the gorgeous wreath is still in my hair. I place it on the backseat. I left the stick there. I call my Mom, letting her know I'm on my way to pick up Ben.

    -Hi Mom!
    -Hi sweetie!
    -How are you?
    -I'm already in the car, I'll be there in half hour. Please pack all the stuff and let Ben know, I'll arrive very soon.
    -Is there any problem?
    -No, just wanted to come home.
    -Ok. We are here. Kisses.
    -Kisses.

-I arrive earlier than I assumed. I need a few minutes before I go up. One can see I was crying but I'm relatively composed. Take a deep breath, smile. They can't notice, I'm having a problem. I walk into the building, call the elevator. 7th floor. I ring the bell three times, briefly. This is our signal for years.

    -You want to talk about it?
    She embraces me, like only a mother can.
    -I don't know.
    -Come, let's sit in the kitchen, I'll make a tea. George can play with Ben in the meantime. Are you hungry?
    -No.
    -I prepared your favorite dish.

We go out to the small kitchen and my Mom warms water for tea. I pick herbal tea, maybe it'll help.

-You really don't want to eat?

-Mom, I can tell you if I want some. Please don't force it!

-Ok, ok. What happened?

-You want the cosmetically enhanced version or the truth?

-What do you think? Honey, tell me, it helps you process it.

-We almost made love. He told me, he wants me completely, not only my body. He wants to be the part of my life. I got scared, I pushed him away and simply left. That's pretty much it.
I take a sip of tea, but it's still hot, so I start stirring it.

-You are a beautiful woman and you are now single. You can't blame him that he tried.

-Yes, but I just got divorced two weeks ago. This is too much for me.

-Not eveything comes into our lives when and how we want them. You can't influence these things.

-I don't want to, but I guess I do. The most important is Ben for me now. I don't think this whole thing would serve me well. And you know what is the best ? He witnessed me being out of it a few times during the weekend, on top of it he had to assist my panic attack, too.

-Oh, honey. I understand you. Do as you wish, as you think is the best. It wouldn't help telling you what I would do, it would not be good if I influenced you now.

-Don't tell me anything. I have to let all these things to sink in. I guess I will go with the flow.

-Mom! Mom!

## Fragments of the Past

The most handsome little boy in the world is running toward me and welcoming me with the biggest hug. With his blond hair and blue eyes, he looks like a little prince. All of a sudden, I forget all my troubles. I keep kissing him, like I haven't seen him for a year. I hug him, hold him tight.

-Mom, it's enough!
-Ok, I'll put you down. I just missed you so bad.
He sits on my lap and gives me lots of kisses.
-Wouldn't you stay for lunch?
-No, thanks. We'll go home and I'll prepare something home.

I won't admit that cooking will be helping me to keep my thoughts busy, in a good way, maybe I'll clean the place, too. That always helps coping with stress and unwanted thoughts. When I'm done, we'll go to the coast with Ben and collect stones adding them to our collection. George is just walking out from the room, waves to me, and I wave back.

-Ok, but I'll pack some dinner for you.
I'll stay quiet, it's better not to argue with Mom, when it comes to food. My accomplice keeps smiling knowing what I am up to.

-Thank you.
She packs the food, George brings Ben's things out from his room. That room was mine before, but since he was born, they converted it for his needs. I'll take my bag, ready to go.

-Take good care of yourselves, I'm so happy my little grandbaby was here with us. You know, he can come anytime, just let me know in advance and whatever is the case, call me!

-I know, I'm very grateful to you to watch him for me. Thanks for everything.

-This is normal.
We hug and kiss.
-Bye Nana! Bye Papa! I'll come soon!
-Bye you two!

We live close to my Mom, that's how I chose the apartment we rented. Sitting in the car meanwhile Ben is chatting away. I'm still missing the beautiful big house, the gorgeous neighborhood where we lived. It was close to the city. It took us half a year to find it from among the houses on the market. I chose the design for all 4 rooms. I painted the walls of Ben's room, I decorated it, I made the garden pretty and that's where I pushed the baby carriage near the forest. I loved the evenings on the patio, loved to listen to the crickets and the noises of the garden parties we threw. We enjoyed tremendously playing in the garden, walking around the neighborhood for hours... I still can smell the scent of the house. I cherish lots of great memories from here. I regret we had to sell that house.

-Mom, do you hear?
-Sorry, I was lost in my thoughts. Can you tell me again?
-What I told you was that I got a water-pistol from Nana and I would like to play with it in the afternoon. Will we go to play?
-Yes. I planned to take you in the afternoon to the beach to collect stones and we can play with the pistol, too.
-Super!

We arrived home too early. It's hard to get used to the neighborhood, although it is a quiet one. We moved here 2 months ago, just before the divorce. We collect our bags and head up to the apartment. I'm walking

## Fragments of the Past

slowly due to the amount of luggage. Ben is behind me. Since there is no elevator in the building we have to walk up to the 5th floor. I hate the stairs. I'm already exhausted at the 4th floor. I take my drink out of my bag, try to balance myself but ending up dropping the red suitcase out of my left hand. We helplessly are watching as it flies down 5 stairs, of course, everything in it falling out. Underwear, dresses. all over the place. Fantastic. I have to walk down to pick up everything. Guess it all need a good washing.... Can't believe it. I notice a yellow note as it falls out in between the dresses.

-In case, you're lost: 917-859-2358, Kisses— Peter.

The little rascal snuck his number into my suitcase. I'll take the note, crumple it. I throw it into my bag.

-Come, I'm ready it's only one more flight.
-I'm coming.

I am taking out my key, opening the door. I got installed on the door 3 locks, safety is number one, especially since I don't have alarm. I put all my stuff down in the entrance hall, will sort them out after cooking. We have two small rooms, Ben's and mine, outside of this a small living room, bathroom, toilet.

I rented out the apartment without furniture, this way we can use my furniture, at least most of it, the rest is in storage. I could not have much variety, to play with the different wall covers here, it's only a rented apartment. It's temporary till I find something better. I, myself, painted all the rooms, using beige color, it needed the hygienic paint, most of my furniture is brown or white. It became homey, but it never will be a home.

-Go, play in your room, but wash your hand before. I'll prepare dinner in the meantime.
-Ok, but I want my chicken with some potatoes.
-I knew that, you always want that on Sundays.
At least this tradition is still ours. I start cooking.
The kitchen is small, the place to work on the counter is really tiny, I hardly can manage. The kitchen cabinets are dark brown, they go well with my white accessories. I put bread coating on the meat, cut the potatoes. I pour oil into the skillet, heat it and I am baking already. I prepare salad for the meal. It's good that I neither make soup, nor cake now. I would not be in the mood for it.
-Honey, come to eat!
The apartment is so small compared to the previous big house we had, we easily can hear each other.
-I'm here.
I bought a small table for 4 people, it hardly fits into the space. Ben is sitting where Gabriel used to, at the head of the table. He winks at me. I love him.
-You're the best Mom in the world.
This is the nicest thing a child can tell his mother, and he knows how to flirt. Just like his father. He really takes after him. Blond hair, blue eyes, wide mouth, engaging smile and confidence. That's what I loved in his father, too. It's hard a bit to see his father in him every day, yet it's fantastic to discover that in his demeanor half is his father and half is me. So, a part of him, even though we divorced, will stay with me forever, connects us to infinity.
-You ate it so fast.
-Cause, I was hungry, playing made me hungry.
He is adorable, I just have to kiss him on his face.
-Can we go to the beach?
-Just a minute I'll finish my meal and then yes.

# Fragments of the Past

We pack some drinks, snacks, two water-pistols, a book, a blanket and a plastic bag for the stones. I love the waterfront, watch the water, read and just to hang around. We quickly jump into the car, and fortunately arrive to the shore when there is no huge crowd anymore. As usual, Ben's first thing is to run to the water, meanwhile I'll pick our spot.

-Mom, I will throw the stones into the water ok?

-No worries, just be careful.

I take my book and collapse onto the blanket. I keep watching him carefully though. This is what I do since he was born. I start to read a crime story, while I hear splashes in the water. Then I sink into the book completely.

-Attack!

A huge splash of water hits my leg. I try to get into safety. I sneak to the water's edge, load my own weapon, too.

-If a fight, then let it be a fight!

We chase each other, take turns in shooting.

He is better at getting me hit, my aim is a bit off the mark, so I keep missing him and he uses that against me. We are having amazing fun, keep laughing sometimes falling down.

-Look, a beautiful green stone!

He points with his tiny finger to a gorgeous emerald green stone.

-Let's put it into the bag and keep looking for special ones.

We walk for hours on the shore, the sun goes down by the time we have our bag full of gorgeous special stones. We can already create a beautiful image out of them. They are like dreams. You can collect them, hide them, keep transforming them for a long time to find the right moment to create something special out of them.

-Shall we, my little prince?
-Yes.

This is always our special time, it doesn't feel great to head home after that. The ratrace will start again tomorrow.

-Are you hungry? You want a sandwich?
-No, I'm not hungry, I ate enough on the beach.
-Are you sure?
-Yep.
-Then make your way to the bathroom.
-Mom, I don't want to take a bath. I'm not even dirty.

-You need to. You can't go to kindergarten tomorrow like this, by the way you got a lot of dirt on yourself around the water. I'll be quick.

-OK.

Our little ritual that we talk through our day while in the bath. The bathroom is with salmon color tiles placed by the owner of the apartment. Couldn't he find a different color in the store? Anyway, I will survive it. Ben starts to chatter away about his afternoon, how amazing it was, how much he enjoyed it. He plays with his toys in the water, I also tell him about the beautiful place I had picnic at.

-Mom, why are you always sad?
-That's not even true, I'm not always sad.
-Many days. You are. Because of Dad?
-That's part of it.
-I love my new room, I love being with you, but sometimes I miss Dad.

Well, yes, we brought his old furniture into his new room, the light blue one, except I bought a new matching automobile rug for him. It reminds him of his old room.

# Fragments of the Past

-I know honey, you'll see him soon.

It hurts me, because I never wanted him to grow up without his father, but I had no choice. I had to make a decision. I know the feeling, when he is not always next to you, when you can only see him time to time. You can't tell him, brag about what you built today, or drew, he will not kiss you goodnight, and he will not put you in your place when you did something bad. This is partially my fault, but I had to get out before we would ruin each other's lives. It was not serving Ben to see how much we argued, how bad the ambiance was at home, how much I cried. We tried to keep this away from him, but sometimes without success, and he sensed everything.

-That's it, now we jump into the pajama, tooth brushing and sleep.

I prepare the outfit for next day in kindergarten, and gently push him into bed.

-Can you tell me some tales?

-Yes. You want me to read or you want me to make it up?

-You.

I lay next to him, hug him and start the tale.

-One upon a time there was a little ladybird boy. He was always sad, cause he did not have dots. His mates bullied him and did not play with him. You don't have dots. What kind of ladybird are you? They pointed fingers at him in the ladybird kindergarten. One day a beautiful white bird flew over. What's the matter? Why are you crying little ladybird? Cause, I don't have black dots on my back, like everyone else. I can help that. Come here. He took his paints and his magic stick and painted 5 black dots onto his back. Little ladybird boy became very happy., he thought they won't bully him anymore, he will be like all of the others. Next day he proudly showed his new black dots to the bullies. I also have dots! The others started to play with him, flew together, jump from flower to flower, but then started to rain...

Ben fell asleep so I won't finish my tale. He sighs peacefully. I step out of his bed, cover him. I place a kiss on his face than put his night light on. I tuck away my red suitcase. Then Ben's toys and the kitchen. I grew tired, I go take a nice shower. I put on my favorite pajamas then I retire into my room to sleep. Here everything is white, ok, the wall is not. A huge white bed, white furry rug, white pillows, white wardrobe and a dresser. On my wall there is a painting that features white orchids. This color calms me. I lay on the right side, this is my place. I pull the cover on me and try to sleep. I can't. I am missing someone from my bed. With Gabriel we always slept spooning. Now my bed is empty, I used to for ten years that he is next to me. I was used to his smell, his snoring, his body. Even when he came home late, he was slipping into bed next to me and held me, except the last period of time. I struggle for few minutes, I open the window, hug my pillow. It just doesn't feel great. Doesn't work anyways. I'm lonely and lost. I do the only thing that always helps me to calm down. I sneak into my son's room and lay next to him. This is the best feeling in the world. I love him so much, and he will be always there for me. I sense his scent, I hug him. His breathing calms me, so I listen to it. I think about what he is dreaming about, I don't want to dream. I close my eyes and slowly fall in sleep.

I wake up to my alarm on my phone. It is another Monday morning. I run to stop it, allowing

# Fragments of the Past

Ben to sleep some more while I get ready. I take my pink suit and matching pink heels. I put my hair into a loose bun, start to do make up. I put my foundation, use my eyeliner, mascara and finally a light lipstick. I wear my gold butterfly earrings. I got it from my Mom with a matching bracelet. I wore it when we met with Gabriel.

## About 10 Years Earlier

-Ann, hurry, we'll be late!
-Alright. Don't worry so much. A party can wait. We are 19 years old not 50, we can go to thousands of parties in the future.
-I know, girl, I just want to go crazy today. Drink and dance with the sexiest guys.
-You know, that just because you broke up with David you don't have to immediately pick a new victim?
-Yeah, I gotcha.
Monique looked awesome in her pink body hugging minidress, her blond hair is curled, her blue eyes are shining. On the other hand, I pick a simple black dress, I put up my hair and use very minimal make up. We are the total opposites of each other inside out. She is beautiful, lean, pushy and sexy. On the other hand, I am unnoticeable, I have few extra pounds and shy.
-Here we are! Welcome in the best club in the world! Enjoy!
She starts to jump around, uses her sexy hip sway and pulls me along herself. The music is pumping, sweaty bodies are clinging to each other on the

dance floor. It's full house. We bump into a bunch of people till we make our way to the bar. Monique orders drinks for us. She screams.

-Get me two cosmopolitans!

She hands me one of them, drinks hers fast than pulls me further with herself. We end up on the dance floor. I have no choice but drink my cocktail quick before someone pours it on me.

-Go, I'll come in a minute, just drink it.

She doesn't get it immediately, so I point at the drink. I drink it slower than I anticipated, because I notice Monique dancing with three guys who are surrounding her. What a bitch!

-Hello, little butterfly!

I turn around and I face the most handsome guy I've ever seen. Blue eyes, blond hair. Tall, easygoing and confident. Not my type. I look deeply into his eyes.

-Hey, I didn't come to meet guys. Sorry.

I leave him. I rather drink the rest of my cosmopolitan and go back to the dance floor. I fight my way to be next my girlfriend pushing through guys. Our favorite number is playing so we sing and crazy dance. We dance to the next three numbers, too, getting warmed up. I lean to Monique.

-I'll get two more of the same.
-Cool.

The counter is close, so I don't have to plow through a huge crowd. The bartender is busy, so I get his attention screaming.

-Hello! I would like two cosmopolitans.

I pay for them and make my way back balancing the two drinks in my hands. All of a sudden, I feel a punch in my side. The drinks are flying all over the place, some of the liquid poring on me.

-Sorry!

## Fragments of the Past

A man's voice is behind me. I turn around and I see the handsome guy I met just a bit earlier.

-You did it purposely, no one can be this crippled.

-If I say yes?

-Play with someone else.

-I want to... with you. There is no excuse, little butterfly.

-What the hell are you talking about? Leave me alone.

I push him away and walk back.

-Can you imagine, a stupid guy made me spill our drinks? He claimed it was on purpose. Arrogant dick!

-I am that arrogant dick!

I turn around and he is offering his hand to Monique. Smiling.

-I'm Gabriel.

-I'm Monique and she is Ann.

Thanks Monique, we'll discuss that. I want to walk away but he grabs my arm.

-Let's dance!

-No!

He grabs my waist and start to sway with me following the beat of the music. I purposely don't do a thing. I don't even touch him. He feels I play head-strong, so he pulls me close with great force. I let him do it, maybe he'll give up soon.

-Ok, I'll dance with you if you promise to leave me after.

-We'll see about that.

Cocky. Dominating. Very handsome. He is still too close to me, pushes his hip against mine. The music is romantic, some kind of a love song's remix. I also start to sway to the rhythm of the music, he likes that. He gets a hold of my face and kisses me.

He sticks his tongue in.... owning me. I enjoy that. He already knows I am his, he got me.

·····

-Mom! Mom! I have to pee!
-I am coming to help, but then we have to hurry dressing up, cause Mom will be late for work!

I dress him, and a quick toothbrushing. It's good that they get breakfast in the kindergarten, because have no time now. I'm already sweating from rushing. We're almost running down to the car. Unfortunately, we're moving slowly, the morning jam is crazy. Do all these people have kids in kindergarten? The parking lot is packed, so I can only park further away. We run again. Finally, we arrive. We walk into the group-room, I immediately start with changing shoes.

-I love you. I'll come soon to pick you up. Take good care of yourself!

We hug, quick kiss. Next stop is work, it's already past 8 a.m. It's not a huge help that my work starts at 8:30 a.m. in the past few months. Like a bad comedy, by the time I get to the office. Fortunately, our company has parking place. I am already breathing hard by the time I get to the 6th floor.

-Hey Monique! Good morning!
-You disappeared on the weekend! I'm mad at you.
-I apologize, I will make it up to you with some nice coffee.

My girlfriend is sitting by the receptionist counter like a queen. Good for her. At noon, I'll run out for coffee, she'll soften up. I hurry into my office, close my

## Fragments of the Past

door. I tried to make it homey as well, since I have to spend a lot of time here. I put family pictures on the white wall. I bought candles, a few ornaments and a brown rug that goes under my desk. The chairs are also brown, so it all matches. My favorite aromatization kit is plugged in to get me a pleasant scent. I use it for years to create good ambiance. A huge pile of paper is waiting for me to be processed, on my desk.

I bury myself in my work, all of a sudden my door swings open.

-You didn't even tell me about!

-About what?

-Peter!

-Excuse me? Don't shout, and please close the door when you come into my office.

-He came to me in the morning and asked me if I know anything about you, because he is worried, since you stormed out from him yesterday.

-There is nothing special, calm down.

-Were you with him?

-Yes, because he invited me to their vacation home to relax a bit, he heard from a gossipy chick, that I just got divorced. I accepted his invitation and nothing happened. We just relaxed.

-Ok, if you say so.

I can see, she doesn't believe me, I will not share the details with her. I'm upset, what is Peter thinking of? He shares everything with Monique? I could choke him to death. That's how he wants to be able to get in touch with me. He can wait for that. He did not reach his goal. I have to calm down, air my head out, get some lunch and coffee for Monique. My company cell is ringing. Unknown number.

-Yes, hello!

-This is Peter.

-And I am not available. Bye.

I start my trip to get lunch and coffee. First stop is my favorite cafe. I buy two lattes then I go to the Italian restaurant for some pasta.
-Such a lovely surprise!
The owner greets me with a smile.
-Hello Lucy!
-You want the usual?
-Yes.
-She wants another one.
I hear Peter's voice but I don't turn around.
-Are you following me?
-No. I just got hungry.
-What a serendipity.
-Ann. Look at me.
-Please leave me alone, I don't want to get into any mess.
-You already did.
We stand quietly. I still can't look at him.
-Pasta is ready, bella!
-Thanks.
What a lucky turn, I don't have to continue this uncomfortable conversation, stay with him any further. I pay and hurry toward the door. I take my leave without even looking back. Finally, I'm back in the office.
-This is for you.
-Thanks, all is well between us.
We grab coffee and walk back into my office. Since there is lunchbreak we can talk for half hour without interruption. I take my pasta, start to eat, Monique is not hungry yet.
-Bon appetite!
-Thanks.
She seems uncomfortable and awkward, I can see she wants to talk about something, but she doesn't know how to start.

## Fragments of the Past

-Tell me.
-Listen, are you attracted to Peter?
I almost choke on my pasta. I cough.
-Cause I am.
Fantastic news. What can I say? If I say yes, I assign him for myself, if I say no, Monique makes her moves on him. I know her for 15 years, whatever she puts in her head she will reach. Do I want her to have him? Maybe they would be an awesome couple. I don't know.

-In my opinion Peter likes you, Ann, and likes me too. Maybe, it would be better for you to be alone. You just got the divorce, you don't even know what you want. I know. I get Peter, but only if it doesn't bother you. He's handsome, smart, great catch. He doesn't have a girlfriend, he's free prey.

I don't have the right to hold him, till I am uncertain about him.
-Try it.
-You won't be mad?
-No.
-Alright. Then I'll get on his case.

She floats out of my office, I've already lost my appetite. I put my leftover into the mini fridge. Above the fridge there are my family photos. I have to take down the ones with Gabriel on them. I don't want to keep looking at them, it hurts. Then my eyes go to a wedding picture. I reach for it and take it down.

### About 8 Years Ago

It is so amazing to be in his arms. I feel safe, he is my other half.
-It was fantastic.
-For me too. As always.

-Don't move my little butterfly, I'll be right back.

I love when he calls me like that, it's when he wants to be intimate and sweet, it always reminds me the night when we met. I would like to go take a shower, we both got sweaty, we need refreshment.

-I'm here.

-Super, but I want to take a shower.

-Wait.

He is smiling like a baby who just got fed. He takes both of my hands and pulls me closer.

-When I met you that night, I knew I was lost. I wanted to have you, and now I do. I want you to be exclusively mine, and I always will. In the past 2 years I enjoyed every minute with you, you complete my life. I don't wish for anything else just for you to hold my hand when I'm old in my last minutes.

My god, now he goes on his knees naked, next to the bed. I will cry.

-Will you be mine, forever, in good times and bad times, in health and sickness, till death do us apart?

That's it. This is the most beautiful confession in the world. I can't believe it.

-Yes!

Naked as I am I jump to hug him, offering my heart. He takes out the most beautiful ring in the world, a golden butterfly with diamonds on it. He puts it on my finger, I admire it for a moment, interesting, it seems as it always belonged there. I kiss him and we start to devour each other again.

....

# Fragments of the Past

Enough of the memories, I have to stop. I put the photo into my bag and add two more. I'll take them home in the evening and will put them at the bottom of the box with photos. One day, when I show memories to my grandchild, it won't hurt. Times fly, I have a huge load of work.

-Let's go home, haven't you heard me knocking?

-No. The time is already up? I can't be late from the kindergarten.

Since Gabriel is not in our lives, I go to pick up Ben in the afternoon, too. So, there is no way to do overtime at work, in extreme cases my Mom goes and picks him up, although I don't want to weigh her down.

-I grab my bag and we can go.

We are waiting for the elevator, this is a very busy time, I'm worried if I get there on time. Peter shows up next us. What can he want?

-My Ladies! Such a surprise to meet you.

- We work at the same firm, it's not complicated to run into each other.

-What are you so snappy for, Ann?

-I don't like this kind of sweet-talk.

-What would you like?

He pokes me and I poke him back.

-Should I list it?

-Ok, stop it. Don't behave like kids. Here is the elevator.

-Hurray!

The three of us standing in the tiny space. Awkward silence. Peter is looking at me, no, staring at me, Monique staring at Peter and I am staring at both of them. I would love to get downstairs as soon as possible. All of a sudden, the elevator stops.

Peter lets Monique out.

-Bye you two!

-Bye! See you tomorrow.

I hurry to my car, would love to get in but Peter stands in my way. He pushes me to my car.
-Would you want me to leave you alone?
-Yes.

He pulls my pink skirt's edge, puts his hand under, slowly touches my thigh up to my underwear.
-Your pink high heels are super sexy. I would love you to wear it when I fuck you.

I get goosebumps. My body gives it all away.
He wants more.

He brushes off my wishes, touches me at the side of my panties. It is very thin. He starts to massage my pussy. It is very enticing like this, through the material, even more exciting. I become wet. He feels it. My back is against the car, from the front his body is pressed against me. He doesn't stop. He forces me to look into his eyes. I do it. I detect in his eyes that fire, his passion. He is proceeding slowly, like he has all the time in the world. We start to breathe hard, sigh. He stimulates my clit with circular movements, easy to feel my unstoppable throbbing, my juice is running down on his hand. I'm close to cum, I just need a little more. I don't care about being in a public parking place, I even like it. He likes it too. We are all worked up.
-Bye you two, have some rest!

I can't even tell who it is, but it puts me off.
-I have to go.

I push his hand away, but he is stubborn and resisting, squeezes my thigh.
-Why don't you give in to your body? It screams for me.
-It maybe, but it doesn't run the show. We are not in the cabin anymore. Good evening!
-Well, then bye.

# Fragments of the Past

He takes his hand away, struggling but leaves, I sit in my car and start. I'm still wet, I should clean up. Why can't I be stronger? I almost had an orgasm at work. This is more than unacceptable. Maybe, if they get together he will not tempt me anymore and I can forget about him.

-Mom! Mom!

Ben is running toward me at the backyard of the kindergarten.

-Hey sweetie! I really hurried to pick you up.

When we get home, we'll play games but before we'll shop.

-Will grilled sandwich be ok?

-Yes, with lots of cheese.

I carry the 3 bags to the apartment, because I was shopping for everything else that was needed. My hands are hurting from the heavy lifting.

-I'll make dinner real quick then we can play, in the meantime please prepare the toys.

-Ok.

I put butter, salami and lots of cheese on 4 slices of bread. It'll do it. It is hard to adjust to prepare much smaller amounts of food, when we were 3 it was different. I prepared food every day, now I make food for 2, days ahead. My daily routine is completely changed since we separated.

-Come to eat!

Ben shows up, running from his room, takes a seat. We eat the grilled sandwiches then we make our way into his room.

-What shall we play?

-Lego, then puzzle.

We play Lego for an hour, then we complete to perfect 100 score the spiderman puzzle. I can see he would be in the mood to play more, but he has to sleep in order to wake up early next morning.

-Don't start this again, you need to sleep a lot, cause you're a baby. If you come now, I'll tell you two more tales.

He doesn't answer, but he knows it's better to come along. He is sulky but starts to walk. I hurry with bathing him. He tells me all about what they played that day, I say nothing. I am tired, it is a challenge to tell a tale. He doesn't fall asleep this timebut waits to the very end.

-Sleep! Sweet dreams! I love you.

- Me too, Mom.

I close his door and go to my room. Before bath I put the pictures I brought from the office, away. I take the little purple box from the shelf. I don't want to watch them all and feel nostalgic. Unfortunately, on the top, there is one that makes me feel uncomfortable, because it brings a very happy memory back. It's the two of us with Gabriel, before we had Ben. We are kissing on it, the gorgeous sea is behind us, as we are standing on the smooth white sand. I'm wearing a yellow bikini with the matching straw hat, Gabriel wears black swimwear. I remember, the sand was so hot, after taking the picture we were running into the water. We dedicated that 10 days only to each other. We were intimate day and night. We couldn't take our hands off each other. Gabriel shot his cellphone down, that was a big deal, because he was a business owner, he was supposed to be available always. He probably delegated running the business to someone at that time, he is very responsible. On this getaway we decided to have a baby together. We wanted more than anything in the world to have our new miracle born from our love. After that we made love even more often, make sure I'll get pregnant, and I threw away the contraceptive. I put the photos into the box, closing the reminiscence. I go to the bathroom. Take

# Fragments of the Past

my clothes off, I can see myself in the full-size mirror. I don't only have stretch marks from weight gain and loss, pregnancy, but also cellulite on my thighs. Awful. And due to the hormones, I got hairier, since giving birth, I have to wax more often and at places never before. On my stomach for instance. I feel ashamed of that. I take a simple razor as I will go to the cosmetician only next week. I put shaving foam on my legs, pussy and underarm. I play my favorite number on my phone- Adele:Rolling in the Deep-this always empowers me... and shave. It feels good to be smooth. I take my favorite red nailpolish too and paint my nails. Why can't I see myself beautiful? I always focus on my imperfections. I don't have the self-confidence, like I had before. It's hard to believe that a handsome guy, like Peter would be attracted to me. Beauty and confidence come from inside, I know I have to nourish it every day, till it comes naturally one day. I can't allow myself to depend on a man's feedback. I turn to the mirror.

-I am beautiful, I am strong, I am independent, I am sexy, desirable! I love myself!

I say these mantras every day out loud, it usually helps. I turn the music off, walk to my bedroom naked, I lay down into the empty bed. I would need to sleep, but I didn't get my satisfaction. From my night drawer I take my purple toy. Gabriel bought it for me with all the accessories . He was always very creative... No one sees me, why not? I touch myself. I spit on my finger. I start to stimulate my clit, like Peter did it, I visualize his hand and face in front of me. It feels good, but I need more. I take my vibrator into my right hand, and very slowly I push up the rock hard phallos, since I'm already wet, it slips in easy. I turn it on. With my left hand I start to stimulate my clit. It vibrates steadily. I imagine it is Peter who is stroking me and my vagina is filled with his hard manhood. I move it with steady rhythm, in and out.

In the meantime, I circle my hips. I feel I'm getting close. My nipples are hard, I stroke it, pinch it, from that my vagina squeezes the toy. I change into higher gear, I move faster. My body trembles, a few times and I cum silently. Too fast... I still don't feel completely satisfied, still not enough. I did not make love in the past six months. It's not good enough to play with myself. I could use Peter to be my lover, but I can't do this without emotions... I put my pajama on and lay on my side of the bed. I have to turn my brain off, I have so much to do tomorrow.

·····

-Mom! Good morning.
Ben jumps on me and he keeps nudging.
-Hey. I'm awake now.
I look at my watch and I see we are running late. I forgot to set my alarm, it's 8:10 am. Dammit.
-Honey, we have to be very fast now. Go to your room and dress up, anything will be ok and brush your teeth. Mom will be quick, too.
I write a message to my boss about running late, promising to stay later in the afternoon. I have no time for makeup, hair either. I quickly put on a light white dress ready to go.
-Come, I'm ready.
-I'm not going.
-Why?
-I don't know where Mr. Teddy Bear is. I don't find him.

## Fragments of the Past

-Find another toy.
-But then he will cry.
-I don't care. Get going.

I scream at him. He starts to cry.

-Alright, I'll check in your room.

He keeps crying. I can't find it. I pick up his toy spider. I hand it to him.

-This is not good!

He screams and throws the toy down. I pick him up, lift him, take my bag, close the door and I am running to my car. He cries all the way. We arrive at the kindergarten.

-Don't be upset! We will find Mr. Teddy Bear in the evening.
-I'm upset.

He leaves me and goes to Sandy, his kindergarten teacher. What kind of a mother I am? He cries because of me, I was screaming at him, I was not behaving like a mother. I arrive to my work an hour late.

-Hello! I can see your morning started awful.
-Yea.

I close my office door, start to work. Later on, someone is knocking.

-Yes?
-It's Monique. Can I come in?
-Come in.
-I brought some coffee for us, thought you would like it.
-Thank you.

I take the coffee from her, take a snip. It's nice.

-What was up in the morning?
-I slept over. I didn't set the alarm.
- I thought it was no more than that. I made a decision yesterday to invite Peter for a date, a little chat.
-Ok.

I was hoping she will wait a few days, but this is Monique. Impatient.

-I'll go back to my spot now.

-Sure, go.

I need to call my mom, to bring Ben from kindergarten in the afternoon.

-Hi Mom!

-Hi!

-Is everything ok? Are you ok?

-Yes, the only thing is I was late this morning and I need to stay later today. Could you pick up Ben from kindergarten? I would pick him up from you in the evening.

-I told you, you can count on me. By the time you get here, I will be ready with dinner, too.

-Thanks. I'll see you in the evening. Kisses.

-Alright. Kisses.

I put the phone down. I don't feel great. The pressure is coming further and further up. My extremities start to feel heavy, spasm chokes me. I'm sweating, I feel my heart will jump out. Oh no. Please, not in the office! I need to think. What shall I do? My colleagues can't see me like that. I need to get out of here. Like a sweaty, crazy person I break out of my office. I won't go to the elevator, there might be a lot of people. I run to the staircase and start to bolt down. There are only 2 flights to the goal. The situation is worsening, this whole sensation is overbearing...I can't take my eyes off his body...He holds me hostage. I feel piercing cold terror. I need to stay in charge. I'm already downstairs. I open the door, almost jumping through it. With my peripheral vision I see Peter, he is holding his lunch in his hands. This can't be happening. Anyways that's not the most important. I am running till I get to the park. It's only a few blocks down. I find a bench and I sit down.

## Fragments of the Past

There is no one around me, it's still early. I close my eyes and take deep breaths. 1-2-3-4-5. It doesn't help now. I'm a pathetic little nothing. What have my shrink taught me? My eyes closed, deep breaths. I visualize that I walk up on some stairs and keep counting. I get to the top and open the large green door. I step out and I feel under my feet the soft white sand, warm breeze caresses my back. Seagulls are flying around me. I walk on the wide coastal path all the way to the beautiful blue sea. Slowly I sink into the water and I go under. It completely embraces me. I simply exist. In a few minutes I manage to walk out of the water. I walk all the way back on the path to the door. I open it and walk down. I'm downstairs and count to 3... I open my eyes.

-Jesus! What the hell are you doing here?

-I protect you and help you.

-I don't need your help. I only want you to leave and leave me alone.

-You need help.

-I can manage.

-Ann, I can tell you're not ok. The panic attacks have psychic reasons behind them and it's good if someone is with you when they happen.

-You are not part of my life and I don't want you to be, doesn't matter what my body says. I told you to find a normal woman for yourself.

-I told you I love the complicated and hard cases.

-I am not your study case, and not your type.

-Don't be afraid of me!

-Don't analyze me.

-Talk.

I can't talk to you about this and I don't even want to.

-Why?

-I don't trust you.

-What would you need to trust me?

-Time and...

My phone rings in a very anxious way. I need to pick it up, it might be important.

-Where are you?

-I'm leaving, just stepped out for lunch.

-The boss is looking for you for a while. He's upset. Come.

I stand up and turn to Peter.

-I need to go. Are you coming too?

-I'm staying, I don't want you to feel uncomfortable if people see us together.

-Thank you.

We look at each other, his gaze is hard to figure out. I'm walking to the office as slow as possible. He saw me fallen apart, again. He is always where he is not supposed to be. I'm not collected yet. I threw him out a few times, but he still wants to be with me. I can't understand. I don't understand him...I should just drift, let things happen the way they want to happen. I just can't. He is too much on my mind, he could give me everything what I've been missing lately from my life, but if I get under a man's influence again, I'm afraid I will lose myself...I was living up to the feminine ideal the past few years. A woman should be gorgeous and sexy at all times; good wife; good mother; amazing lover; a working woman who is also independent. I wanted to be adequate to so many things that I lost myself in the process. I didn't let my passion drive me and the things that make me happy, instead always considering what would be good for others, what is expected of me.

I didn't want to fail, but I did... I failed as a wife.

-Thanks for calling me.

# Fragments of the Past

-No worries. In the meantime, the boss told me that he sent you your to-do list in an email. Take care of those quickly.

-I will be on it.

I sit by my computer and take a look. The list is too long, and the deadlines are too close. I have to hurry. I need to focus on the job, I can't daydream about my problems. Everyone have problems, but this is a workplace. They are not paying me to feel sorry for myself. I have to get a hold of myself. I am proceeding nicely, I already completed 3 assignments, I put in 4 more hours. I am not even in the mood for lunch. I check the time on my laptop. 10 minutes after 7pm. I didn't even notice how late it is. I close my computer, take my bag and step out of my office. I'm tired.

-You still here?

In a body-hugging tight blue dress, high heels, and an updo she is like a queen.

A dangerous, killer queen.

-Yes, I'm going with Peter for a drink. He was ok with meeting. So, I stayed, there was not enough time to go home to change.

-Enjoy!

- Thanks, I hope I will go home satisfied. Bye!

-Bye!

I encouraged him to try with other women, still it hurts. What if he sleeps with her tonight? I'm sure she won't hesitate, like me. Peter told me he used to have a lot of quick affairs. He only sees me since we've met? Right. If that was the case, he would not have said yes to Monique for a date. He's a man. He's driven by his basic instinct, too. What was I thinking? I should not worry about this anymore. I would love to be alone. I chose this. I'm a strong, single, independent woman. At least I will be. It still is bothering me that they will spend time together. I can't wait to get to my mom and ask her advice. I quickly get there, there is not much traffic in the evening. I ring the bell 3 short times, as we always do.

-Hello. Sorry for me being this late. I know you're also tired, but I can't count on anyone else. I had a lot of work in the office.

-No worries, I told you we watch Ben anytime. They're in the bath right now, he is playing with his toys. George is watching him and now they're pretending to be pirates on the sea. Shall I get you the healing tea?

-Yes, but I'm not hungry.

-I told you, I will cook for your guys, we already ate an hour ago.

We go to the kitchen, sit down by the table.

-You know, in the morning I was late, but this was only the beginning. I had a panic attack in the office, of course, Peter was there again, and before I came home Monique told me they are going out for a date since he said yes to her invitation.

I buried my face in my hands and started to shake my head. As I was explaining it, the whole story sounded even worse.

-Why did you have the attack again?

-I think stress and the emotional instability are behind it.

-Very possible. Here is your tea. Drink it.

-Mom, I will not be better by drinking the tea.

-Don't worry, just drink it.

I'm not really enthusiastic but I start to sip the tea, better to obey.

-What shall I do? Did I lose my mind? Why can't I accept the fact that they date? Am I not handling the situation well?

# Fragments of the Past

My Mom is very beautiful, every time I look at her, I think, I want to look like her when I grow into her age. Blue eyes, blond hair, skinny body type, soft features. I inherited my looks from my father.

I look into her eyes, so calming. She exudes inner power. She always knows what I need. She is my rock. She looks at me and strokes my face.

-Ann, you're amazing. You're not crazy, only confused, but this is normal in your situation. You have to calm down. We all are afraid of the unknown. Remember we discussed before the divorce, that it is better to be alone than suffer next to someone. Just take a look at yourself as an outsider. See your life from outside. See Peter from outside. If you would need to give advice to yourself, what would that be?

I need to think about this while sipping the tea. It tastes awful.

-I don't know yet.

-Can we stay here?

-Of course. It would be lovely. Let's get the guys!

We stand up, she smiles. We walk into the bathroom, surprise the two pirates.

-Get ready for launch! 1,2,3!

My little pirate is launching a water-cannon by hand, hitting George with it.

He holds his hands up and keeps laughing.

-I won. I hit the enemy, Mom.

He's so adorable enjoying his victory. Carefree happy childhood.

-You did great. We stay with Grandma for the night, ok?

-Hurray! So, Granddad will tell me a tale about the pirates. Do we know where Mr. Crabby is?

-No. I didn't have the chance to go home, but tomorrow evening by the time we get home, we'll find him.

-How about sleeping with the green parrot tonight, like a real sea bear?

George is smiling.

-Fine, and his name will be Pip.

-Good name.

He nods. I put my hand on his shoulder and squeeze it. He handled the situation very well. I couldn't even think of that. I take the little one out of the water. His skin was already soaked on his hand. I give him kisses, I embrace him, I dry him and put his pajamas on.

-There you are, ready, let's get to bed, Granddad is waiting for reading you tales. Goodnight, sweetie!

-Goodnight, Mom.

Ben walks into his room, and we walk back to the kitchen. George is a hero volunteering to help Ben get to sleep tonight.

-Let's eat chocolate.

-Fine, you talked me into it. Mom takes my favorite chocolate out of the cabinet and she serves it to me.

-You want me so fat that I roll? I'm sure no one will want me than.

-Silly. This is full of happiness, there is no calorie in it. By the way man like if there is some meat on a woman. Your figure is super, your lines are sexy. Gabriel told me many times how he loved your body.

Mom is right. He loved, when I became pregnant and started to be round. Gabriel loved that my breasts became bigger. He looked at me with devotion, admiring that I had our son under my heart. He wanted to please me constantly. I enjoyed so much how he stroked me for hours and talked to our little one. After Ben was born, I saw my changed body appalling, but he loved it even

## Fragments of the Past

more. He said I became a real woman now. He kissed my stretch marks one by one, kissed my folds, and he pampered me till I had orgasm. He always told me he was grateful for me to give him the most beautiful thing in life. He made me understand that these little signs are reminders of the most beautiful memory, so don't focus on them negatively. He desired me the same.

-I know, but since I'm single, my inferiority complex came out again. I'm ashamed to undress in front of another man. My imperfections are illuminating in my eyes, like neon ads in the dark. Look, there is a sausage!

-You're silly, Ann. You are beautiful and your figure is great. When you get together with a man again, believe me he will not check these, what you consider huge flaws. Men don't care about these tiny details. They only see the essence. We, women, give huge importance to these things, but this way unfortunately, we become frustrated and they do pick up on that. They have great senses. If they feel weakness on you, that you don't appreciate yourself, they can use it against you easier, they can rise on top. They can take the lead. See yourself as the most beautiful, the sexiest and you will exude this. Female power. This is the biggest man-magnet in the world. Focus on what is gorgeous on you. Only that.

-Ok. I will try.

I pick up two little squares of chocolate, eat it, Mom also takes some.

-That is not enough. You need to feel it.

-You handle the relationship with George so well, for so many years. What is your secret?

-I have no secret. You know with your father it was very different for me, I was also very different than. Next to George I've been able to remain a woman. Many years passed, that counts too, I gained experience, I became wiser. Many things I would treat differently today.

-Why do they cheat on women in your opinion?

- I could say that only men are guilty of that. I could say it's easy to seduce one who wants to be seduced. I could say we can't trust any man really. I could say they only fight for what they want till they get what they want. I could say they always look for new prey, they need it, it's in their instinct. I could say, the same woman after a while becomes boring for them, they need something new. But these are half-truths. We, women are also guilty in being cheated on.

-Why? How could you say that?

The chocolate keeps shrinking. I take out of the cabinet another serving of happiness and I put wine glasses next it. I take white wine out of the fridge, pour some for us. I'm angry, it's written all over my face, like everything else. This is one of my shortcomings. I wish I could wear pokerface. I need to practice.

-Let's leave this thing, honey. We'll discuss it another time.

-I just wanted to suggest it, Mom.

-When is coming Gabriel to pick up Ben?

Another super question. I make a face. I sip some wine, Mom follows my example. If we keep drinking, we'll drift into analyzing even more touchy subjects.

-This Saturday is the first time since the divorce that he will take Ben. Everything became so hard and difficult. If I could turn the time back, when I met him, I would not go to that party. Although I would, I still would go. Ben is the biggest treasure in my life, and I am grateful for him for that.

# Fragments of the Past

## Before Giving Birth

Can you feel he is kicking? He is fidgeting. He wants to come out to meet his parents or just to tell his father that his scruff stings.

I turn to the most awesome man in the world, I kiss his face. I lean back on the sofa, I love it, cause it's big and U shaped, I put my foot up on an ottoman... I love our living room, it's dominated by earth colors, just like in the rest of the house. It's simple, cleancut, friendly, yet it's still special. On the walls there are paintings I painted. There are objects all over reminding us the beautiful moments, and wherever I look I can recall where we made love. If the walls could talk. Unfortunately, all the positions are uncomfortable already. The baby is heavy, unfortunately, me too. I am most likely like puffed rice - I constantly get watery. He puts his hand on my tummy, he strokes it and leans close to the baby. I hope he inherits his father's beautiful eyes., his great lips and his hair color and everything else. He doesn't even have to look like me. He can be absolutely like his father. A mini-Gabriel.

-Hello my little son! Stay inside a little more, just about a month. I'm so waiting for you. Mom too, but you know that. When you come out, I will take real good care of you, I will teach you everything what a boy needs to know. Target pissing, drive a car, flirt and thousand other things. Men know everything, you will too. I will have an accomplice, two boys versus Mom, we take over. But this should stay between us.

I punch his shoulder and he smiles from ear to ear.

-Ouch. I was only kidding.
-I hope so.

.....

He kisses me, we embrace and he puts on a romantic movie. Lately I only watch those, although he feels sorry about that. I became overly sensitive. A little relaxation in the evening, the two of us before it will be three of us. We'll have less time for each other, at least in the beginning.

-I asked you for the third time, what are you doing on Saturdays?

-Sorry, I was lost in thoughts.

-I noticed, honey.

-I don't know yet. Maybe I will cry my sorrow into my pillow. Can you recall what Gabriel said when Ben was born and he held him in his arms for the first time?

-Not really.

-He said he was the happiest man in the world, and he will always take care of us. His tears were rolling down. This was the first time I saw him cry. He promised, he will do everything for his family, he will live for us, because he feels truly what we mean to him. His life became complete. He said he loves us the most in the world and he will never leave us...It didn't happen like that. He lied, Mom!

The tears are rolling down on my face, but I don't even wipe them down. I'm Just sitting and falling apart. Mom is embracing and cradling me, as she did when I was small. I love her fragrance. My Mom's fragrance.

-Shh. I know it hurts. It will be easier with time, the pain will slowly fade away. The memories are staying but they won't sting us from the inside. When you cry and talk more about it, it becomes easier a bit. Every day will be less and less painful.

# Fragments of the Past

-When will it go away, Mom? I thought I am over it, I wanted to be strong, but I felt inside that this is behind the panic attacks. It doesn't work. Sometimes I'm strong and sometimes I'm weak. You know I let him go, but not yet of my identity and my life I had back then, I couldn't yet.

- You don't have to let it go completely, whom you were then. That helped you become who you are now. Your life then had magical and not-so magical moments. Check what the past ten years gave you. What can you learn from it and how it made you better. Analyze it and file those thoughts away. You grew up next to him. He provided everything through the years for you guys. Maybe he was too controlling and protective, he is 6 years older than you. That's no problem, but you are on your own now. There is no man next to you, but you are stronger than you imagine. You can solve all your problems on your own. Remember everything has its own reason behind it, even if we don't see it immediately. Every chapter of life has us grow, teaches us something. You have to find your own self and your own path. You will feel which way you need to go. Meditate, that will also help with the panic attacks. And something else: Live, don't only sink into the illusion of life!

-In my opinion, don't stress over it! Be cool!

-Jesus, you scared me George. Since when you are standing here?

-In a while. The little pirate fell asleep.

He pulls a chair and sits by the table, pours wine for himself too.

-Let's talk about some lighter subjects. By the way you women tend to overcomplicate everything.

-Hear the voice of a simple man who knows everything.

-Ann, darling.

-Mom, don't correct me, I'm not a child anymore. I'm right by the way. I don't like when we women are portrayed as the ones who overthink things, making all kinds of relationships more difficult and complicated. We don't overcomplicate things, we only analyze them, as women. We think differently from you, men. You shouldn't try to figure out how we think, cause it's hopeless. You simply need to learn our language of love. Your simplicity asmen, we women can't get anyways. Sometimes we can be empathetic with you, but...

-You will list now food, sex, sleeping? Gosh, Ann.

-Yes, George, that's exactly I wanted to explain later.

-It's enough darlings. Before you get entangled into this treatise let me tell you that's exactly the reason why women and men are a good match, complete each other.

Let's pick a different subject. In the kindergarten in the past few days we practiced with the kids test pages, cause those will be used for age-appropriate exams and tests. I would have Ben practice with the new test pages.

-You are the best in your field, Mom. Ok.

-You are aware that Ben is extremely smart boy. He beats many kids.

-I know.

-Can you prepare him before he'll be leaving with George?

-For what? He's his dad. I need to be prepared.

-You don't need to wonder about things further, find a new hobby.

# Fragments of the Past

-Maybe lonely, brokenhearted women's sewing club every Wednesday?

-Funny Ann, but I thought of something else.

-Then what dear ever-clever George?

I'm smiling at him from behind my wine glass, he smiles back. Mom is looking at me with a question in her eyes, what can she advice now.

-Go to jog, to release your extra energy. Sport always helps.

-What would you say when? At 5am? Or after work? I can't leave Ben in the apartment alone.

-I will go with you in the afternoons, and your Mom will watch Ben. She will be entertained and I will get back to exercising. I may not be in such a great shape like your father but there is some secret reserve here. Would you help, Marge?

-Why not. I will not ruin anything cool. Honey do you want it?

They want to help. I don't want to reject them, but lately I became lazy, I did not work out for years. George is not same either like before but it is very sweet of him. I became a couch potato. So, this was the big opportunity for a fresh start. I have to start somewhere.

-Let's do it!

We did a high five, the three of us, we were happy about our new agreement.

-Such great ideas can be inspired by a glass of wine, right?

Of course. George, of course. You and your always genial ideas.

-Like always. Let's get to bed, it's past 11 pm already.

Mom is sleepy or I bore them? I guess she's right, we need to rest.

-Goodnight! I stay a bit, pack my stuff away.
-Ok. Have nice dreams honey.
-Thanks for everything.

I am not in a hurry, I'm not sleepy. Thoughts are floating all over in my head. I start to wash dishes, but the hot water burns my hand, cause the regulator is not working properly. I can feel, Peter will burn me the same way. Why George can't fix it? Why can't they buy a dishwasher? I cleaned up nice. It's time for me to go to sleep next to Ben into the small bedroom, it will be best, shower before it. The small bed is not comfortable, I'm irritable. I don't feel good anywhere really. If I'm home in my house that's the problem, if I'm here than that. I miss the sense of a home. I feel like a plant without soil or a little beetle flown around in the wind, looking for a flower that would be the perfect landing place. Everyone says home is where you feel comfortable and calm. Last I felt this way was in our house. I miss it.

-Honey, wake up!

Someone is shaking my shoulder. I don't immediately know where I am but then I realize it. I climb out of bed where my son is sound asleep.

-What time is it?
-It's almost 6am. I made breakfast too.
-I can't eat this early, but I will take it with me. I'll go get ready.
-I'll take care of Ben.
-Thanks, that's huge help.

I'm done everything, Ben is ready too. Finally, I will be at work on time and there won't any jams either.

-Hello. You seem to be tired. Is there any problem?
-Nothing, I just had a long night.

# Fragments of the Past

She's smiling. I feel like someone punched me in the stomach. I hope it's not what I'm thinking of. Monique is running after me to the office, she seems very excited. I'm not prepared to things like that early morning, although I'm not ready for this later either. She sits in the chair, I put my bag down on the top of my cabinet and open my computer. I don't even have coffee. Damn.

-You're so beautiful today. This dress looks so great on you, and your make up is awesome. Is it new lipstick?

Diverting technique, no problem, we need a bit of warm up. In the meantime, I open my emails.

-Thanks. And I bought this lipstick a few days ago.

-I can see she's waiting for me to ask about things. Ok then. Better to know.

-So, what happened yesterday with you guys? Neutral face. Neutral face. Neutral face. Maybe I can pull it off.

-I thought you will not even ask me. I wowed him, but it's no surprise. I'm irresistible..

-Of course, you are.

-So, we went out for dinner to a nearby Italian restaurant. Small place but very nice, great food. It's not overly elegant, but I didn't care about that. After the usual basic questions, we had a nice conversation. Then we had wine. He was checking me out. Did you know he had clients outside of the office too?

-No.

-And that his grandparents live abroad, and he sometimes visits them?

-No.

-He said maybe he can take me with him. I could tell you so much, I don't even know where to start. Oh, this is a good one. He's so sweet. He told me, he had many women in his life but he found the one he can imagine a future with. Can you believe it? Her smile is victorious.

-Yeah, maybe.

Great news. What is so surprising? He told her the same lines.

-And he goes to the same gym I'm going to, only he goes other days. We agreed we can work out sometimes together, too. We spent two hours in the restaurant, he paid for it - of course. When we said goodbye, he asked me if I wanted to grab a drink at his house too.

-Did you go to his house?

-Go figure. He has a spacious three-bedroom apartment in the upscale part of town. Real spacious, beautiful, a real bachelor pad with great view. You can imagine, I liked him even more. We sat on the sofa, he put music on, got champagne for us. He French-kissed me, we hardly could hold it back till we got to the bedroom... He was in bed as I expected him to be. I wasn't let down. And his size? Yumi... A great bite.

-I see. I'm happy for you guys. Listen, I'm still working on deadline projects, we can catch up later.

-Thanks. I'm out of here.

-And she marches out. Let's see my tasks for today, at least my thoughts will be averted. Two hours later I stand up from my desk and start walking up and down. I wanted this right? Yes. I let Monique to make a pass at him. Yes. Why did they sleep with each other? Why did I believe he was attracted to me so much? It was too great to be true. He told me he sees me only. He lied. A disgraceful man. He did not have me so he used the opportunity that was offered to him. He is not different from anyone else.

# Fragments of the Past

Ahh... I can't believe it. I have to calm down. I take a few deep breaths. There was nothing serious between us, I still felt that extra between us when I looked at him. It wasn't just desire that was dominant. That's it. Another disappointment. I was hoping he would demonstrate how can I trust a man again. He brought feelings to the surface I buried some time ago. The truth is, I pushed him away. More than once. I told him to look for someone else, he said he won't. Still. Maybe if I didn't let Monique to make a pass at him. He wasn't forced to sleep with her. I need to forget him. All my illusions are gone. I don't even want to see him. It's better. Ahh. I don't know what would be good. Only thing I know, I hate him. There is knocking on the door, I stop the pacing, start to feel dizzy.

-Who is it?

-It's Monique, you want to come for lunch?

-No, thanks, I will go out in the afternoon to eat something.

I close my door from the inside. I take my earphone out of my bag, I play Adele's "Someone Like You" song loop, I'm listening to it at maximum volume. Slowly, my emotions are brought out by the song, I start to cry. I don't want to think about anything only unload the extra steam. Oh, those beautiful old times...I listen to it ten times, I'm feeling better. I correct my messed up make-up, afterall they shouldn't see me like that.Thank God my make up kit is always here. My bag is always heavy, it has many survival items in it, clean wipe, a few rocks and Ben's other treasures. A mother's bag is like that. I pat down my long emerald-green dress, it fits my mood. I open my door and I smile at the colleague from PR division who walks by. Everything is fine, mask is on! My phone rings. Who can that be?

-Are we going in the afternoon?
-Where? Why are you so excited?
-To jog.
-Let's go, now I would need it.
-Your Mom will bring Ben, go home for your stuff and let's meet by the bicycle road at 6 p.m.
-I'll be there.

At least George is so zestful. The time when I finish work is far away, I'm restless. I feel like a child who was cheated, who did not receive the promised gift, I would love to throw a tantrum out loud. I'm walking down for coffee to my favorite place, this will pick me back up, or not?

-Hello. I'd like a cappuccino with two sugars and a chocolate muffin, please.

I pay the order, it is a real calorie bomb, but I need this now. I open the door, finally I'm on the street. I hold the coffee in my left hand and the muffin, with my right hand -I'm putting my valet back into my bag. Ouch. Suddenly I sprain my ankle, the coffee splashing all over me. What the heck? I look down, I notice I stepped into the only one pothole on the sidewalk, the heel of my shoe broke off. It was my favorite. Can this day be any better? This was the only thing I needed. I need to think. I will not take it off, the bottom of my feet will be dirty. Fine, so then what? I have chewing gum. It will do it. I take four into my mouth, chew it. I take them out and I fix my broken hill. Masterwork. I will try to clean the coffee stain when I get back to work. Like someone who's walking on eggs I'm walking so carefully back to the office. Please don't fall out, pretty one, please. I probably look ridiculous like a doddering penguin. I just took 5 steps, hurray. No. I feel the chewing gum starts to get loose, I fall. My ankle is hurting very

## Fragments of the Past

much. Sitting on the ground I'm trying to check the size of the damage. It's not broken, but I when I try to stand up I can't. I guess it's a strain. I'm on the verge of crying. I somehow need to get back. I call Monique, trying to ask her to come and get me. I find my phone. I punch the numbers in, it's ringing but she doesn't pick up. People are walking by, looking at me but no one is asking what's the matter. I dial my other colleague I'm friendly with, an automated message comes in that he is in a meeting, he'll call me back. I make an attempt to stand up, again, but it doesn't work. There is only one more person comes to mind. Out of question. I won't call him but I need help now, this is a different situation. It's a must. I hope I still have his number. I move my stuff out of my bag and place them around me. It has to be somewhere here. Bingo. A bit crumpled but clearly can read it. It's worth a try.

-Hello. Finally, I hear your voice, did you get lost?

-Hello. It's worse. I'm sitting on the ground in front of the cafe cause my ankle went out. I called a few people for help, but I couldn't reach anyone. Could you come and help me?

-A few minutes and I'll be there.

-Thank you.

In reality, I couldn't be more pathetic. If I asked for handouts, people may throw me some change. 5 minutes passed. Where can he be?

-You look so great in the middle of the sidewalk, maybe I should leave you like that.

I turn around. He's standing in front of me, I have to look up. His lips are about to smile.

-Then leave.

I turn sulkily around.

-I was just joking.
-I'm not crazy about it.

He touches my shoulder, starts to pull me up, holding me by my armpit.

-What happened?
-The chewing gum is guilty.
-What chewing gum?
-The chewing gum that was holding the heels of my shoe. I stepped into that pothole and fell while I was fixing my bag. My heels were broken, I didn't want to walk back without shoes.
-It was bad idea from the get-go. Next time when something like this happens I'll rather
-Ok, I figured by now. You want to lecture me or want to help?
-Both.

I put my weight on him, he's holding me.
A live crutch. We are walking slowly but surely.
It feels so great to be next to him. No, it's not good.

-Let's just get back quick.
-Are you mad at me for a reason?
-No.
-I can feel it on you, your body is so tense, your anger comes accross.
-There is nothing. I'm only mad at myself and the pit.
-If you say so.

He stops. Why is he stopping? He turns me around.

-Don't lie to me.

He strokes my face with his right hand. He's holding my chin and looks deep into my eyes.

-What's the matter, my beautiful?
-There is no problem.
-When a woman says that, there is a big one.

# Fragments of the Past

He's holding eye contact, his gaze hypnotizes me. I see desire in it and myself.
-Now I will kiss those beautiful lips of yours.
-No, never ever again. Kiss Monique's.
-What are you talking about?
I see he doesn't get it. Is he surprised? Good actor.
-I know everything. Let's go.
I turn around and keep balancing on one foot, waiting to the moment he is willing to move. He doesn't do that. Since I have no better idea, I start to jump around on one foot, he is holding my bag at least.
-Wait!
I stop, look back.
-No, you feel sorry for me?
-I'll help you, I can't stand watching you jumping around like that. So, what is with Monique, what were you talking about?
He comes back next to me.
-Don't pretend that you don't know. I know you two were together yesterday.
-Yes, but
I put my hand on his lips. So soft.
-Don't say anything, it doesn't make sense.
It takes 15 minutes to get to the office, we don't talk. We get into the elevator. We have time till we get upstairs, I need to tell him what I would like to. I break the silence.
-Listen, Peter. Thank you for helping me. I would like to ask you to scratch my number out of your phone.
-Why?
-Because I will never look for you, and you should do the same. Avoid me in the office, I will try to do that too.

As soon I say this, he suddenly punches the elevator wall with his fist. It is scary and too loud in this small space, at least his hand is not broken. Angry, ready to jump, will explode in a minute. Only two floors left. He is breathing loud, blows the air out with a sound, steps in front of me, his two hands positioned around my head and pushed against me. He is too close to me.

- Are you aware what you are doing with me?
- No, but I'm not even interested.

I push him away. Thank God the elevator door opens. I put my bag on my shoulder and keep jumping till my office door. Monique gives me a scared look from behind her computer.

- Nothing.
- Can I help you with something?
- No, please leave me now.

I sit in my chair, I put my legs onto the footrest. I rest them a bit, maybe the pain will go away. I have no change of clothes, the spot doesn't even bother me anymore, I will go home with naked feet. How unlucky I am. I made a decision about Peter, this should be the right one. He slept with Monique, he only played with me. If I gave myself to him, it would hurt much more. I was right to listen to my brain. Unfortunately, I did certain things with him, but I don't regret those.

I look through a few statements and financial propositions. Maybe the pain lessened a bit, I just realize I have to call George.

-Hello.
-Hello. I am calling you to let you know I can't go to jog today.
-How come? You already backing out?

# Fragments of the Past

-No, I'm not. But listen to this, my shoe's hill broke off, I fell and my ankle is hurting. There is no chance to jog like this.

-It's so you. I understand, but I will push you to the point of actually coming with me to jog.

-Ok.

-Don't you want to be alone in the evening? You Mom already planned out to be with Ben. He could sleep here, we could take him to kindergarten in the morning, and you could rest your legs peacefully. You could just come and pick him up tomorrow afternoon.

-I don't even know. He was there yesterday, he has no extra clothes now, I don't even want to burden you with this.

-I offered it, and don't forget he is our grandson.

-Well...

-Don't be too brainy about this, he is coming here, period. We'll see you tomorrow.

-Tell him I love him.

I wait for the end of the shiftthen I am leaving for home a half hour later. I don't want to see either Peter or Monique. I pick up my bag, I leave my shoes there. Go barefooted, I will fix the shoes tomorrow. I peek out my door if there is someone else in the office, but fortunately everyone left already. I am slowly dragging myself to the elevator sometimes hopping, it still hurts. I only have a few steps to my car. I open the door and I am ready to start the car when I discover a little note on my windshield. What can this be? Who left it there? I lean out half-way, I can reach it.

–Please give me another chance to explain.

-He can wait for that. When chocolate donuts fall from the sky. What is he thinking? He fucks her, then comes to me to beg for forgiveness? It wasn't what you think, I didn't even want it, I was drunk, blah-blah. I am not interested to hear that. So, he still doesn't understand that I asked him to leave me alone. I get home quick. Oh. I did not consider how will I get upstairs. OK. It will work, it's like training. Guess old people can feel this. By the time I got upstairs I am bathing in sweat, my ankle is hurting a lot and I have to pee. Why did I put up so many locks? I still have to open two. No. I am squeezing my thighs together not to pee in my pants. I can do this. Only a minute and I am inside. OMG! Let's run. It's the icing on the cake that some pee came out before I was able to lift up the lid of the toilet. At least no one has seen me. I take a shower then jump into my favorite home outfit. Black sweat suit bottom and pink top with the picture of a donut. It is fuzzy and worn out but super comfy. I have a little free time now that Ben is not home. What shall I do? All of a sudden, I don't even know. Should I clean? Or cook? Or should I iron the freshly washed clothes? Or arrange things? No. I will be selfish. I will watch a romantic film, munch on some stuff, put on a facemask and drink a glass of wine. This is much better idea. It will be the two of us, me and my relaxing self. I love our livingroom. I had the big plasma TV installed onto the wall, my books are on the bookshelf in the corner, all the accessories are grey. I had to buy a new sofa, cause the one from our house could not fit here. It is brown, the pillows are grey, and my carpet is grey too. I pick a film, sit back and take a sip from the wine. Typical love story. Gorgeous woman and a gorgeous man. They make love, I can't watch this. I change the channel. We were like this too.

## Sometime Ago, When I Was Still Happy

I hear the front door opening. Finally, he is home.
-Hey, my cute little wife.

# Fragments of the Past

I am cutting vegetables, he embraces and kisses me.

-Hello, my cute little husband. Where is Ben?

I left him at your Mom's, the evening only belongs to us. Surprise!

He touches my thighs and grabs my butt.

-Huh. OK. Right now, I am preparing dinner, I am not done yet, approximately half hour. Wait till than!

-No. Shut the gas, put down the knife, take off the top with the donut on it, leave the panties on. I will taste your donut now. Do it. Now! I obey. It turns me on. I am excited, what does he come up with. I am standing there wearing only my pink lace panty.

-Turn around, lean on the counter, push your upper body on it. Spread your legs. Curve your back. My God, you are gorgeous. Stay like that. I don't want to. He kneels and kisses my right leg all over. He also throws soft ones on my left leg, purposely leaving out my pussy. He tortures me. I am throbbing. I can't see from this angle what is he doing. Finally, he takes my panties off, throws it away. He licks me from the outside. I want more, so I push myself closer. With his warm tongue he flaps up and down for minutes. It is so good, I start to move my hip, he also starts in circular motion on my clit. We move to one rhythm. He knows what I love. He grabs my butt, holds it strong, then forces his tongue into my vagina.

Ahh... He moves it in a certain rhythm, as it was his cock. I am sighing, my juices are flowing. He takes out his tongue, suddenly puts his finger into me. I am waiting for it to move, but he pushes it into my mouth.

-Do you understand why I am crazy for your little pussy? I lick his finger, then I take it into my mouth and suck on it.

-I love the way you taste, the perfume of your skin.

-I love also yours.

I want to turn around to take off his pants, but he pushes me back.

-Stay like that.

I hear him unzipping his pants. I want to reach for his penis, but he holds my hand back. He moves his hard on between my butt cheeks, and sometimes moves it away. Plays with me. He stimulates my pussy from the outside with his penile glans. This is it.

-You want it?

-Yes-yes. Please, put it in, I can't wait anymore. I push my pussy to his body, I sensually sigh. He can't hold back anymore, suddenly he enters into me. He fills me out, he is the perfect match.

-I was waiting for this, my little butterfly. He strokes my back. Starts to move faster. He holds my head, lifts it up, then pulls my hair back. It hurts a bit, yet it is exciting. My God! It is so good, the perfect angle. I am getting close, every fiber of my being is expanded. I can only feel him. He is getting close too. He thrusts one more, my pussy tightens around him.

-Gabriel!

My body is trembling, I am floating in the clouds, only the two of us exist, him and me. I cum, in the meantime he screams my name and cums too. Then slowly pulls out, turns me around and kisses me.

-Now we can eat, but then we will have some seconds. He smacks my butt. You will be the dessert too.
-I can't wait.

·····

## Fragments of the Past

I need to think of something else, but I can't help it, the past comes to mind very often. I am angry and it is hurting. I take scissors from my sewing set, I take my top with the donut off, I make the first incision. Then there is another one, and another, and I cut it into pieces. I did not even realize, my tears started rolling. I throw the scissors to the wall, I brush all the rags off the couch. The little pieces are all over the rug on the floor. I slowly collect them and throw them into the garbage... like my last ten years. I feel better, temporarily. After all this would be great a meditation session, maybe it would bring me a sense of calm, I try. I start some peaceful music on my laptop, I light three white fragrant candles, I put them onto the coffee table. I get comfortable, close my eyes. I have to force myself not to think of anything else in the meantime. I open my familiar green door, and I find myself on the beach. There is no sign of the idyllic picture. The sky is cloudy, it's silence before storm, the air is damp and suffocating. On the path I arrive to the water. I dip in then I encounter a giant wave. I have no time to react. I disappear under the water, can't breath, it is pulling me down. Someone grabs my body and drags me out of the water.

·····

It is Peter. I get so scared, that I immediately open my eyes, I am already sitting in my living room. I am covered with sweat. I will not meditate for a while, for sure. I was hoping for peace, and now my subconscious is playing with me. I blow out the candles, shut the music. Peter again...Why can't I get rid of him? Why does he have to pierce through my thoughts?He is everywhere. I can't influence my feelings. It is a fact, he started something in me, then he destroyed all my illusions about the two of us. Why did I have to meet him? Why did he have to hurt me? If we have to be together and if he will be my next life partner, why can't everything be simple? And if he is not my man, then why did he enter into my life? I get into embryo pose, I pull the plush cover and continue reading my favorite book. I need to escape into a different world from mine.

 In the morning I wake up feeling more energetic, the relaxation yesterday was helping. I let my hair down, I put on a long dress. I put makeup on, I choose the rose-gold jewelry to match, but instead of high heels I can only do the flat, ballet dancer shoes. My ankle is still hurting, but I can stand on it normally. I get ready in only half an hour. It is so much faster alone. Before going to work I stop by in my favorite cafe, I buy a big cappuccino, learning from yesterday.

 -Good morning, you arrived early. How is your leg?

 -Yesterday you seemed very angry, are you mad at me?

 Monique is looking at me with innocent eyes, comes out from behind her desk, she hugs me and kisses my face. Kiss of Judas. I don't hug her back like before.

 -There is nothing wrong, and I don't have problem with you either. I was mad at myself yesterday and mad at the damn pothole.

 -Alright, but if you have any problem, please, let me know. I will be right here outside.

 -Certainly.

 I finished with the deadline project, so I dig into the preparations of our PR campaign. An unknown perfume company's first fragrance needs to be

## Fragments of the Past

introduced. To shoot a spot, press-media coverage, online marketing etc. But my first task is to create an action plan for the PR campaign. I love this part of my work. I have a few tough weeks in front of me, I guess. I don't even stop till 3pm, but because I got hungry I have to go down to grab something for lunch. I get my purse and go to the Italian restaurant. That is the reason behind my love handles, the good Italian pasta.

-Where are you going?
-For lunch.
-Can I go with you?
-Come, just hurry.

I wait for Monique in front of the elevator, but in the meantime, I stomp with my feet, to make her understand I have no patience. In my entire life, I always wanted everything immediately, to wait is not my strength. What is positive though, I am fighting for my goal till I reach it. I dare to dream big and the impossible. I think if can visualize, I fight for it; I believe that I achieved it already. We finally get into the elevator.

-I wanted to talk with you, before we go home.
I am looking at her with surprise. She is a beautiful woman, it's only her nature that is a bit undesirable. Ouch, this doesn't sound good.

-Tell me.
-Peter would love to see me again, he told me at noon. We will have a date tonight. This is good news, isn't it? We get out of the elevator, at least she doesn't see my reaction.

-Sure.

I am trying to hurry as much as possible. I need to change this subject to something she loves.

-And tell me what did you buy lately? Did you buy new perfume? Cause it smells very nice.

Her eyes light up. She weaves her arm around my arm.

-This is the new product, everyone is working on, didn't you get some from Marc? You weren't in the office when they were giving it away, for sure. But imagine, I got some deals. For instance, I took a designer bag at half price and bought some sexy underwear. All lace, they are perfect for deployment. I also found a new nail salon, the new girl is doing a better job. Check it out, how pretty!

She puts her blue flowered manicured hand in front of my face. I don't even have time to do mine, she only has time for herself. Sometimes I'm jealous, but I would not switch with her.

-It's pretty, really.

-But you tell me nothing.

-Nothing interesting is happening with me. I either work or I am home with Ben. Although yesterday he slept by my Mom's and I was able to rest.

-Is Gabriel coming this Saturday?

-Yes. I forgot it already, I told you about it. I have to pull myself together till then.

-You'll be great.

-I hope so.

We order two giant dishes of carbonaras, then we hurry back to the headquarters. Only one more hour and I can see my little love.

-Mom, Mom!

My sweetie is rushing to me. I kiss him, hug him and don't let him go. He is still my arms as I go to my Mom. We sit down.

-Hi sweetie. is your foot better?

-Yes, thanks. Resting yesterday helped a great deal. Please, don't ask if I want tea or food.

She makes a face.

# Fragments of the Past

-Why are you sad?
-I am not.
-You can't lie to me, I am your Mother.
-It's just some little nothing.
-I'm listening.

She can look at me like she sees through me. This is some kind of motherly superpower.

-Monique is having another date with Peter tonight. Outside of this when my shoe's hill broke off, I asked Peter to help, because there was no one else available. After we arrived back to the office, I asked him to scratch my number from his phone, and asked him to forget about me existing. By the way they slept together.

-I wouldn't have thought that, by what you told me this seemed unlikely.

-I wouldn't have imagined that they will jump on each other. He took Monique to his apartment, that's where it happened. I guess they are both beautiful people, single, too. I don't even know why would I be surprised by that. Maybe I enjoyed it too much that someone treated me like a woman.

-I understand. Try to forget about Peter. He does not deserve you, if he appreciates a little fling better. I know Monique too, she is how should I say, a little too easy to get. I have to smile thinking about this. She is more than that.

-Let's talk about you instead. How are you Mom? George?

-As you can see, we are great. Me and George are living a bit old fashioned next to each other. You know we agree on many things, we know each other's whims, we don't go anywhere. Maybe that bothers me. Your father at least tried to make up for the hours he was away working. I was worried about him all the time, scared, when he went to capture some criminals, each big crime scene made me fearful. His job is his love, even now is in the first place. It was one of the reasons it did not work out between us, but I told you all the other reasons too, many times. I don't tire you with that.

-Then you talk with George about this.

-I will.

-It's great to hear, but now we are ready to leave.

-Are we going to take a walk to the beach? Let's go home only after that, please Mom.

He is looking at me with those big blue eyes, his lips are curling down. He knows he can get all the results what he wants with this.

-Ok, but we won't take a big circle, cause Mom's leg is hurting. We will sit down on a blanket, you can collect and play with the rocks, but you have to stay in front of me. We will just sit around. Does this sound ok to you?

-Yes.

Today I pick a body-hugging dress with black and red stripes to wear, I put on red lipstick and let's get the matching gorgeous red shoes.I feel provocative and sexy this way. Sometimes we need it, it helps the self-confidence. I arrive to the office a bit late. I drop my stuff, turn on the computer and storm out to get perfume from Marc. I need to become familiar with the new product. I don't like him much. He is arrogant, always hyper, he thinks a bit too much about himself and his position.He looks just like a groundhog. He has the biggest office on the floor, he could fit a sofa and large table in there, comfortably. The meetings are held most often in his office. The products we dealt with and dealing with are all lined up on a big circular table, next to the window.

## Fragments of the Past

I ask for one sample, but I won't stay to chat, I need to be in the solitude of my office. My little space compared to his is a tiny mouse hole. I sit down comfortably, I turn my chair toward the window, I take the top off the from the perfume and I close my eyes. Let's see.

I take a big breath. It is a flowery scent, there is vanilla and cherry in it, too. It is not pushy but has character. It is feminine and an exciting combination. I am not a specialist but it is good for a start. Hm... I need to imagine it. There is a beautiful summer night, an adventure, a stolen kiss, the scent that stays on the man's clothes from the woman, a dream, a desire that overcomes you, erotica, a real woman. There are the immediate associations that come up smelling the fragrance. I spray some on myself, maybe I get inspired. The perfume I use in the past few years is the same, maybe it's time to start using a new one. You need to be in love with your perfume. When you are choosing one from a few hundred in the shop, it needs to stand out, you have to feel this scent is you. This is it- choice. I have the key. I am upbeat as I start to get to my work. In a few hours my table is covered with papers and little yellow notes. I take a small break. I am walking out to the common kitchen. It's at the end of the long corridor. All the other offices are facing the same long corridor. In almost all of them there are more than one people, I'm lucky to have one on my own. When I arrive, the kitchen is empty, it's not lunch break yet. About half past noon all of them will come in, they will line up for the microwave, or they eat in a standing position, if they could not get a seat by the table. I don't like to eat here, it is too small and there is not enough air in it. I make a cup of green tea, not in the mood for coffee.

-You look super sexy today!

I turn around. It is Matt, a sweet guy from marketing. He is standing by the door, checking me out.

-Thanks, you're sweet.

-Would you like to go on a date with me?

I almost drop the cup with the red dots from my hand, being surprised. He is too cute. Brown hair, blue eyes, freckles, baby face, athletic body. He is handsome on his own way, but not more. I smile at him.

-You are kidding, right?

He comes closer to me as I lean to the counter.

-No. I like you, we could spend a fun evening together.

I am just staring at him not knowing what to say. I should get rid of him politely. Ouch, whom am I seeing? Peter is coming toward me, angry, but stops in front of him. He puts his hand on Matt's shoulder, squeezes it a little. I can see he could stifle the poor guy. He heard everything.

-Don't even try with her, bro.

I don't want to be with him in the same space, why did he come here? I rather would go. Ha, take a big breath. I start walking toward them, using my sexiest stare, I give Matt a flirty smile. I slow down when I get to him leaning to his ears, whispering loud enough for Peter to hear.

-Maybe.

From here on I walk like a queen. I close my door, sit down to my computer. I continue my work, although I would rather just be home watching a movie with a big bowl of popcorn. He still turns me on. On what right he talks to whom I'm seeing? He doesn't own me. I am not his toy. I can still remember the happy memories but immediately comes the anger. Maybe not even anger, sadness. I wish he would leave the firm. I wish we would have never met. I would love to be ice cold, maybe it would not hurt me than. Monique is peaking in the door.

# Fragments of the Past

-Are you in the mood to chat?
-Sorry, I have a lot to do.
-Ok, then I'll go. If you change your mind, come out.

Ok.

I don't miss hearing how she is swept from her feet by Peter or talk about fashion or anything else that doesn't interest me now. I immerse myself into work, the end of shift comes soon.

I arrive to the kindergarten with the speed of light. The kids are playing in the backyard.Some in the sandbox, some collecting leaves. It is spacious, has a lot of toys. All the groups have a separate part of the backyard, our group is the Yellows. Fortunately, there are lots of trees, they offer shade when there is a hot day. I find Ben under one of those, as he is drawing images into the sand.

-Hello sweetie.

I hug him, crouch down next to him. His lips are curling down, his eyes are shining.

-Hey Mom.
-What is the problem? Is anything hurting?
-Yes, my tummy, since lunch.
-Then we will hurry home, and I will heal you there.

We change, say goodbye to the others and rush home. He is crawling on the stairs and lays down the couch as soon as we arrive home. My sweet little one is sick. At least he can tell me what's the problem, when he was smaller I had to guess it. I bring some pills to him, I cover him and lay down next to him. I stroke his tummy, this usually helps. He is resting for a few minutes than jumps up and runs to the toilet. I'm sure he went to pee. He is a big boy, he can manage.

-Mom, I threw up.

As soon as he says that he starts to cry. He got scared.

-Oh, don't worry. It happens to everyone sometimes, at least your tummy will be better. I'm sure you ate something that caused this.

-Maybe.

-Come back to the sofa. Tomorrow you will not go to kindergarten, we will stay home for you to be ok.

Other times he would be doing the happy dance hearing that, now he just sits without much reaction. I am writing a message to my boss, saying that I have to stay home with my little boy. All evening is a struggle. The medication gets to work slowly. He is holding Mr. Bear, thank God I found him fallen behind one of the storage boxes. He is throwing up a few more times and falls into sleep after all the challenges. My heart breaks when I see him sick. I wish to be in his place. I only sleep few minutes at a time, want to stay alert in case anything serious happens. My motherly intuition is 100% working, I feel all of his vibrations on a much deeper level. After just a few hours of sleep I wake up moody. I climb down the sofa, leaving the little patient to rest. Resting is the best in these types of cases. I'm still groggy, walking like a zombie to the kitchen putting on coffee. Fortunately, it is ready real quick, I drop few cubes of sugar into it then I prepare a sandwich with some jelly and butter. I eat breakfast alone, I better get used to it. I take a shower, I don't even put make up on, jump into a sweater. This will be a lay-back day. I look into the mirror. I am strong, I am beautiful, I am happy, I am smart, everything works out for the best. I smile at myself. I have to practice. After strengthening my confidence, I walk back to the kitchen, take the book in my hand that I started to read earlier, I continue reading and sipping my coffee.

# Fragments of the Past

After a few pages I get bored, can't focus on the book. Best if I clean the shower. I get the cleaning stuff, start to work around. After the toilet, it is the tub, then the faucet, finally the mirror. I am still distracted enough, so I start to work on the tiles. Finally, I wash clothes, we have a few portions piled up through the week.

Hi Mom.

I suddenly get scared as the door opens.

-Hi honey. Are you feeling better?

-Yes. I'd like to have breakfast.

-It's very good, that means your tummy's better. You should eat toast and I will make some tea with it.

-Okay.

I make the breakfast quickly, he eats it slowly.

-Just eat as much as feels good.

-All right. Shall we look at a story?

-Of course, we pick something we've seen a long time ago.

We choose the cars. I'll start the story. I hug him, he hunches over to me and watches the events excitedly. He loves cars. His father made him love them.

## Sometime Ago, I Saw He Was a Good Father

We are driving from work on the dirt road, it's faster than driving through the city. Our black SUV is very durable. The jazz is softly playing from the music box.

-Want to drive Ben?

-Yes...Yes!

He enthusiastically screams from the child seat. I get out, get him out of the seat and put him in Gabriel's lap. The fun starts.

-Grab the wheel, I'll put my foot on the gas. We're going slow, you just watch the road.

They are so sweet. Ben concentrates deeply, and I see Gabriel is so proud. My two guys!

-Avoid that pit. Good. Now a little left. This is it. Look they are facing us, now we'll be on the right side of the road.

-I push the horn.

-No. You only need it if you want to signal something to the others.

-Only once, Dad, please.

-Okay.

Of course, he presses it three times. The Master teaches him patiently, we get home quite slowly. I open the gate and they enter the garage. This is where the kitchen opens to. I like it because after shopping, I can carry packages straight away without having to walk through the whole house. I pour drinks for us, we sit down by the table.

-Mom, did you see how well I drove?

-Yes, you are the best.

I kiss his face. Gabriel gives him high five.

-From now on you drive home every day, when we come together in the afternoon, and when you will be 18 years old, I enroll you in a course.

-I want the course tomorrow.

-You still have to wait, little pilot. Close your eyes, I have a surprise.

He closes his eyes, stretches out his hands and waits. My little husband puts two pieces of papers in his hand.

-Can I open?

-Yes.

-What is this?

He looks at the tickets. He doesn't understand, he looks back with a question in his eyes.

-We and the boys are going to a vintage car show.

-What's that?

-Old cars are there.

-Super!

## Fragments of the Past

He jumps up and down in his excitement. He hugs his dad.
-And me? What about me?
I look at him with big kitty eyes.
-Honey, in the meantime, you can entertain yourself, or go shopping, or get a massage, or go with the chicks somewhere.
-You convinced me.

·····

Well, yes, whenever he could, he has taken him to many places. So, I just loved him even more. He always tried to do exciting programs with Ben. They also went to drive go-karts several times. The Formula One races they always watched together on TV, cheering loudly on their current favorite. I hope the strong father-son relationship between them can remain still. Unfortunately, it's up to Gabriel not me. I will make sure that this is successful, and that they do not move away from each other because of the current situation. The tale is slowly coming to an end.
- Mom, can I watch part 2?
-Yes, this is your day to rest.
As long as he is enchanted by the cars, I will start cooking. I'm making some light soup, second is tomato pasta. The two of us do not need a large portion, and the little patient's stomach is not advised now to have too fat, heavy food. Most of the evenings it feels like I have to do the cooking, so I tend to be reluctant to do it, but if I'm in the mood, I present more special dishes. I like to experiment. Anyway, I can make anything, but the cookbook sometimes comes in handy. I find it most convenient when you order food though. This saves you from leaning over the stove. You just pick something and do not take

hours from your life. Price often comes out the same as if you were buying the ingredients for the food you choose. I also miss going out to restaurants. Gabriel and I used to go out to dinner at least once every two weeks, while my mother took care of my little prince. We felt like we were dating again. I dressed up, we talked about all kinds of things, but as usual with parents, mostly about Ben. If I started dating a man again, I'd go out to a restaurant. The beginning phase is exciting, and the novelty charm is all-encompassing. But I don't want it now. In these types of cases, everyone shows their best side, they are promising false illusions. Then ... I built too many air castles anyway, I need no extra complications. It would be nice if I really accepted Mate's invitation. Hm ...

-Ready for lunch, wash your hands and sit down at the table.

-I'm coming.

We eat the food in silence. My little love is too silent.

-What's wrong? Does your stomach hurt again?

-No.

-Then?

- I'm a little sad.

-Why?

-Because I'd love to play with Dad with the cars now. I'd give him the favorite black sports car, which I always want. But now I would be with the red, which is like Lightning Mcqeen.

-Oh ..

-I know how bad is that you can't play with him right now.

-I have to tell him he'll come for him tomorrow, but I don't want to get him excited if Gabriel doesn't take him. Ok, I'll tell you since you already mentioned it.

# Fragments of the Past

-I have good news for you. Tomorrow Dad will take you with him, he will come for you and then you can play together.
-Really? Serious?
-Yes.

His face gets rosy immediately, he rushes into his room and I hear as he is searching. I'll go after him. He is packing his favorite cars in his favorite little bag. He stuffs at least twenty into it.

-Isn't it going to be a bit much?
-No. I don't know which one I want to play with.
-Good, as you wish. Don't want me to help you pack?
-Maybe.

We put into a bigger bag his pajamas, a change of clothes, coloring book, his favorite storybook. I hope I don't forget anything, but I think his father may have bought a couple of things for there too. I'm feeling bad because I will miss him much. I wouldn't let him go if I listened to my heart, but I have to. I don't want him to turn Ben against me or anything like that. Why did we have to get this far? I'm not missing this at all, but I know he needs his dad.

-What? I wasn't listening, sorry what did you say?
-Can we go to the pastry shop? I would love to eat a chocolate cake.
-Let's go. I, too will enjoy a bit of sweetness and we need some exercise too.

The pastry shop is located five streets away, surrounded by brownstones. Everybody from the area comes here to shop because the products are fresh, prices are affordable, the pastry is delicious. There is once again a long line waiting for eating a slice of calorie bomb. We get to the end of the line.

I hate to wait. I can only just hope that by the time we get there, the seats will become available. Ben is checking people out, I'm just lost in my thoughts as we move a few inches forward, my little one is pulling me. Finally, I order a creamcheesecake and he gets a chocolate cake. Not far from the cashier, one corner table has been freed up so we can occupy it quickly. We eat slowly, it's good to be out and just be together. He is just chatting about what he was arguing with his little friend at the kindergarten. All of a sudden someone pats me on my shoulder, I turn back reluctantly. Oh, no. Big brown curious eyes, long brown hair, the trendiest and most expensive clothes, chattering voice. It could be just one person, but her hair color was different.

-Hi Ann. Hi, Benny.

-Hi, Emma.

She smiles, so I feel I have to smile back. She sits down on one of the chairs.

-I was standing in line when I saw you. I thought I'd come here to say hello since we haven't met for thousands of years. How come you are here?

-We live here. Your new hair color is looking great but suddenly I couldn't recognize you.

-Thanks, sometimes we need a change.

-Where did you leave Gabriel? I haven't seen him for a long time.

-He's not with us anymore.

-What happened?

-Listen, I don't want to talk about this now. How are you anyways?

-I'm always in the hurry. You know how it goes. Chuck is out in the car waiting for me to pick up some pastry for Tommy's birthday.

-Happy birthday to him.

# Fragments of the Past

-Thanks. Don't you want to meet and chat tomorrow? We became so distant. I have time in the afternoons, we could meet sometime.
Wonderful. I have two choices. One is that I stifle myself into my pillow and alcohol alone at home, and the other one that I do it with someone at a bar. I choose the latter.

-I don't even have a plan yet so I'm game.

- Ole! Do you have the same number?

-Yes. Yours is the same too?

-Yeah. Let's talk in the morning. I'll call you and we'll figure out when to meet.

-Ok, bye.

-Bye.

She stands up and rushes through the door in a split second. She was always like this. She was always hyper, rushing everywhere, talking fast, and her favorite word was ole.

-Ole, ole, ole –Ben is chanting, swaying left and right.

-Ok sweetie, it's more than enough to hear this once.

-Will you meet her tomorrow?

-Looks like Mom, at least, goes out while you're away.

This plan is better now than nothing. At least I hope I don't regret it. On the way home we stop at our favorite playground. Big green space, the coolest toys are all here. As usual, it's packed with kids. Unfortunately, there are more kids than available toys. Parents are sitting around and talk to their parent friends, sometimes shouting at their kid if he is up to something no good. It's a strange little community. I think they ostracize you if you don't mingle with them, or if your kid isn't a friendly type or you're not very communicative. As if it were obligatory to make friends there and show a smiley face. I think, they usually share the ins and outs of parenting, which is nice, but they also gossip and are all ears. They are listening to the current gossip so they can talk about it the next day, make it very colorful, enlarge every detail. I heard things about myself, too, a lovely mom told me what they talk about me. Horrible. I'm not like that. That's not what I'm used to. We had our own garden, we played there. Our friends' children came there for fun, or sometimes the kids from the kindergarten. destroys a sand castle.

I see a bigger boy coming up to him and borrowing his black shovel. He gives it to him and they are ready to build together. We're here for an hour and a half. I'm already bored. I'll call my Mom.

-Hi Mom.

- Hi sweetie. How are you?

-As usual. Ben got sick last night, his stomach was hurting, he vomited, he was depressed, so I stayed with him today.

-He is doing better?

-Yes, thank God. Now we're on the playground, and before that we went to the pastry shop.

-You didn't give him too much food, did you?

-No. Mom, I know what to do in these types of cases.

-What will you do tomorrow afternoon since you will be alone?

- Can you imagine, I will be drinking and talking with Emma.

-Don't tell me that?

-I do. We ran into each other at the pastry shop and she asked if I wanted to meet her tomorrow. I said yes, because it is better than being home all alone.

-But…

# Fragments of the Past

-Mom, don't start. I know it too.

-Well. Be smart, and with Gabriel just be relaxed. Don't show him you're still crazy about him. After he is gone, or in the evening, if you have time call me. You have to get over this, and then each time gets easier, you'll see.

-Thanks, I'll try and will call you. Kisses.

-Kisses.

I'll pick up the little rascal, let's go home. On the way, we run into the store for a few little things. In the kitchen, I unpack everything I bought and start making dinner. I wish it would be tomorrow night, I'd be over with meeting Gabriel. Ben is bouncing around, running between the rooms, he is high energy now. I can't calm him down. It was not a good idea to tell him where he's going tomorrow.

-When will it be tomorrow morning? How many hours is till then?

-Many.

-But mom, I want to go now.

-You can't yet. Wait, be patient.

He starts pulling my clothes. He is whining.

-Come play then with me.

-I'm coming.

We bring out the Lego, I come up with new stories for him. This does not hold his attention either. I'll try something else.

-Should we draw?

-No.

-Should we play with Mr. Crabby and his friends?

-No.

-Are you hungry? You want to eat?

-No.

-What do you want than if nothing is good?

- Playing with Dad.

Tantrum. I'd love to scream at him but he doesn't deserve it because he is a kid and he senses everything differently. He doesn't understand the concept of time either. This is sometimes a blessing, sometimes a curse. Often, I would like to feel his heart and to see the world through his eyes. Kids are so pure. They have not yet been distorted and transformed by society, they do not want to look different from what they are... A wonderful few years are these for him.

-Tomorrow is approaching quickly. That's the last idea I come up with for him. Would you watch a story?
-Yes.

He falls onto the couch and I start to play Toy Story to him. He loves it.. He often pretends his favorite characters come to life. A few minutes of rest. I go out to the kitchen and eat my dinner. I can understand if he's not hungry. A big slice of cake after lunch. He'll eat later. I toss the food from right and left, with my fork I am drawing images on the plate. There is no one to talk to in the meantime, it's sad. I start to feel lonely. Of course, Ben is here for me, but it's a different emotion. I blame myself often for the current situation. It could have been otherwise, but maybe it would have been worse. Part of my soul died anyways. Now is the time of mourning. According to my psychologist, this will unfortunately be longer than I had hoped. I'm not trying to hurry anything. I have to go through all phases to be completely fine. I can't exactly tell where I am in the process, but it didn't start with the divorce, I'm sure.

## One Year Before Divorce

-Hey. It's so good you came. Ben is playing in his room, he's waiting for you.

He takes off his black jacket and throws it on the couch next to me. He leans over to me, but only gives a slight little kiss. He doesn't sit down beside me, he keeps

## Fragments of the Past

standing, he is looking tense. Poor thing.
-Now I'm not in the mood.
I step close, my closeness maybe soothes him.
-Is something wrong, honey? You look very tired, you came late.
I gently strike his face.
-No, it just took a long time to negotiate with the investors. The new project now consumes all my energy. You know what that means.
-What would you like to do? would you like to eat something?
-No, I've had dinner.
He is answering while pushing buttons on his phone. I hug him, maybe. He gently pushes me away.
-Why did you push me away?
-There's more to do, I'm just sending emails. It's important and you distract me.
I'm stepping away. I turn away my face, I don't want him to see that I am offended. I know when he has an important project, he is tense, and he handles it poorly, he usually projects his tension that builds up, on me. Maximalist and a workaholic. Difficult combination. In these cases, I have to let him be.
-Understand, I'm going to read.
He retires to his study, I continue to read my book on the couch. An hour later, I take Ben to the shower than I put him into bed. I got sleepy too, it's time for me to go to bed, too. I take a quick shower and get a robe. I peak into the office to see if he's going to join me. He is leaning over the laptop in deep concentration. He turned off the lights, pulled the curtains down, this way the room looks darker and more unfriendly. The walls are blue and all the furniture is black. There are abstract pictures on the walls.

Too modern and cold. Not my style. Next to it is a wine glass and a half-eaten chocolate bar. There are papers lying around him. But he always makes sure that there is order, everything has its place. The file holders are in alphabetical order on the shelf, and any clean-freak would envy his desk.

-Are you coming to sleep?
-No. I'm still staying up.
-Good night then.
-You, too.

I'm in bed alone, missing him. I'm watching TV for a bit, but my eyes are closing.

I can't wait for him to get into bed next to me and take me in his arms. At night, I wake up from a nightmare, I see he is not next to me. He's still working probably. I choose to sleep, keep my eyes closed, the feelings begin to fade. It was just a dream, just a dream. It was just a dream.

·····

I'm writing a message to Gabriel. Nothing fancy, I'll be on point. "I hope you will come because your son will be very disappointed."

-Hey. Will you come for Ben tomorrow? The answer will come in a minute.
-Hey. I'll be there by 11.
-Amazing. Be calm, calm, calm. I already have stomach cramps, what can I expect tomorrow? The story is over, I go into the living room.
-Are you hungry?
- No, Mom.
- Okay, then we go for a bath. You need to get to bed early to get some rest, because tomorrow Dad will come for you.

# Fragments of the Past

-Then hurry.
We never got to bed this fast ever. I'm covering him and climb into bed next to him.
-Should I tell you a story or read from a book?
-A book...
I'm starting to read Peter Pan to him. I'm half-way when he falls asleep. I turn on the night light, sneak out and am about to take a bath. I also wash my hair and apply a moisturizing facial wrap. Meanwhile I iron some clothes. I hate it. From all the house chores I hate this one the most. Let's say the quantity has dropped significantly, since Gabriel's shirts and suits are no longer are my concern. The cream has completely dried on my face by the time I finish. I brush my teeth and jump into my pajamas. The ironed and washed clothes I put in the closets. That reminds me of what to wear tomorrow? I can't be a sloppy, but I can't be too sexy either. It's not a date, but I want him to see how good I look. This is what my self-esteem needs. Notice, I didn't slip into self-pity so much that I wouldn't give up on myself. I'm a strong, beautiful, independent woman who might go crazy about seeing her ex. No, I don't even like to look at clothes right now, and in the morning I'll decide what I'm going to wear. I'm getting into the cold bed. I have to force my mind not to spin. I have to rest. No way. Okay. I'm going to count sheep, cute white jumping puppies. That'll work. 1,2,3,4,5 ... 200... The cruel beeping of my alarm clock makes me jump out of bed. Now I don't need to snooze like other mornings. It is promising to be an eventful day, but it's just one of many. I had worse. For instance, the day of moving or divorce. Ok, I can't start thinking about the past right now. It's over. I'm trying to

positively embrace this damn day.

    Ben will be with his dad, I'll step out of the house, I can be alone. It will not work. Still terrible. I turn on my favorite musical number, set it to repeat. Not too loud to avoid being heard in the other room. I open my wardrobe, it's time to choose my outfit. Black is too sad, pink is too cute, red is too defiant. I push the hangers around but nothing catches my eye. He knows almost all of them. I need something that is perfect for meeting Emma in the afternoon. Got it. I lay my eye on my favorite royal blue outfit. It is knee-length, has a belt at the waist and a finger over my elbow. It highlights the beautiful curve of my waist. Dress check. But I'll wear it later. I leave my hair out, but I create soft waves with the iron. Well done. I do not overdo my makeup, it should be pleasant and almost invisible. Primer, eyelid, mascara and nude lipstick. I'm ready. I wake Ben up to have breakfast. He sits down by the table and feverishly gobbles up two pieces of bread with milk. After he's done, I'll get him dressed. Thank goodness we packed up yesterday. I look at the clock, it only shows 10 am. We still have one hour. I decide to dress up. I choose a blue stone earrings and necklace for jewelry. I look great, I think. I still have my inside slippers on my feet, but I can't be in high heels at home. A little weird for the dress, but still better. My phone's display says 10. 15 am. Time is not passing. I have to keep myself busy until then. I'm tidying up Ben's room. Damn it is still only 10.20 a.m. I don't want to eat because I still have nausea. Time is just inching forward, although other times it rushes 10:30. This is not true. I'm sitting upon the chair like a dove. Ben is watching his stories. My phone is ringing.

    -Hey Ann. Didn't wake you up, did I?
    -Hey, no, I've been up a for a while.

# Fragments of the Past

-I told you I will call you. Where should we meet? Want to have something for lunch too?

-Yes. Let's meet at Pepita restaurant where we used to. Does that work for you?

-Of course. Then we go over to one of the bars.

-Good, then one pm. Bye, Emma.

-Bye.

I'll hang up the phone 10:35 a.m. It's incredible. I get up from the table and make some coffee. Even this is getting done too quickly. As slowly as I can, I sip. My stomach is lifting up and down. I sweat. I look over the apartment to see if there is mess somewhere. I put a few things away, but that's it. Needless to say, I'm not calling him, he's not coming home. The bell is ringing. 10:59. Of course, he's always on time. I ask Ben to turn off the story. He is rushing beside me. I look into the mirror in the hallway. It's acceptable. Huh. With my sweaty palms, I grab the handle and open the door. Ben immediately jumps into his father's arms, he holds him. They hug each other for a long time and then he puts him down. He looks at me.

-Hey.

I should say something. Just a greeting. I can do that.

-Hey.

It was a bit too quiet. Now I'm looking at him closer. He looks tired, with circles under his eyes. He wears jeans, a black shirt, and matching black shoes. His hair is shorter than it was. But it's perfect in appearance. His posture does not show the usual confidence. He puts his hands in his pocket, stepping from one foot to the other, checking me out. Don't check me out. He looks from bottom to top, then his gaze settles on the lips. It reminds me the way he used to look at me when he wanted me. His lips slightly open. It can't be, I misread something. We are looking at each other... but for what?

I'm not breaking the awkward silence for sure.
-You look great.
-Thanks.

Are you surprised? You were expecting a wreck to open the door. You're mistaken. I see he wants to ask something. He takes one step toward me, I step back.

-How are you?
-Well. - I squeeze out a half smile. And you?

I see the sadness in his eyes flickering but who cares. Just be sad. He deserves it.

-I'm fine.

He says so sadly. He bows his head like a sad dog. Fortunately, Ben saves me from this awkward moment. He begins nudging Gabriel's arm.

-Dad, are we finally going?
-Yes.

I go into the apartment and bring his little bag and the bigger one. My heart is about to pop out of its place. I take Gabriel's belongings in my hands, carefully, try not to accidentally touch them.

-I packed a whole bunch of stuff in the bags, I hope you got everything you could need. There is no toothbrush cause I thought you bought one, but if not I bring it now.- I don't need it. I've got a couple of things, just for when he's with me.

-And what are you going to do?
-We'll eat somewhere, then we'll go to see a movie and later whatever we like.

-Understand. Before bedtime, please put him in a bath and make sure he pees. Read him a story, too. Yeah, and don't forget the night light. And in the morning

-Ann, he is my son too. I know everything, don't worry.

# Fragments of the Past

I hug Ben as if I was seeing him for the last time. I give him thousand kisses.

-I love you baby.

His face is so happy, I'm about to cry. I swallow my tears. Gabriel puts the bags down and touches my shoulder. He wants to comfort me. He strokes me and leans slightly closer to my neck as I lean closer. I can smell his perfume. Not this. It's all too familiar, yet alien. I instinctively shrug my shoulders. That makes him realize the moment. He moves his hand. And turns away. Me too. I can't look at him, I don't want to see his gaze, because then who knows what I would read. Let's wrap up the situation. I want to go inside, cry and scream. I say good-bye.

-See you tomorrow. Take care of yourself. Have fun with Dad. If anything wrong, just call me right away.

I have to say goodbye to him too. Deep breath.

-Bye Gabriel.

-Bye Ann, he almost whispers.

They go down the stairs, a terribly painful sight. I am left alone. I walk into the apartment before I collapse from all the stress. I fall onto the ground. I feel suffocated, I feel a lump in my throat and my chest tightens. I'm starting to tremble. I feel helpless. I press my face firmly against the floor, my body collapsing. I can't let the panic attack come over me again. I have to calm down ... It's good to be just laying here. I feel the lump is getting smaller in my throat , my tears running all the way down to my neck. A warm feeling. Can I sink lower than that? ... My body is forcing me to finally get up from this cold place because I'm shivering. I don't want. I wish I could stay here all day. It can not hurt that much. I am so weak. My son's in good hands with him. I know that, but it stirs me up to see him again.

When I was together with him, even if the last period was bad, at least I knew what was going to happen tomorrow. Same as yesterday. Painful, suffocating but always still water. Now everything is uncertain ... I'm strong, I'm strong, I'm strong ... I'm getting up. I stretch out my limbs. I look at the clock. 12:15. I have to go to the meeting. I refresh my makeup, put on my high heels and take my bag with me. I don't have time for more. In the car, I turn the music on maximum volume - Eminem: "Love The Way You Lie" - and until I get there, I have it playing loud ... I've been in this restaurant long time ago. It is in the center of downtown, an elegant, quite upscale place. I am neither hungry nor thirsty. I don't feel like anything. It takes me a quarter of an hour to park my car, but I still have to walk three streets back. The air refreshes me. Entering the door, I see that the restaurant is full. The whole place is black and white. You would think it is distracting, but its not. It's rather clean-cut. Silver chandeliers hang from the ceiling. The furniture is modern, with large white round tables scattered throughout the room, the floor is black stone. The ornaments are the same.. Fortunately, they leave enough space between the tables, so they whole spot feels spacious. In addition, five boxes are available if you want to hide away. Silent lounge music is coming from the players. Pleasant. I take a look around to see where Emma could be. I don't see her by the tables, so I walk towards the boxes. She's sitting in one of them.

 -Hey.
 -Hey Ann. You look pretty.
 -You too.

 She is wearing a yellow dress and has her hair tied up. The jewelry is elegant, on her, expensive. We don't kiss each other, I just simply sit down across from her.

# Fragments of the Past

The waiter immediately appears. She orders a soup and a second dish. I only order a tomato soup with mozzarella balls. I gotta eat something.

-I'm glad we ran into each other last time, we'll finally have a chance to talk. How long have we not?

As if she didn't know, but I answer.

-More than three months.

- It's been a long time.

-Sure. Why did you want to meet? I thought after what happened you would realize that we would never be the same close friends again. We can spend time together as two old acquaintances, we can chat, but you need to remember, that's it.

-Ole, you always get to the point.

-It is always best to clarify, start with the embarrassing situations head on.

-I wanted to explain to you, believe me. I just didn't know how.

I raise my eyebrows. You could have tried. I'll be curious to hear that.

-I didn't support him. He didn't tell me what he was up to. If I knew I would have tried to stop him. But

-Indeed?

-Yes.

-It doesn't change the facts, Emma.

-I know. I'm sorry.

-And you really didn't know or did not hear about that we were breaking up?

- Just at the gossip level, but I didn't believe it. You were so good together. Gabriel also cut off communication with Chuck roughly a month ago.

-Why?

-Chuck said that he told him one morning

that he did not want to see each other anymore and that their business relationship was over. He didn't explain it deeper.

-This is weird.

-It was. When did you get divorced?

-Almost three weeks ago, but even before that we separated, that's how we could meet in that pastry shop. It's still fresh.

-How are you holding up?

- Surprisingly well.

It's none of her business how I'm doing. She has no business knowing about my struggle.

-Tommy already misses Ben. We should arrange getting them together sometime soon.

-Ok. Now tell me. What has happened to you since I haven't seen you?

They are just bringing out our soups so she can't answer right away. We both dip our spoons into the soups. It's quite delicious, although it could have more spice.

-I opened another clothing store. Do you believe this? The third one. You could come and check it out. Chuck started a new venture, and Tommy started to go to karate.

-This is amazing. How does he handle all these after school activities?

-He loves it. You know, he's like me. He is hyper, can't stay in one place for a long time.

Yeah, all three of you are wonderful ... We just ate our soups. The waiter is taking the plates, but here comes Emma's pasta.

-Are you used to your new apartment? Don't miss your house?

-Yes I do. Moving from a house with garden to a regular apartment is a sacrifice. I feel squeezed like a matchstick in the box.

## Fragments of the Past

-I understand. Ben likes the new kindergarten?
-Luckily. And we can see his friends in a different settings.
-Do you have any help? All alone, I wouldn't be able to do it.
-My Mom.
-Of course. Hats off for doing it alone.
-Need to. What is most importantly is Ben.
-How often do you meet Gabriel?
-Every two weekends. He took Ben today so I could meet you now.
-Ole. You see, it has it's upside.

Of course, you don't even know what you're talking about. You should face the same problems and try to solve everything as I do. We are silent for a few minutes while she is finishing what's left of her pasta.

-I'm done We can leave for the bar.
-Which one should we go to?
-To the "Green."
-Ok, though it's a little early to start to drink.
-Ann, it's Saturday. Nothing is early.
-I did not realize.
-What?
-That we're going to drink and I don't know what to do with my car. I drove here.
-You'll drive home.
-Are you joking? Drunk?
-I usually do that.
-Well I'm not surprised. I will not. I'd rather not go.
-But come on. It will be good for you I can feel that. You'll be back for your car tomorrow afternoon. Come on. Just two drinks and you can take a taxi home. You were not able to relax for a long time now.

-Ok, it would really help me and I could possibly manage to get more info out of her.
-But then you leave your car here too. You can't be drunk behind the wheel. Don't be stupid.
-Good. If this is the only way you come. I'll call Chuck to pick me up. He will.
-Let's go.
-Ole.

Just don't say this word again, it drives me crazy. I would be happy to tell her that but I don't. After today, I don't want to see her again, so what for. I want to shut things down with her, too. We walk to the place. The bar is two storeys high, we hung out here with Emma several times. The upper part is the VIP section. Nothing special about it. Long bar counters and fewer tables. Plenty of large green plants are placed everywhere, making it cozy. The walls are green and beige. Because it is afternoon, it has not yet been populated. There can be a maximum of 20 people around. I feel a bit awkward that I drink so early. I know I shouldn't care about who thinks and what. I'm drinking in the afternoon period. We settle on a table next to the bar. I'm asking for my favorite cosmopolitan, Emma is getting mojito. I taste it. Yummy as always. Not overly strong.

-You never want to try another cocktail?
-If something works, why would I replace it. I don't like experimenting with drinks.
-There's truth in it. I do like experimenting, just like with my clothes. No wonder I studied to be a designer. And you're so full of yourself, I don't even know how did I endured you so far.
-And tell me you still have someone else outside of Chuck?
-Well, there is . Only you were always monogamous.

## Fragments of the Past

-I see the athlete most of the time. But sometimes it's a different person.
 -Aren't you afraid of getting caught?
 -It can't happen, Chuck is crazy for me. He also never at home. You witnessed that, too. Good combo.
 -Main thing is confidence. Do you still love him?
 -Who?
 -Chuck.
 - Love is gone, but we are good together. I'll get the extras somewhere else you know ... I'm out of drink, so I bring us another round.
 She drank it quickly. She gets up and hurries to the counter. Overwhelming. When we used to get together I used to like the juicy stories of how she hooked up with her current boytoy. And what kind of stuff they do. They used to meet thorugh her kid's private lessons, or I should say, still do. They always met in the guys' apartment or sometimes in a hotel. I could tell all Chuck what I know, but I'm not going to betray her. I have no right to interfere with their life. Sometimes I envied her, but I despised this whole thing, too, because it disrespected marriage. No, her husband, Chuck is blind. I better not judge others. Unfortunately, I can imagine they had and have a good reason. We also pretended in front of others that everything was fine with our marriage. They have been perfectly functional white liars for years. They swiped everything under the rug. That's also how people can live side by side. Maybe it's still better than abusing each other.
 -Ole, I'm here with the next serving. Drink it! She forces mine into my hand.

-Ok, I'm drinking. Tell me some fresh juicy story.

At least she'll talk about herself. I'm waiting for the right moment.

-You want to envy me?

She smiles. She pulls her chair closer as if anyone could hear what she is saying.

-Maybe.

-You know me. I do like extreme sex too. So, once I got to the hotel purposely earlier than the guy. I wanted to something more unusual. And do something new. I took a leather costume with me, kind a slutty. Black shoes with very high heels. I slipped into it. I looked like a domina. Grrr... I also brought some accessories. A whip, handcuffs and a new attachable dildo. I waited for him sitting on the bed. He immediately threw himself on me. Not surprised. I took his hand and ordered him to undress. He did. I asked him to call me mistress. He was a good boy, so I let him eat me out.

-And then?

-Well, there was everything. I got on top of him and rode him, I handcuffed him to the bed. I was playing with his brain. I sucked his cock. I didn't let him cum. Finally I tried the dildo on him.

-What did you do?

-Just what you hear.

-Good, don't want to know all the details. It probably was humiliating.

-He enjoyed it. In sex, there is no taboo between us.

- You should try it.
- To fuck my next guy?
- No, it's not you.

-Then?

## Fragments of the Past

   -To push your own limits. And if both parties are enjoying, then there is no problem. You're a prude.
   -Not really. We also used toys, but nothing like that.
   I drink my cocktail quickly. She drinks up hers too. For Emma it's needed, a very interesting woman. Whatever she knows is always the best and what she does should be an example to follow. She will find your weak point, and use it to her advantage.
   -You may have been not enough anymore for Gabriel.
   I must have heard incorrectly. I drank a lot, I misheard it, cause I'm aging.
   -What?
   My eyes opened up wide immediately.
   -You heard that right.
I'm about to slap her. If one could be killed with a gaze, she would be dead. I stand up.
   -How dare you? Who do you think you are? Are you aware that
   -Oh, Ann. You're naive and you always were.
She shrugs her shoulder, superiority radiates from her face. She looks down on me, I can feel it.
   -You could have kept him, right?
   -Yes, I could have kept him.
I am about to explode. I hit her. I lift my right hand and it moves by itself. By the time I realize it, I've already slapped her. I shout.
   -Go to hell! I never want to see you again in my life, neither you nor your family! I thought
She jumped up, too. We stare at each other, the tension is unbearable.
   -What?
   -Let's not waste any words on each other! You're a cheap slut and you will always be!

I turn around and am not waiting to any reaction. Would love to hit her again. I'm leaving the bar. Walking slowly, majestically. Where should I go? This can not be true. I was stupid for coming here. What did I expect? I thought I could get some info I wanted to know. Home? No. I'll go somewhere. I walk a few streets until I see another bar. This is downtown, there will be plenty of open bars. My leg hurts in the nice high heels. I walked three streets. People are walking around, talking, laughing. Couples are holding each others hands. They enjoy the day. Brr .. Finally. A little secluded spot in the side street. I enter. There's no one inside outside of the bartender. I wonder why? The place is pretty rundown, but it'll do now. Scrappy looking chairs, graffiti on the walls, crappy music, weird smells. I imagine what characters going on debauchery here.

-Hey, I want a cosmopolitan.

-Hello. There's nothing like this here, I can only serve hard liqor, cutie!

What I imagined.

-Then a whiskey please.

-We have that.

He looks at me with boredom. I'm like a pink dot on a surface among many blacks. It doesn't fit there. I pay him and find the table farthest away from him. I feel like a looser. My plan failed, I'm feeling worse than after the morning meeting. All right, the panic attack is a bit different. This whiskey is strong. My throat is already burning. On top of everything, I drink it after the two cosmopolitan. Bold, I don't mix usual. It will hit. Besides, I ate almost nothing. I made sure Emma would never reach out to me again. I should have slapped her a long time ago. In essence, I successfully scare everyone away. Or just not the right people surrounding me?

## Fragments of the Past

Who knows. Anyone but a loser would not drink on Saturday afternoon. Do I have a problem? I trust everyone and then they push me over. I don't have a real good girlfriend. Monique? Forget it. Emma? She never was. From now on, I'll pick the good ones. When I was with Gabriel he filled my days and I spent most of my time doing housework and raising my child. I didn't miss a girlfriend much. Now I do. Talking with a true girlfriend for hours honestly. But I can't rely on anyone else. I don't go to see my psychologist anymore. Money is wasted, my panic attacks are are coming even when I see her. I need to heal my little wounded soul myself. The first whiskey went down already. One more please. Time is passing. I feel like I'm drunk. I feel hot already, unable to divert my thoughts to one direction. One can see it from the outside. I'm probably blushing. What does the bartender think of me? A down-on-her-luck lonely thirty something. That's true. I'll drink the rest quickly, head home. Fuck, I can't drive the car. I get up from my chair, I'm a little dizzy, but at least my anger is gone. I don't think my steps are straight. The bus stop is close so I don't have to expose myself in public in such a state for long. The busride takes longer to get home, and I don't have a seat. My stomach is upset and the smell of alcohol was pouring out of me. Half an hour later, I'm finally out of this horror vehicle. A few steps to the house. But why so many? I dig in my bag for my key, I can't find it. The large front door is open. I'll go in there. I don't care about my key right now. I'll get through the door. Stairs. Oh, no. One-two-four-seven. Infinitely long. How long has it been? On what floor do I live on? I need to lean to the wall. Supercool. Everything revolves. I stumble upwards. What did I want anyways?

Yeah, get to my apartment. It's just one turn and I'm there. What the hell? Would I be smashed that much? Yes, I am. I don't believe my eyes. He is sitting in front of my door and looks very much like someone.

-Peter?
-Hey. It's me.
-What are you doing here now?

I can't stand straight, fighting for my keys. They must be hidden at the bottom of my bag.

-I'll help.

Without my consent, he takes my bag out of my hand, finds the keys and opens the numerous locks.

-Are you afraid of something, that's why so many locks?
-From you.

Damn, I said that out loud.

-That is, from burglars, we used to have an alarm. Thanks for opening the door, goodbye. Sweet Dreams. I'll go inside. He stops me, puts his arms around me.

-You don't get rid of me now. Why do you think I'm here?
-You are bored you have nothing better to do.
-You are funny, as always Ann. We will talk now.
-You can command someone else, but not me. No, and that's final.

He doesn't care about my argument. What's up with him? He pushes me inside the apartment, he comes in and closes the door. He takes off my shoes, puts my bag down, and he gets rid of his. We are standing around in the hallway. I'm glad I made some cleaning earlier.

-Since you were so aggressive welcome in my house. Feel free have a tour in the apartment, but there is no guide.
-Are you drunk?

# Fragments of the Past

-You got it big boy. You are an intruder, an aggressor, a liar, a pompous person who thinks he is the king of the jungle , it's hard to get rid of you, a handsome person.

-It was nice, now it's my turn.

-You Ann, you are an unforgettable, annoying, childish, timid, self-confident, wounded, beautiful woman. Whom I need.

Amazing. This is normal? What does he want? Ok, I'll neglect it. Let him stand alone there for the night. As if he wasn't here. I need to shower. He can do what he wants. He shouldn't be here either.

-I'm going to take a shower, find the couch, or do whatever you want.

-Indeed?

-Yes.

I'm going to the bathroom. This evening is terrible. I hope he leaves. I do not need him. I'll let the water run. Dazed. I'll take my jewelry off. I put my have my hair up. The door opens.

-Get out.

-No.

-I say so.

He grabs my two hands, holds me down. Male power.

-Do not fight. I'll bathe you. It'll help you.

He begins to undress me. Didn't he just talk about bathing me? He slowly takes off his green T-shirt. Oh my God, I can't stand this. I could watch this every day. He is taking off his socks, pants. The white boxer too. Jee.
I stare at his perfection. He is so beautiful.

-Your turn.

He squats in front of me. Slowly stroking my feet with his hands. Carefully peels off the blue dress from me. Oh, no. I enjoy this. No more escape. I'm standing there in my panties and bra. He steps behind me and unhooks my bra.

-Ann, you drive me… crazy! That's what I want!

He leans over and starts to pull off my thong with his teeth. He accompanies it with kisses. I desire sex much more from alcohol. My body is on fire, I'm melting from the touch, I step out of the thong. He looks at me as if he wants to tear me apart. He wants to devour me with his eyes, eager. I don't touch him, I have to stop somehow. I don't want him drunk. No and no. He ruffles his brown hair and grabs his neck.

-Hmm… come on and I'll bathe you now.
I don't mind. We enter my big tub. We sit down, he settles behind me. With warm water he sprinkles my body and then his own.

-Relax.

He starts massaging my shoulders. I bend my head back. I lean on him. Do it a little more, I'm going to calm down. It feels so good. He takes a small amount of chocolate bathing foam and puts some on my two breasts simultaneously. My nipples immediately show him the results. He grabs them and takes them in his palms. Just squeezes them tight. I feel he is ready, his body is pressed to me.

-I can't stand it, my beautiful. I've never wanted anyone like you before.

He kisses my neck, panting in my ears. He flows the sponge bath foam over my back, slowly rubs on it, then on my stomach, very thoroughly. No … Now my pussy is next. I am cray with desire for him to touch it. I'm pushing my body against him, sexual tension is palpable. There is only two of us, our heart beats at the same pace. Can it be a little good for both of us? That's allowed… I don't cross

## Fragments of the Past

any big border line with that. Toying with his cock at my back. I'd sit up but he stops me.

-Not yet. Turn around.

I turn to him. We are facing each other. Can't touch my pussy ... Oh how much ... His size is ideal, I watch him holding it in his handing, pull it up and down. This private number is only mine. He is playing, waiting. He looks defiant. Licks his lips. That sight is worth everything.

-Wow... this is... Now it's my turn. I take my hand from the sponge bath and apply it to his chest. I go down in circular motions. Slowly, taking my time. Torturing. He moans. I don't give him the pleasure of going down, even though I want it to. I'll continue with my hands. Next is the right side. The shoulder and then I get to his fingers. I take the index finger into my mouth, only the tip. I start licking, gently, like ice cream.

-Don't do this. I'm gonna lose my mind and oh yeah ..

I won't let you talk any more. I see his jerking his cock I take his finger deeper and start sucking and sucking. It's yummy. We are moving to the same rhythm. How erotic. I am really worked up. I am touching myself, my performance comes.

-Do it. I want to watch you. I want to cum from watching you, and you will cum from seeing what you do to me.

We are panting. We seem to run out of air in the bathroom. I see nothing but him. Just one more move and I cum just like him. He grabs my hand and places it on his hard dick and puts his hand on my pussy. Heavenly.

- Let's cum at the same time.

He puts his two fingers into me, we move our hands in one rhythm. We look at each other, it's crazy that I don't have his cock in me. It is a sweet delight for both of us. I don't even know whose panting I hear. Too good, too different, too much.

-I almost am...

His voice changed, his body trembling, mine too. Everything disappears, I simply am flying... We clean each other, I wipe him, and we come out of the bath naked. After a few minutes of cuddling, I snuggle up next to him on the couch. I don't...

-Ann, now... nothing else is missing.

That's what I want to do with you every day.

-Peter, it doesn't work. I was irresponsible now cause I was drunk but that's it. It wouldn't work. You have Monique anyway, and I don't want that. Not like this.

I get up and am going to get my clothes. He is following. He is looking at me confused.

-What are you talking about? You think I took Monique to bed?

-Don't play the innocent.

-Nothing happened between us. She is not my type. That's what I wanted to explain to you. Let me.

-I'm listening.

I get dressed, he picks his clothes up too. I am sitting on the bed, he is standing, walking up and down. All my focus is on him.

-We went to dinner because she kept asking me a bunch of times. I said yes because I wanted to know more about you. That's it. I asked her all about you. Then I got her in a taxi and she went home.

-She said she went up to your apartment. Your villa in Rose Garden because you invited her for a rendezvous as well. Yeah, and she stated that you have been

## Fragments of the Past

inviting her back to dates since then. And that you went to work out together, and to visit your grandparents abroad, and that swept you off your feet.

-I could have guessed.

-What do you mean?

-Monique is nuts. She made all it up to rip us apart and so you get disillusioned about me. Hate me.

-That is impossible. She is a girlfriend of mine. I told her she could meet you because I don't know what I want from you yet and she liked you a lot. I wanted to give you two a chance to be happy together. But I can't believe that. You met her, you had meals together. You gave her the basis for all this.

-But that's it. I told her about my grandparents and where I live and where I go to work out. She made up the rest.

-Why?

-Because I didn't care about her. She noticed that I was just there for you. I inquired about you, I knew your girlfriend could tell me a lot about you. She couldn't bear to be rejected. Revenge.

-It's disgusting. To make such things up. Unfortunately, her plan was successful.

-I have noticed. I would not have been able to bear it if this would have break us up. I had to explain the situation to you.

-Good.

-What's good?

-I believe you. I think. But I can't really trust any man anymore.

-How can I prove I'm telling the truth?... I need you.

He holds my hand.

-You know yourself, you've had many adventures. Women are after you. Monique is very pretty. You are a man, and when we know what stands, the mind rests. I had some disappointments in my life.

-You didn't give us both a chance.

-I know.

-Let's date.

I don't want to overthink this now. Here's the chance. It may be worth a try. On Monday, I will be discussing this issue with Monique, and that will give me more confirmation.

-All right.

He throws a kiss. Very gentle, not too intrusive.

-Finally.

-Say something that is in your living room, striking or distinctive.

-I like your way of thinking. I have a big sculpture next to the sofa that depicts a female body. Conspicuous.

-I wasn't surprised. Typical. This will be good.

-Why do you say that ? The female body is real art. For example, yours is one.

He grabs my waist and pushes me down on the bed. His eyes have that little sparkle. I shrug him off and give him a kiss on his unshaven face.

-Enough. Come on, you sculptor. I'll make some quick dinner.

I pull him up from the bed. We go out to the kitchen touching each other. He doesn't even want to let me go.

-What shall I cook? I tell you the options that are quick 1. carbonara 2.milano 3. sandwich

-Carbonara. Do you have wine? I didn't dare bring, you would have misunderstood my intentions.

# Fragments of the Past

-For sure. Yes, on the shelf above. Take one that is sympathetic and pour. You'll find the glasses in the closet next to it. And look the corkscrew is right next to it. I don't dare to drink much in light of what happened in the past few hours. As he is taking out the things he is constantly touching and pressing himself to me. He kisses my shoulder. He smells me and enjoying the fragrances. I missed this so much. I like him to be in my kitchen. I like him being here. I can't and I don't want to be a kitty yet. Just pamper me, show me your feelings if they really are there. In time, I will open up more. I hope so.

-Your apartment is nice. It expresses you.

-Thanks, like how?

-Simple, clean, homely and such a delicious scent everywhere. One would love to stay here, it's peaceful.

-You should see when Ben is in a fiery mood.

-He is with his father now, isn't he?

-Yes, he took him today. That's where all the bad things started on this terrible day. Nothing panned out as I hoped. He pours the wine, puts it on the table, then sits down and looks at me. I put the pasta on the cooker and chop the ham. I'll have the sauce soon ready too. Suddenly he grabs me and sits me on his lap.

-Hey.

-Tell me, is it still a bad day that I'm here? Stroking the curve of my face. He has an attractive scent. I'd kiss him, but I won't.

-It is better this way. You divert my attention.

-About what?

-About my ex-husband, my ex-girlfriend, the fact that Ben is not here. By the way, how did you know I would be home alone? Or did you just come here by chance? What if Ben would have been home?

How long have you been waiting?

-That's a lot of questions at once.

-I know, but let go of me or else you will go hungry.

-Good if you have to. I knew Ben wouldn't be home. I've been waiting here for two hours now, boredom has almost killed me. I would have waited for you at your door for any amount of time. And I'd love to get to know Ben, if you let me.

-Who told you?

-You told me about it during our weekend together. I remembered.

-I forgot.

-Shall we forget the past, my beautiful? Let's start with a clean slate.

He offers his hand.

-I'm doctor Peter Pataky, 33 years old, single, with a background of strict parents, a lot of bad experiences, by the way, I'm crazy for you.

I extend my hand too.

-Ann Daray, 29 years old, divorced, mother of a child, a lot of bad experiences, by the way, the pasta is ready.

We shake hands playfully, good to see his beautiful smile. I flash him a smile, too. I serve dinner. I take the food out. I light a scented candle for the mood.

-Thanks, looks good. Next time I'll take you to a restaurant.

-All right. Enjoy your meal.

-You too.

We often steal gazes from each other while eating, I'm enjoying his attention. I didn't think this afternoon that the evening was going to turn out like this.

-Tell me what was most terrible today? How did you get drunk?

# Fragments of the Past

-Ben left before noon. Weird situation. I've seen my ex for the first time since our divorce. After that, I met one of my longtime friends I had lunch with her and had a drink in a downtown bar. She drove me crazy so I slapped her in the face and walked away. It was a good feeling. Finally, I drank all alone in a no-name pub. All of these, both individually and in sum, were terrible. And at the end of the day, you were waiting for me here. And I drove home drunk. This is not me.

-You were cute and then daring and wild. Why did you slap your friend? Who is she?

-You're lying but it's fine. Her name is Emma. The wife of Gabriel's business partner. We used to get together in the past, our kids are the same age, and we used to have a lot of fun – chick entertainment. Completely different character than me, but she's entertaining. Until now, unfortunately, I didn't realize how much she could hate me. How this relationship was only a matter of convenience for her? The bottom line is that we had a break in our relationship three months ago. It was disgusting. Today I got the full picture of what it was that day. So, I met her in the afternoon, hoping she would tell things herself. There was no time for this because she said I couldn't keep my husband, I'm naive, she would have succeeded. Forget it.

-What was three months ago?

-Enough to say now, that's when my heart broke apart for good.

-I'm sorry.

-No, it's better to see clearly, for some reason it must have happened. We always get answers to why later, but again, it will turn out.

We break our dough and go into the living room with wine. I turn on soft jazz music, now it's Nina Simone's Feeling Good song, I really enjoy listening to jazz. Only minimal lighting remains on. We only gaze for a minute at each other ... But I'm curious about a lot, so I have to break this magic.

-I've talked a lot this evening, I'm curious about you. How about an unpleasant topic. Former relationships. However, it is better to clarify something at the beginning. If I allow you into my life in any form, I expect you to be completely honest.

-I understand. So it will be. Let's start. I was 16 when I lost my virginity. It was a teenager's love, lasting a few months. It was a full purple haze. After that, no one was serious, but I did not long for love again. I went to university, lots of mischief. Studying, parties, booze, sex. I seduced a lot of girls into my bed. We competed on who succeeded more. I used them, now I wouldn't. After college, my bed was always warmed up. There was only one girl I had cared about at that time. She stayed with me for 2 years. At that time, I was building my career, staying little at home. Everything else was more important than creating a family nest. I couldn't really love her. The career was over, and we were getting distant and letting it go. Since then, I've had some superficial adventures, and then I met you and since then I do not want anything else.

- Did you regret letting her go?
-Yeah, but I learned from it.
-What?
-I know how to appreciate what she could have done. Security, home, true love. In the past, I didn't need that. Now yes. You caught me.

# Fragments of the Past

-How romantic someone has become. Is the skirt chaser getting on the right track?
-You and your reposts.
-Did you see this in me?
-Yes. You're different than what I've been dealing with so far.
-Uglier? Fatter? More Divorced? more hurt?
I put the accent on the end of the words.
-No. More beautiful, smarter, kinder, more erotic, more complex, more inferiority complex.
He also adopts my style while smiling and holding his head.
-Do not smile. Not funny.
-You made a joke of it, Ann.
-You look like a lone wolf me.
-I said, I was bored. I want permanence.
-How do you see yourself in the future?
-With you, as a real family. I said it on the meadow.
-These are phrases you don't really think about. At the moment, the desire drives you because you haven't got me yet. I'm not stupid. That's what every woman wants to hear. Words too nice. There may be truth in what you say, but it hasn't been possible for you to develop in such a short time. Don't say what you think I want to hear. You know I got out of a marriage, obviously I'm starving for an adventure, you've already figured it out. But that wouldn't be enough for me, you sense it right. That's why you talk like that. That's right. Somewhere, You are not far from the truth, but you will not...
-Enough.
-Truth hurts?

-No. Don't be cynical, don't try to explain what I feel about you. You have a lot of hurt, so you don't believe me. Look into my eyes. What do you see?

-Warm brown pretty eyes.

-You dare not really see me, but you will.

-Peter,

-We'll make small steps.

I don't answer that, I hug him instead.

-I'll give you a massage Beautiful.

-I'm not sure if it's a good idea.

-Why?

-Because we shouldn't excite each other again. The less physical contact the better.

-I feel like we could fall for each other at any time.

-This is true. Then do it, but nothing extra touching. Just a strict massage.

I'll get some oil to lubricate. I lie down on the carpet, leaving the seductive lingerie on me. Of course, black lace. Pleasant jazz that just adds to the mood. First he drips the oil over my body. He starts with my neck. Massage with gentle movements. My shoulders and then my hands are next. He has a strong hand, but he can give delicate erotic movements. He continues in a spiral line along my spine. He works too long at my waist and at the curve of my butt. He starts kneading my butt like a dough, passing through my inner thigh. I can only concentrate on the throbbing of my pussy. It doesn't reach that point, but circles around it. Then he raises my head with the other hand, gently pulls my hair, then pulls me to him and kisses me with passion. Starving, rough. Contrary to the subtlety of his hands, he has a demanding tongue. Turns me into doggie.

-How desirable and beautiful you are. I love your feminine lines.

# Fragments of the Past

He goes down my thigh with his hands to the bottom of my feet. He stays there. Than he goes backwards, but skips my butt and other parts. Lies down, unhooks my bra. He throws it away. He rubs my breasts from below. All my willpower is needed not to lie on him immediately. He holds them together and puts both nipples in his mouth. He sucks and licks them as if his life depended on it. Ready. I cannot stand it anymore. He needs to take me now. The control is gone. I lean over and French kiss him, biting his lips. We touch each other where we can passionately. Oily pleasure... I see nothing can stop him. Like a wild bull, he wants to get me right away. We excited each other too long. I, too, just want to be fulfilled, want him to fill me completely. I start to undress him, he's constantly kissing throughout.

-Wait, Peter. Stop it please. Do you hear me?
-What? I'm only listening to your groans.
-Someone is ringing the bell and keeps knocking.
-We're not home, let him do it. You can't leave now.
-I need to, what if it's Ben, or if there is a big problem? I have to go.
-Fuck it!

I take off his hands, I leave him there, run off for a robe. I have butterflies in my stomach. I quickly open the door. Thank goodness it's not Ben. It's my middle-aged neighbor who lives above me.

-Hi, Leslie. What's wrong?
-Hi Ann. I'm sorry to break in on you. I came to tell you, don't be scared if you see the damage.
-What damage?
-About an hour ago, my washing machine broke down and soaked my whole bathroom. It was old.

You will see the water damage, but of course I'll pay for the cost of the repair. I'm sorry. Tomorrow tell me how much I owe?

-Oh, okay. I haven't noticed yet. We'll talk tomorrow, I'll look for you in the afternoon.

-I'm sorry once again, goodnight.

-You too.

I close everything again. I find Peter sitting on the couch. He is angry and frustrated simultaneously.

-Do not be angry.

-This was our moment, but something crossed it again. I want you so much that it hurts. But I already said that. Come here and let's continue where we left off. You can't leave a man worked up like this.

You're right, I've experienced this. It really was our moment, but maybe it's not time for sex. It would ruin everything. Is it possible only this expectation hold him next to me? Then, when he gets me, he'll evaporate..

-Don't think, come on.

-I think you should go home.

It is very difficult to say. I rarely see anyone so surprised.

-Are you serious?

-Yeah, let's continue some other time..

-I will not go home. I came for you. If you won't be mine today, I'll still stay with you. Sleep beside me, like in the little house, and let's be together tomorrow. Let's spend Sunday just us alone until your son comes home.

-Why not? I would be glad. So what's your plan for the rest of the evening?

-Tasting your pussy till dawn.

-Pig.

-Honest pig.

-Let's direct our attention to a different direction.

-It will not work.

# Fragments of the Past

-Let's try it. A good movie?
His eyes light up.
-Porn?
- No. Sex-free action or horror.
-Well, ok. Let it be horror. At least you will cuddle with me?
-Yes. Do you want some snacks?
-Only you!
-Not an option. I'll bring you chips and some soda. Get comfortable, I'll be right back.

I pick things up and look at my forgotten phone in the kitchen. Mom called ten times, but no one else. I'll call her back tomorrow. Why didn't Gabriel tell me everything was ok? He could have signaled. I guess that's not what he was thinking. My little darling must be sleeping. I'll tell him about it tomorrow, so be sure to do it next time.

-Are you coming, Beautiful?
-Yes, I was just sidetracked.

I'm snuggling up in his arms. His presence always calms me down.

-Where?
-I thought of Ben, and how lucky you are to have no ex you should always see in connection with your kid. You aren't very injured.
-It's really good for you, because I'm not starting our relationship with you with as much prejudice as you are. It'll be enough to put you back together.
-There's some truth in it. It may be a long time before I let you in my heart. I've opened it to you a little now, but don't abuse it. Ben always my first, can you accept that?
-Yes, that's natural. You're a mom. I'll only ask the other half of your heart in exchange for mine.

-How romantic. We do not know what the future will bring. Anything can happen. What do you expect from a woman in a relationship? Expectation is not a pretty word, what do you want?

-That she loves me; cooks well; be a sex maniac; be able to handle me; create warmth at home; be a good mother; behave like a woman; I should be the only man for her; respect me. These are the most important, the rest will develop. And you?

- Love me from his heart; he needs to be honest; accept and love my son; be terrific in bed ; I should be the only one, he should not be selfish; treat me like a woman; behave like a man; be a good father; do everything for his family. The rest, as you said, will develop.

-I'm a very close match, if you see.

-We'll see, time will decide.

-Ann, what is time? Time is subjective for everyone. It never passes the same way. Only the product of our perception. Illusion. I think. For example, Einstein's theory of relativity is... Let's put this philosophical conversation to a later time, please. I would just like to add one thing: "The difference between the past, the present and the future is only an illusion, even if it is so stubborn."

-You quoted Einstein. You sweep me off my feet, Beautiful.

He places a kiss on my face.

-Let's start that horror flick. I will close my eyes on some parts, and I may shiver.

-I'll protect you from all terrible fears, my dear Lady.

-A promise is to be kept, Sir Peter .

The movie is horrible. He likes it. Too scary. They chop each other up, torture. I indeed close my eyes through some scenes. I don't watch horror anymore.

## Fragments of the Past

A few corpses later finally over. I stretch out, became sleepy.

-It's been a long day, let's put ourselves to rest till tomorrow. Before that I go take a shower, strictly alone. I am hurrying.

-Okay, I'll wait for you in bed.

I'm really in a hurry to take the shower and get ready for the evening. I walk into the bedroom, but I see him on the phone in the kitchen. When he notices me, he says goodbye to someone in a bouncy voice and let him know they'll talk another time. He is even harassed in the evening. It's bad for him.

-It was one of my clients, we can go now.

We get into bed and I lie on my side automatically. How natural it feels that he is here in my home on my bed. I'm starting to let him into my little world. He strokes me and then hugs me tight. Our mouths are very close. We immerse ourselves in each other's gaze. I caress him too. The moon's light illuminates his vivid face, his beautifully arched mouth.

-Do you believe in destiny?

-I do not know. If there is one, thank him for driving me to you, my lovely Ann. You?

-I do. I think they are no coincidences. You'll meet everyone when you need to. You are together as long as you can give to the other. Every encounter teaches you something, brings new opportunities to your life.

-Nice thoughts. I'm more realistic.

-I could spend hours explaining examples from my life, but now I'm not going to bore you. I'll tell you another time. Good night, Sir Peter.

-Good night, Lady Ann.

He cuddles up to me, we fall asleep in each other's arms.

## Trust Me

What is this delicious fragrance? What could it be? I try to sit up, but it is difficult. It rips, pulsates, beats my head at once. I deserve it. If you can't stand alcohol, drink moderately. I get to the same conclusion every time. I climb out of the warm bed. It's ten o'clock. I put on my robe, straighten my hair and sneak to the kitchen. Peter is making our breakfast. Scrambled eggs. He makes the same dish what I prepared in the little house.

-Good morning. I did not expect you to be a busybody this morning. When did you get up?

- Good morning, Beautiful. Half an hour ago, I wanted to surprise you.

-Thanks.

- Have a seat at the table, while I prepare the table. I'll take care of everything.

Music to my ears. So sweet. He's in a boxer, rushing, spinning, getting organized. I would kiss his muscular back, grab his round butt, hug him from behind. I don't, not yet. He kisses me, sets the table, then he serves the delicacy.

-Enjoy your meal. Hope it will be great.

-You too, it sure will be tasty.

At the first bite, I feel some spices are missing, but I won't tell him. I won't offend him. I eat it this way, I don't want him to be discouraged. Slowly goes down.

- It was fine, thank you.

-It was tasteless, you know it. Thanks for not criticizing.

-The intention is what's really important, I'll teach you how to spice it up. It is not difficult.

-What would my Lady say if we had our coffee by the Danube, sit down somewhere?

-I couldn't have thought it out better. Weather is nice and we still have a lot of time. Let's get ready and let's go.

I wear a black maxi dress with sneakers since we are going for a walk. My cleavage is beautiful and it is narrower where it is beneficial. I let down and straighten my hair, make smoky makeup for our date. He's dressed too, but he wears something different than yesterday. Blue striped t-shirt and jeans? I didn't even realize he had brought a change of clothes with him. I did not notice how sophisticated his bag was. Whatever. He is waiting in the living room, on his phone. Immersed in something.

-I'm ready to go.

-You are sexy, I want you. Let's not go anywhere.

-But I want to. I deserve my coffee and my walk.

I reach my hand toward him, wanting to pull him up some can leave, he pulls me back onto his lap.

-Let me just pamper you a bit, let me feel your body. Your warmth.

He turns my head, kisses my neck. That's not enough, meanwhile he is putting his hand on my left thigh and touches me. It feels good, I can tell he feels the same way. We cannot go deeper than this, there will be no stopping. We always dance on the edge. Just one last stroke on such an occasion and it's over.

# Trust Me

-Let's go. A great walk, divine coffee, to calm down this whole feeling.

-Ok. I can't stop. I try hard, but I can't tell how long I can take not to take you just anywhere, even on the street.

-I'm the brake I know, but it's very hard for me already.

The sun is beautiful, the wind is not blowing. Walking, hiking time. The proximity of the water and the sound still soothe me. We, too, stroll along the waterfront like a real couple. I am not alone in my thoughts or just the two of us with Ben. Although that's good, but this is better. Lots of people have come down to the beach now to romance or play. Some of the women passing look at me with envy. Yeah, he is an attractive guy. When others look at me while beside him, he notices and puts his hand on my waist. We are not in a hurry, we prefer to walk slowly along the water. He throws a couple of flat stones to the water, I also show him a few tricks. He finds a big white heart shaped stone and gives it to me.

-Put that in your collection.

-Thank you, I'll save it.

Well, he remembered what I told him about the collection too. He's really paying attention. We sit at a place directly by the water where we can see all the beauty from the terrace. We order the two coffees along with 4 different cookies to choose from. We're eating, during which we tell nice little stories about our childhood. He is a good narrator, he makes me laugh often.

-I love your smile, your eyes are shining when you do. I don't want you to be sad anymore. I see it too often in your eyes. I want to protect you from everything.

-Sir Peter, the hero knight, savior of ladies, protector of virtues, killer of dragons. I accept the nobleman's offer to be my protector.

-I stand by at your service, at the cost of my life, Milady.

And bows as far as the table allows. We share trivia from our daily lives. He is interested knowing me, just as I am about him. I'd like to peak into my everyday life.

-What are you waiting for? Tell me.

He is pestering. Somehow we always end up at this topic.

-No. It's too intimate.

I look down blushing.

-You keeping it a secret from me?

-Yes.

-How much do you do?

-Since I know you, I have to ease myself almost every day otherwise I'd go crazy. I don't want another woman. How about you?

-Twice a week, or so. You know, my sexual appetite decreased lately. And that alone is just a substitute.

-We need to fix this problem. Let's go back.

I smile at him flirtatiously, I reward his idea.

-Ok.

We're going back a little faster than we came. We know what's waiting for us when we get back to the apartment. It's a pleasant, tingling wait. He walks on the stairs, behind me, grabbing my butt, groping, teasing. We are only one floor away I purposely don't run. We arrive, he grabs me immediately and we start French kissing. With such energy that I can barely breathe. Vehemently, with a crazy speed.

-Wait, I'll just get the key out.

## Trust Me

-No. Here.

He puts my bag on the floor and presses me to the door. He pulls my dress up and puts my left foot on his hips. I look around, but there's no one here. Luckily for me, there is only one apartment upstairs. There is no large passageway.

-Ann, I said so. Now just enjoy what I'll do with you.

He kisses the middle of my chest, strokes my naked leg. I feel his erection, I touch it. I stroke it through the pants. I focus all my senses on him. I feel tingling. He grabs my pussy and massages it from outside, so I do it harder for him. What a foreplay. Than he pulls my other leg up, I hold onto him. He holds me. He places both of my arms over my head, squeezing me more to the door. I hear our moans, "What the hell is this?" Somebody yells from next to me.

I turn my head to the side and see Gabriel standing there shocked. Dear Lord. Immediately I move out of Peter's arms and pull down my clothes. I could sink right here on the spot. I feel guilty. I move closer to him. Peter stands by my side and grabs my waist. Oh no... That's not a good idea.

-It's not what it looks like.

-Ann, do I look stupid? I've seen you like this a thousand times when you lost your head. You're my wife!

He doesn't lower his voice, so I speak up too.

-Not anymore! We have nothing to do with each other! Would you have forgotten? Are you questioning me? What the hell do you think about yourself? How long have you been here?

He's so angry he is about to lose his mind.

I know him. He doesn't look at me anymore, but Peter. He doesn't care what I'm talking about. There's a red cloth in front of his eyes, he can't see, he can't hear. I see he's ready for fight.

-Be calm...

All I can say as he pulls in a huge punch to Peter. Peter didn't expect it, his head is thrown backwards, he is out of balance for a moment, but remains on his feet. He moves towards him, preparing for the next blow. I have to stop him. He will not stop himself. He could hurt him real bad! I grab his arm, but pushes me away. Yelling at me.

- Get out of here now!

He jumps on Peter, they land on the ground and he is hitting him where he can. Peter also punches back, but he doesn't really fight, though they are similarly strong. Why? I can't watch this. I have to do something. They went crazy.

-Stop it! There's no point in hitting each other! Gabriel, please stop! Please!

By my words he stands up and leaves Peter on the ground, his posture suggesting he has not done with him.

-I let your lover live.

It almost spits words. I don't provoke the fire any more I stay silent for a few moments, though I'd love to scream. Gabriel breathes hard, Peter gets up from the ground, but he doesn't come closer to us. I have to solve this situation. I have to think what would be best.

-Gabriel, where's Ben?

I see now he is starting to calm down, grasps what I asked. He doesn't look at me.

-In the car with my mother. He's waiting for you downstairs, I just planned to come up to you in advance to talk about the weekend. It was a pity. I see you had a better program with your boyfriend.

He looks at me with pity, he has no right. Why did they have to meet like this? My fault. I look at my watch. No, he came too early.

-Let us go down to the car for Ben now, and Peter, please go to my apartment and wait, we'll come up with the little one soon.

-I won't let this happen, Ann. He can't see my son.

-Gabriel, on the way I'll tell you what I'll tell Ben about him, come on. Take it easy.

I signal Peter to go through that damn door, otherwise Gabriel won't stay calm. He opens the locks, I start pulling him down. Suddenly he tears himself out of my hand and steps back to the door.

-If you dare him!

He steps in as a threat, but cannot finish the sentence because Peter screams back at him.

-What will happen? She is not with you anymore, you have given up on her! You didn't want her! I do!

- You Motherfucker!

Gabriel raises his hand again, but I am faster and pull him away from there. I drag him down three steps and stop.

-Look at me—I'm asking him.
-I can't.
-You don't have to, but I'll talk now. You can blame this situation on yourself. Fuck it, we're here because of you. You can't claim me, you can't talk into my present life, which you are no longer a part of. You could have struggled a few months ago, but you didn't. You gave up then.

He turns to me and comes closer. That smell.

That face. That... I can't become soft. He's a jerk, a disgusting man. Nothing else. My past. He's already dead to me as a man.

-My little Butterfly!

He wants to touch my face. He radiates immeasurable pain. I still feel him. His soul. Something still connects us, a thread. This is incredible. I hold his hand because I feel I need to. I'm going to cry right away, his eyes are teary as well. We hug each other. I close my eyes, he as well. He clings to me closer. I'm starting to be sick. Jesus, I've never felt like this. Everything is spinning with me, my heart rattles, I see a blurry picture appearing in front of me. Feelings come from nowhere. I can feel him again, he was my other half. Whatever we lived together comes back now. The enormous love. Suddenly I see myself in my head like a movie, crying on the ground, screaming and crying and feeling like I want to die. The pain tears me apart. This duality is unbearable. Seconds later, I open my eyes because I don't want to see and live this anymore. Who will be in trouble? Me? Ben? Him? I look at him, but now I see wisdom, not pain, in his blue eyes. That can't be... I had a vision? Or only my suppressed feelings broke out of my subconscious? I break our hug, I'm a little dizzy.

-Listen, you can never call me that again.

-But I...

Don't say anything, I beg you! Let me go! Stop!

No answer, nothing to say, we quietly go down to the gate. I have to tell him what I referred to upstairs. I hold him under his shoulder, hold my hand soothingly.

-I'll tell Ben that he is my co-worker, imagine he is anyway, and that he came to work with me because we had a very important deadline. I thought we

## Trust Me

will be done by the time you guys arrived, but unfortunately we couldn't. ..He'll stay with us for a while when Ben plays in his room. I also need to talk to him about the present. I may need to reassure him, too. Don't worry, he won't take your place, I won't introduce him that we are a couple. Don't worry.

-He came to work on you!

I take my hands off his body.

-Finish this! You don't know anything.

We are facing each other, almost in an offensive position.

-I do, what do you want from him?

-Enough, don't start over. Let's finally go to Ben, but please let's try to smile, pretend we'll be at peace with each other. H shouldn't feel anything. Anyway, I never want to see your mother again, only to wave hello to her . You take Ben out of the car. And let's give each other a kiss for the sake of pretense.

-Good!

We walk out side by side at the gate. He parked near the house with his black jeep under a large tree. I loved that car. We arrive there and my former mother-in-law and my little dear come out like doing a favor.. I wave to my dear ex mother-in-law. What a hypocritical, malicious old woman. Evil energy is radiated from her. Fortunately, Ben rushes to me right away so I don't have to go closer. Gabriel takes out the packages as I asked for and hands it to me.

-Say goodbye to Dad, we're going up.

-Hi Dad. See you soon.

-Hi son, I love you.

-Me too.

They hug each other, we move closer with Gabriel and give two kisses to each other. We both smile afterward cause that was the plan. My baby can't detect anything.

-I'll call you, Ann.
-All right.
-And Ann, take care of yourself.

We get upstairs while I tell Ben what was happened with me yesterday.

-And imagine, Mom has one of her co-workers right now upstairs, because we've been doing an important job all morning. We need to work a little more, and then he'll go home. In the meantime, please play in your room.
-And you play with me afterwards?
-Yeah, and you tell me everything that happened to you and dad.
-Good!

I worry while opening the door. I don't know how Peter will receive us. I think he might be waiting in the living room, so we are heading there. How smart he is. He took my laptop and now it is in front of him. He anticipated my explanation, although it wasn't difficult to figure out.
He gets up and comes and say hello to my prince.

-Hi Ben, I'm Peter.
-Hi. Are you Mom's colleague?
-Yes.
-What happened to your face?

Jesus, I haven't noticed until now. He has blackeye, his mouth cracked and bloated.

-I defeated a dragon and got hurt.
-Really? Was it very big?
-Yes.

## Trust Me

-If you come into my room I'll show you I have it from Lego. We can play.

-Another time, I promise, we still have to do some work with your mom.

-Well, then another time.

Disappointed he goes into his room to play. I let him know if he needs anything and I will be there in a drop of a hat. We sit back down on the couch. I don't know what to say, there are so many things in my head. Then I start,

-Peter, I'm sorry. Gabriel behaved terribly, I couldn't stop him. I wish he would have come later. Why didn't you hit him back?

I have so many questions. I stroke his face and give him a small kiss on his swollen mouth.

-It's not your fault, you couldn't have stopped it. This is what I would have done in reverse situation.

-What? You would have beaten him up?

-Yes, I understand him. It was a terrible feeling for him to see us. I'm jealous of you, too, so what could he feel. That's why I didn't hit back, among other things. It wouldn't have made sense to get into the fight deeper.

-You're too understanding. Don't you feel bad that I didn't stand up for you more? I know I didn't confirm things in front of you. But then I told him to get out of my life ... Shall I bring some ice?

-I don't need ice. You did your best, you didn't work him up further. You did everything right, believe me.

-And how do you like my ex? I'm ashamed of this whole thing.

-I'm going to have to see him with you, unfortunately, if I'm going to be a part of your life. I'll

have to fight him several times, of course, verbally, but it's worth for you. With Ben, I feel I'll be fine.
  -With him, sure.
  -Ann, I think neither of you really got the other out of your systems. The way your ex-husband was behaving today is clear.
  -I think I'm closed this chapter. See, that's why I said my life is complicated, my relationships ... Will you always fight? Do you accept that you may see me for a limited time? Can you adjust to my parenting responsibilities, which are the first for me?
  -Yes. I want to adapt, otherwise I have no choice, because they come with you.
  -But there is. You can go now by saying goodbye and closing this whole thing here. Better now than later.
  He holds my hand.
  -You really want to send me every problem?
  -It is not the case.
-Then what is?
  -I don't want to be hurt more. Another complication in my life. Please, if you don't take it seriously with me, you just want to sleep with me, go now. Look for someone else. I don't ask you to promise that you will never lie to me, but then have the honor to walk away. Last time I'm asking you...
  -Ann, if you just needed me for sex, I wouldn't be here with you right now. I could find anyone juts for a fuck.
  -You don't just work hard until I spread my legs?
  -No. I need your whole being. And the fact that you have a pussy? It's just a bonus. I'm about to cry. It's not allowed. Deep breathing, deep breathing. I turn away from him for a second so he doesn't see.

## Trust Me

-Just so you know what you have to put up with if you are with me, I'll tell you, there's a lot of unresolved things around me.

-I'm not a kid anymore. I can realistically assess situations and what I gain if I am persistent. I'd give you a kiss now, but if Ben comes out and we'll be caught twice today. Couldn't explain that to him.

-No. Don't risk it. Thanks for everything.

-Now I go, be with Ben, I'll rest for a while.

-Good, tomorrow there's work anyways. Try to fix your face by then, with some cream maybe. I don't want people asking you ho has beaten you.

-I try.

With difficulty but we stand up. I'll accompany him to the door. He is holding my hand.

-Beautiful, don't worry too much today, and I promise we'll continue this conversation. Yeah, and I'd like to spend so many eventful weekends with you.

-Silly.

I walk out the door with him, and we exchange a stolen kiss like a teenager.

-Bye Peter.

-Bye Ann. I'll see you again tomorrow.

I'll wait for him to go down the stairs and then I lock up. I'm strong, I'm strong, I'm strong. I can't crash right now. I'd rather go play with my little darling.

-What are you playing?

-Pirates. Will you be one?

-Yes.

We play at least half an hour. He doesn't behave any differently from when he left, though I was afraid of it. I am cross examining him.

-How was it with dad?

-Super. We went to the movies, watched a Lego movie, and then went to McDonalds. And he also has a new room for me. It's green, there's a lot of things in it. Jigsaw, Lego, plush, games.

-Your father's apartment is nice? Large?

-Yes, bigger than ours. It also has a giant TV and an Xbox.

Somehow I suspected it was bigger, but at least he made him a room of his own.

-You slept alone?

-Yes.

-Were you scared?

- No, he was reading to me and I fell asleep.

-And you played too?

-Little because he made a lot of phone calls.

-And today?

-Granny came, I played with her a lot.

Hope she didn't say bad things about me. How strange life is. I've come to this. I am asking my child how his father was. I'm afraid what if he felt better there than with me. What happens if he comes to me asking he wants to live with him. I wouldn't bear it.

-I am glad.

-And imagine Dad said he would take me on weekdays, too. We're going to the playhouse, hiking. I'm getting new cars. A lot of them. And everything I want.

Oh no. He promises everything he can, otherwise Ben is disappointed. Or does he want to influence him with gifts? Unfortunately, kids can be influenced this way. What is its purpose? It doesn't bother me so much that he is with him, but it does if he wants to manipulate him. In these type of cases, it's good that they do not yet understand time and cannot assess when they will meet again. In the meantime, this great longing for his father can subside The

## Trust Me

problem is that it will start all over again every two weeks. It's going to be a cycle, but I can't stop it. That's what I accepted.
-It will be super. Did you guys talk about Mom?
 -Little. Dad asked a few .
 -What?
 -What do you cook, what do we do in the afternoons, where do we go, do you cry?
 -What did you say to that?
 -You are sometimes sad and upset.
 -Did Dad tell you what he was doing?
 -I don't know. He told me he loves me but he has to work hard, so he can't see me all the time. He's got a big white cloak that he covered me with after bathing. I ate candy for breakfast, is it ok?
 -No, the point is you had a good time there. I playfully wrestle him to the ground, hold him down and cover him with kisses.
 -I missed my little treasure.
 -Me too, but I only went there for a week.
 So sweet he always says things like that. Let's just go down to the playground. Mom. Well yes, the time perception ... I wish it was tomorrow and I want the conversation with Monique to be over. Now I want to clarify all my relationships. And to banish bad things and people, as I did with Emma. Monique is coming.
 -Are you hungry?
 -No.
 -I'll order a pizza just in case. I'll get your favorite!
 I go out to the kitchen and order our pizza. I move things around than put in one round of laundry. Oh no. This reminds me of the spill. I forgot it. I look up at the bathroom ceiling. Really huge.

About a man's size. Great. I think I only need one coat of painting, but I'm not a professional. Tomorrow I'll call the guy who painted for me what is his suggestion and what would be the price, then I will talk with George. I forgot something else. To call my mother, I promised her. I dial quickly, but I make a calming tea in the kitchen. She picks up on the first ring.

-Hi Mom.
-Hi sweetie. I was already terribly worried. How are you?
-So-so. I wouldn't go into the details now, but don't worry.
-Ben?
-He is all right, he's here, he's playing.
-Something was this bad?
-Mom, I'll talk to you in person. Now I don't want to remember things.
-Well. I understand. Call me, let me know when you come.
-Good, bye, kiss.
-Bye.

I'm sure she got upset that I did not go into details. I heard in her voice. Then she will be reconciled. I'm going back to Ben. I see he's drawing some black circular horror on the wall, he doesn't notice me.

-What is that? What are you doing?

He throws the chalk away, runs to me, hugs me. He looks up at me with those big eyes.

-Mom, don't yell.

So I shouted, even though I just wanted to speak firmer.

-What's on the wall?
- I'm sorry, don't be angry. I just wanted to paint a pirate ship there. Beautiful?

## Trust Me

-You can't draw on the wall, forbidden. Strictly on paper.

-But on the wall is nicer.

-No, I told you. I'm angry.

-No please don't. I will erase it.

He starts to cry, with a small gesture pushes me away and sits back at his desk. I'd rather leave him alone now because I'd yell again. I can't speak to him right now. I'm angry. My calming tea will help. I sit back in the kitchen and sip the tasteless smelly liquid. Am I projecting my anger on him? Am I normal? Ok, he painted a black thing on his wall, but I shouldn't have reacted to that. What would I normally do? If his father were here, what would I say to him? Would he scold him, too? No. He would say Ann, he is a kid, they do things like that. Think about how you can reverse the situation so that you act as a parent and teach. And he would say don't act from anger, patience, my little butterfly ... Thanks Gabriel.

-Listen, Ben.

He doesn't pay attention...

-I have an idea. Although I told you before that you can never paint on a wall, but now we make the exception once. Either I have the painter paint your wall again or we paint there whatever you want.

He looks at me, smiles, barely believes his ears.

-Indeed? You are the best.

He brings all his chalk, pencils and put them all in front of the wall.

-You can't.

-Mom, I want a pirate ship, parrots, sea and island. May I?

-Yes, let's try.
He kisses me.
First we start with the black spot. I draw around it and turn it into a pirate ship. This will be the hardest part of the job. Then we draw all shapes with a pencil and paint or color them with chalk. You could draw the little things, but we color everything together and talk about it. You're in?
-Yes!
He jumps up. I'm not a great artist, but it will be our creation and it's more important. I'm looking for a picture of a pirate ship on my phone, that's how I begin. In the meantime, Ben makes a big green hill. That will be the island. I'm proceeding, it's not that hard. Ok, I'm just working on the big lines. We can work together well, he listens and follows what I ask for. Meanwhile, the pizza arrives.
Come on, little artist, take a break, eat.
-I want to eat here.
-Ok.
This is an exceptional time. I'll lay down a blanket in his room, put the pizza and refreshments on. The picnic is ready. He enjoys eating in his room and being together. Me, too. These are happy moments. Hours later, all figures and shapes were drawn on the wall, but not yet colored. It was quite good compared to where we started from. There will be water at the bottom of the wall. This is where the ship is. Little pirates lined up. The pirate flag has a sun icon, Ben wanted this way. Two shark fins hang out of the water. We continued to draw the island as a continuation of the sea. Pretty big.. There are parrots on the island and many palm trees. On one of the smaller hills he drew me, his Dad and himself. We are waving. That's what he wanted, I wouldn't have

## Trust Me

stopped him.

- God, Ben, I just remembered. I forget.

-What Mom?

-I forgot our car downtown, we have to get there right away. Otherwise, we go everywhere by bus tomorrow, and who knows what happens with the poor car if I left it there for another day.

-If you have to.

-Sorry yes, but we will hurry. I promise.

It takes about an hour and a half to do this, but I finally have my car. Nothing was wrong and we were back home safely. He storms into his room, I'm after him. He stops in front of his new decorated wall, we're standing side by side admiring our work.

-Mom, it's beautiful, but I'm tired. I want to sleep.

-We didn't color it yet.

-Tomorrow. Let's go for a bath.

He never asked for that. It's an improvement.

-All right, let's go. We'll finish it up gradually. Give me high five because you were talented and persistent.

He hits my palm. I bathe him quickly and put him in his bed. He pulls the blanket tightly, embraces Mr. Crabby. By the way, I tell him a story in which Mr. Crabby scarches for a pirate and treasures with his companions in the endless sea. Sometimes he corrects me, sometimes he interrupts telling what really happened. The two of us complete the story.

- Good night, my Prince. I love you.

- Me too, Mom.

I should get to bed too, but it's not late enough yet. What should I do? In these type of moments, it's bad that I don't have a partner to talk to about my feelings or make love as a glorious closing of the day.

I get upset. Someone's missing. But who am I missing? Just the feeling? Or does he have a face? Peter? He was so sweet with me through the time we spent together. We'll date. I don't dare yet to enjoy it. I surrendered to him , but I have some bad feeling that is hard to explain. Gabriel? It's not him. It's just my family like we used to be. Three, in unity. He surprised me today as we hugged and I felt his soul. Or not? I do not know. Feelings swirl in me everywhere, I should put my mind in order. I'm alone, but that's what I wanted it.

## 10 Months Before Divorce

Coming home, I want to please him so I cook his favorite steak with steamed vegetables and potatoes. Real masculine food. An hour later, I set the table, light a candle. I take a delicious dry red wine out of the fridge. Sex can come after dinner, of course I'll put Ben to bed before it. I put on a beautiful red lace bodysuit. He'll love it when he sees it.

-Ben, honey, come out of your room, we're waiting for Dad at the table.

The two of us sit down and I can't wait for him to get home. He'll be surprised and he'll appreciate it, We're restless, he should have been here 10 minutes ago. The wall clock is just clicking and drives me crazy. In the morning he said he would be home by seven. Half an hour late and he is nowhere. Should we still wait? Ben is hungry and impatient.

-When's Dad coming?

- I don't know, but eat, baby, I'll eat with Dad later.

He eats his dinner, I'm getting nervous.

-Go play some more or watch a story.

# Trust Me

He goes back to his room, I go to the living room. Where can he be? I call him. It's not good it would piss him off. But I still call. There is no answer the phone, it is turned off. He's been home late in the past two months, it feels like he is a nervous wreck. Sometimes he's relaxed, then he cuddles with me. But that is not enough. That's not how he usually is. Luckily sex is fantastic but I'm also tense because his feelings come through. This stupid new project. Why did he start it if it consumes him? We have enough money. We do not need it this much, especially not at such a price. He doesn't play with Ben either. It was the last month when we had dinner together. When he gets home I 'll talk to him... The food's cold already. It's nine o'clock. I've called five times since, but nothing. I'm hearing he's arrived, I feel a punch in the stomach. He enters the door with a sour face. Ok, I'll be nice anyway.

-Where were you, honey?

-Does it matter?

-No. We were waiting for you, I cooked your favorite, your phone was off.

-Ann, as you can see nothings wrong with me. Sorry, I was in a meeting. This is important now.

- Everything more important than us? You could have send a signal. This is the minimum.

-Don't start it. I said sorry.

-It's not enough. I understand everything, but we've barely seen you home in the past two months. What about the weekend? Are we planning to go somewhere?

-Please understand, I work so hard for you guys.

-I miss you. You're starting to get far away from me.

-It's not like this. You are my everything and Ben. Only two more months and the project will be completed.

He kisses me and hugs me. This hug is not like it used to be. I can't explain why, but you can feel it. Maybe more reserved. I ask again about the weekend, he and we need the relaxation, the quality time together.

-Well, Dad, are we going somewhere over the weekend? We really need it.

-We'll see.

.....

Oh well. I remember there was no sex after this conversation. He walked into his study and left me alone. I couldn't tell him what's bothering me, how do I feel. I don't care anymore. I'm hung up on the past again. I'm just getting worked up. The best way to deal with this is distraction. I'll start reading. I manage to distract my brain for an hour. My thoughts go astray, so I stop reading, instead I start to think more about my strategy with Monique tomorrow. No, why do I need strategy? I'll be straight forward. No, not quite. At first, I trick her and then attack. I will be tough and determined. Maybe she will get a slap from me if it's true what Peter described, she deserves it. Although there is no reason to make plan, things can't be calculated anyway ... I take a shower and go to bed. I lie down , turn on Beyonce's "Listen" on my phone, I need it now. As I listen, I start to cry. It feels good. I'll play it three more times until my tears have completely dried up ... I miss Peter's warm body. His body also fits mine. Surprising. I thought it could only be one person that has the perfect fit. My mate... It's like a puzzle... Life is like that.

# Trust Me

The big picture is not predefined. You already have the most important pieces of the puzzle, but you are still looking for the remaining pieces, you do not know in advance which tiny item will fit where. How is the right way to fit, how does it come together, what comes out of it at all? I wake up ready for a battle. I don't spend too much time getting ready. A purple dress with black high heels and black accessories. I look in the mirror before leaving. The mantra can come. I'm pretty, I'm beautiful, I'm strong, I'm good. But that's true. I thought yesterday I was going to have a panic attack again because of the many things I had experienced, but it didn't come. Am I improving, too? No. Not so, because it was Ben on Saturday when he left. But even though, yesterday was rougher, it did not happen. Maybe I'm starting to get tough. We get to kindergarten quickly, the traffic is not so bad today. This is it. That's a good omen for today. When you start the day well, you feel better about going to work. And today, a lot will be revealed. I can't wait to get to my workplace, my stomach is constantly feeling butterflies, I'm sweating.

-Hi Ann.

-Hi, Monique.

Her hair is coiffed, she is wearing a red dress, she has spotless makeup and is visibly bored. She's browsing some newspaper. A fashion magazine for sure. She never has to work? I'd rather be a receptionist. Maybe I have a bigger smile than I should have. Not a great choice.

-I see you're happy, what happened?

-I had a great weekend.

She is picking on her nails while having the conversation.

-Nice, Ann.
-And you?
-Me too.

She gets up from her chair and stands in front of me.

-Shall we chat?

It's good that she offered it, I did not have to insist. Another good sign for me.

-Of course. Let's step into my office.

I put down my bag and open the window to let in fresh air. It's needed. I'll sit down at my desk. Monique is doing something on her phone. I'll write a short email to Peter regarding what he needs to do if the conversation turns a certain way. I'm nervous ... I have a lot of work to do but now Monique is more important. Let her start it. She sits down in front of me on the chair, waiting for me to speak. I hypnotize her to start... You start.

-Haven't been chatting for a long time.

It's good that she started, that's it. Can I influence others the same way? Do this, do that ... I just have to be relaxed when I answer and everything will be fine.

-Yeah I know. Unfortunately, I have a lot to do lately.

-I see. Are you mad at me? You find excuses, often.

-I'm not angry, I just had a rough couple of days.

If you knew...
-It's OK then.
-What did you do this weekend? Shopping? Workout?

She ruffles her blond hair and throws it back.

-Well, I bought few nice things, but other great things happened too.

## Trust Me

I'm curious to hear about that.
-What?
She looks remorseful and keeps adjusting her red mini dress.
-I didn't want to tell you first because I saw it bothered you. I was with Peter all day yesterday. We... We got together again. I couldn't hold it back anymore. It was so good.

Is this woman this stupid? I have to keep myself from laughing, I quickly drop my pencil so she won't see me grin. I'm looking for it a little longer than I should. Poker face up. She is giving me the right cues.

-This is amazing. At least you got together with him. That's what you wanted ... His puppy is cute, right? Did you guys take him down for a walk?
-How do you know he has one?
-Oh, well, he told me at our weekend together.
Her face is motionless. Not surprised.
-Very cute fluffy thing. He was digging me immediately, I played with him too.
-Ben should have a dog, but it's not great in a brownstone. It would be alone often. And we need to walk him in the mornings as well, it would jeopardize us getting ready.
-It may not be for you.

I'm mentioning the living room, but not the female statue, something I can tie to Ben ... I got it.
-And you noticed what a good collection of little car-models he has in his living room showcased on the bookshelves? Ben also loves small cars. He would love it if he saw it. You know, Gabriel took him often to car shows.

I'll quickly write another email to Peter asking him to come to me in three minutes and do everything as I asked.

-I find it a bit childish to collect those. But it doesn't bother me.

-Nothing is bothering you? Nor his many sexual adventures before you?

-No. He is a great guy, I longed someone like him. He is also pretty talented in bed.

-I don't know about that. You know, it's good that you've finally found each other. I'm really not ready for a serious relationship yet. You were right. Good luck with him.

-Thanks. And what did you do this weekend? That's it for you.

-I met Gabriel, my old girlfriend, and even had a date.

She's surprised. I move to the chair next to her. I smile at her trying to radiate power from within.

-With whom? New?

I look at the clock. Now. Suddenly, the door opens. We both turn that direction.

- Sorry, honey. I thought you were alone still. I just wanted to check with you, are we going tonight? And of course wanted my morning kiss. He is so handsome today. He's wearing a white shirt, black suit pants and a black striped tie. His hair looks perfect, he probably put some foundation on his face cause I did not see the spot. He's using some fine perfume that fills the air ... I don't answer his question immediately. He leans slowly towards me and places a kiss on my mouth.

-I'm going to leave you, talk later. Bye sweetie, hello Monique.

He closes the door, his scent stays there to remind me. I look at Monique, she is about to explode.

## Trust Me

Anger and something else is coming across, but I don't know what that is. She gets up, so do I.
-I have to go.
I'll grab her right arm. Elevate my voice.
-You're not going anywhere!
She is trying to pull her hand out, I hold her tight.
-I have not finished yet. What do you think about yourself? Do I look so stupid? How conniving and how simple a woman you are. This is not what I expected from my girlfriend, whom I have trusted for years. Tell me, why? Why was that good for you?
-Let me go!
I'll release her arm. She turns her back on me.
-He's yours too! Like everything! I hate you! She's very angry, her hands are shaking. She turns to me, looks at me with hatred. I haven't seen that face yet. Doesn't stop. Her hand motioning around like chicken dance.
-You got Gabriel, now Peter. Money, a kid.
You've got all the good stuff, you're lucky. Poor little Ann, poor little innocent creature! You're always feeling sorry for yourself! You're not pretty enough, not good enough. Is it difficult for you? You got all the best stuff from life. You took it from me! Gabriel should have been mine! At the nightclub, I should have gotten together with him. I'm prettier and better than you. I stayed with you because I was waiting for the right time, for my time to come... I hate you more every day. I longed for your life for ten years, after all I was glad that you were alone. Then I realized that Peter liked you, again, he didn't notice me. I had to do something! I can't find words. This is incredible. I didn't expect that. This is terrible...
- Curse on you, Ann!

She is so angry, her head turned red. I point my hand toward her, I may strike her in a minute, bring her to the ground, and tear all of her hair off.

-Get out of my office! Never come near me again! You'd better look into yourself! I can only feel sorry for you!

I can't continue or hit her because she turns around. She grabs the door handle and slams the door so loud it almost falls out of the frame. Everyone must have heard that. Now I have provided a good reason for rumors. This is incomprehensible ... She is not normal ... She wanted my life? My husband? Peter? Hates me? How much wickedness and hate had accumulated over the years in her... I don't have time to think about these things, later. I can't sink into lethargy. I need to work now. I close my window and sit back to my desk. I won't get up until lunch time. I'm doing a great job. A slightly evil idea occurs to me. I look out of my office and see Monique's desk is empty. She went down to eat. I have time. I'm going back to my place and start looking for a picture of the Oscar on the net. I find one soon. I print it on a color printer in A3 size. It looks pretty good. I put the paper in front of me and write next to the picture with my finest writing, using big red letters: - Dear Monique! I give you the Best Actress Award. You deserve it. You deserve it. Put it on your wall to always remember me. Hugs, Ann. - I fold it nicely and put it on her keyboard to make sure she finds it when she comes back. I may be childish, but I had to do this… I just head out of my office, I feel like leaving and I'm craving sweets. I deserve a cookie. I'll go down to get one. I take my bag and am heading to the elevator. My accomplice comes toward me.

## Trust Me

-Beautiful, I came to you catch you to have lunch together.

He grabs my waist.

-You were almost late, thank you for your morning help anyway. I just am going for a cookie, but come with me and we'll have a coffee too.

-Anything good with you.

-Good to hear that. Next time, I ask you to iron with me.

He starts laughing.

-If we do it naked, I'm in. That board can be good for many things.

-Is there anything that doesn't remind you of sex?

-In connection with you? None, and neither will be.

-I almost guessed it. You seem a little sex-centric to me.

-Why do you say that?

Going to the cafe we don't meet colleagues. It's good, because we are holding hands. I'll let him do that. If I saw someone I know, I'd automatically would let go. I don't dare to go public yet. I think he would. The waterfront was different. We order two cappuccinos and two double chocolate muffins. Our table is close enough to the serving counter so we move closer to hear each other.

-And you seriously said I had a dog?

-Yes. And she said what a cute fluffy thing. I even told her about your non-existent car collection. I heard all this from you on our weekend together. She didn't get it. She didn't think that you knew everything?

-Exactly. But don't interrupt me. The point was, when you came in, everything became clear to her. She was destroyed. She started to flap her arms around. She blamed me that I took Gabriel from her. She hates me and envies my life. She is wishing me bad.

-I didn't think her hate for you was so deep and lasting.

-Me neither. She played the role of girlfriend so beautifully. A lot of things connected us, and I've lived through many things with her over the years. I still don't really believe it. Monique screwed me over. After Emma, I had to cut her out of my life... Yeah, and gave her a prize.

-What?

-Wait, I'll tell you, let me just bite into my well-deserved cookie... So, I printed her a photo of the Oscar award and wrote next to it that s deserved it. For such a long time to play the role of a girlfriend like that, not everyone would be able to. Put it on your wall and remember me. I wrote something like that.

-That was nice. You stomped her emotions even more.

-Why, what would you have done?

-I do not know. I've never been in such situation, confrontation with a jealous, idiotic woman. If you would've beaten her, she would hate you less. Now you had the last say again, she can't stomach it.

-You don't have to feel sorry for her, she deserved it.

-I know. I'm sorry about all this that you had to go through today. Why did you want to find out what's going on between us?

-It was a bigger bang. I really can't comprehend that she hates me that much, and her lies. I'm not like that. I wish not to see her anymore, I wish

## Trust Me

she would leave this job. Tell me, do I deserve this?
    -No. You are a good person, except you choose bad friends.
    -I can only misunderstand people like her. I'm a bad judge of person, and really naive.
    -Oh, Ann. You'll have new girlfriends, just choose better.
    -Thanks, I'll be on it.
I put my head down, I think I'll start to cry.
    -What would cheer you up?
    -Now, this cookie does just that, but that's not enough. Let's say ... a weeklong vacation away from everyone and everything.
    -It can't be solved right now
He starts whistling and tap his finger... I know this song. Bobby McFerrin. I can't believe it.
    -Don't worry... Be happy... uuuu uuu uuu ... don't worry, be happy.
    I put my hand on his mouth.
    -Enough, not so loud. Everyone is watching us.
    He pushes my hand away.
    -Here's a little song I wrote, you might want to sing it note by note, don't worry, be happy.
    Becomes louder... I'm blushing more and more.
    -In every life, there is some trouble, When you worry, you make it double, Don't worry, be happy!
    He has a pretty good voice. Deep and pleasant. He's so sweet, gazing at me all the time and smiling, even with his eyes. This is the way he wants to cheer me up, and I feel I'm a little ashamed of the singing. But he really can't continue singing for me, I have to silence him. There is one method, I kiss him...
    -You're so sweet, thank you, and by the way, your voice isn't bad either.

-You feel better beautiful?
- Definitely, and I think the other guests agree.
- You're blushing, I'm just saying.
- Just the unexpected attention. I like to stay in the background, but you just made them look at us.
-Willingly.
And he sits up, places a kiss on my forehead.
-You are crazy, but I like it.
-After all, something that pleases you.
-You know there are other things too, but I'm not starting to list them now.
I drink my coffee, and his drink is running out. He looks at me with his big brown eyes , like a puppy waiting to be pet by his owner.
-We should get back slowly, though I don't have much of a mood, especially because of Monique.
-Can't we stay here all day? It's so good to be sitting with you just to be by your side.
-Unfortunately not. Let's really get going.
-But before let's set a date again.
-We met yesterday.
-I'm asking for a date. Tomorrow?
Of course I want him too, but wouldn't that be too soon? Shouldn't we postpone it? Not too fast? Who would look after Ben? Just mom, but should I inconvenience them? I do not know. Waiting would be a good idea, we were together for most of the weekend.
-I don't know which evening I could do, I have to ask my Mom to be with Ben. I'll talk to them in the afternoon.
-Ok. We will only get together as soon as possible.

## Trust Me

We reluctantly get up from the table and head back. He wants to hold my hand again, I'll pull it out.

-Give me your hand, I need your touch.

- No, and if anyone sees us? They come down to eat often around here.

-What do you care about the opinions of others? You don't want to touch me?

-Yes, I just don't want them to talk rumors about me, that I am already having an affair.

-Silly talk.

He reaches for my hand and grabs it, starts stroking the inside of my palm with one finger. I don't pull it away now. He is right, it is not the rest that really concerns me, but this is another step, if they see us they will know. Nah, it doesn't matter. I'll be brave, what can I lose? I have to accept him, our relationship that is beginning ...

-It's nice, Beautiful. Your hands are in mine. He doesn't let it go as we arrive all the way to the office, we enter the door like this. As we arrive, our two male colleagues come across from the marketing department. Murphy... Okay, relax. They may not have noticed us. My knight grabs my hand harder so I don't accidentally get it out if his grip. They're getting closer to us. Super!

-Hey guys.

Welcoming them, Peter. They look at us slightly surprised, and then their gaze immediately slips into our hands. Great. They both crack a half-smile.

- Hi Ann, hi Peter.

-Hello!

I turn my head and start to walk a little ahead, signaling Peter, let's get out of here before getting into a conversation with them. He realizes this and we rush to the elevators. The colleagues, passing by us, hurry to the door. We board the elevator, fortunately empty.

    -Why did you need this now?
I raise my eyebrows, standing a distance away from him.

    -Ann, don't say that. You start to offend me.

    -I don't want to, but now everyone will know that we

    -Are dating? We are together? You belong to me?

    -Something like that.

    -After all, they should know. Isn't that what you want?

    He comes near, caresses my face, then gives me a soft kiss. What do I want really? Do I want him? It's all so confusing. ..If so, I have to give in.

    -Yes.

    -That didn't sound too convincing.

    We almost arriving upstairs. If we get out of hand in hand, it will be seen by Monique and by anyone who walks by. I have to decide now what to do. I mean the other two colleagues pass on the news anyways. My workplace is like a small village. Everybody knows everything. I hold his hand and we get out. It will be what it will be. Monique notices us, gets pale, and starts to look at her monitor quickly. She doesn't dare to say a word, though she must have received my gift. An older colleague was just explaining something to her, standing right next to her. She looks at us too, suddenly becomes silent, she gets it. She looks at me with pity and gives Peter a forced smile. Fantastic. She probably thinks that the divorced sex-hungry woman quickly fished out the best catch in the office. And who knows what else she thinks, but her gaze betrayed everything.

## Trust Me

I look at Peter, I can tell he wants to say something and I stare at him not to do it.

- Hi girls, I hope you're doing great. I am, thanks to Ann. And as you can see, Ann and I are together.

-Congratulations! Monique says.

At least that's what she managed to squeeze out of herself. Peter rushes to my office after me. I drop my bag and stop in front of it. He bypasses me and then throws himself down by my desk and invites me to go there and sit on his lap. I will not. I'm angry. I look back at him being sullen acting like an idiot. He stands up, grabs me and puts me on his lap. I don't look at him.

-Ann, don't be childish.

-I will be. What was that good for again? Ann and I are together as you can see. Are you going to carry me around like a bloody sword? Am I this year's trophy?

-If everyone needs to see for understand it, yes.

In a moment, he lifts me up from his lap and puts me on his back. My head hangs down, my purple dress slides down my back, he holds me under my butt. I'm like a sack of flour.

-And now, the showing-around can start.

I start tapping his back with both hands.

-No, enough, put me down. You are childish, Peter. You don't have to prove anything.

-But I have to.

- Oh no.

-You can't do this. It's a place we work. Our workplace.

-Yes I can.

He pulls my clothes back and opens the door. Jesus. I'm trying to free myself somehow, leaning left and right, but all in vain. He just holds me stronger. Nobody supposed to see us this way. He starts right. No. Does he take me to the kitchen? Or? I see nothing only that there is no one behind us. I hear clatter of shoes. As we moved forward, Monique is passing by, she probably was in the kitchen. From her eyes a lightning may strike me, I think she would kill me on the spot. In response, I raise my hand, smile at her, and wave to her. Here you go, stupid cunt. After she's leaving, I lower my head. I don't want to see who's passing by or who's behind us. I'm about to sink. I can't hear another knocking of the shoes.

-Enough, put me down , please. I understood all.

-No.

We are still moving ahead, we are by the kitchen. I see some people eating and staring at us. I believe they think they went blind. As we move on, I notice our other colleagues have come out to the hall to watch the show. I can't stand this.

-Dr. Peter Pataky, Ann Daray! It's not a playground, and it's not prehistoric times to carry ladies that way.

-God, this deep, humming voice is the boss' voice.

-Peter, stop now.

He stops, takes me off his back nicely, I turn around and I see our boss standing in front of us. Now, not so sweet, old teddy bear as usual. He's angry. He ruffles his gray hair and puts his hands in the pocket of his gray suit. He's about to fire both of us. For sure. I have to come up with something. I need to squeeze something out right now. I cough a little.

## Trust Me

-Boss, excuse us for this scene, we're doing research, we're practicing.

-What do you practice?

-I asked Peter to help with our latest perfume campaign. We were just trying to see what a similar scene in a commercial would look like and how people's reactions would be. I'm looking at Peter for help, now he's talking. Fortunately, he opens his mouth.

-Yes, because this would be one of the takes, that there is a mass of beautiful women in a meadow, or in a hotel, or in a workplace. Based on the fragrance, the man selects the most beautiful woman, grabs her and playfully throws her over his shoulder, carrying her out from the crowd of women. After

-Stop it, Peter... I like the idea.

The boss starts smiling. I can't believe it, I'm about to collapse. Huh.

-Ann came up with the idea.

-It's great, whoever had the idea. In two hours, you should both be in my office and bring the synopsis with you. You know, what the message is, the cost, the target audience, etc. Let's go to work now.

-Thanks, we'll be there! (we say at once).

The boss turns around and heads to his office. We can't go back to my office now, we should go to Peter's. It's in a quieter place and I'll be able to kill him there easier. How should I do it, what method should I use?

-Let's go to your office.

-That's what I thought, Ann.

-Super!

We go through the big glass door, don't go, we're rather running. This is what connects the two corridors and the two divisions. By the way, each floor is designed like this. Three offices later he stops and points to the door on the left.

-We are here.

-I know which one is your office is, can you imagine I know our levels, but I've never been to yours.

-It's time.

He lets me walk forward, puts his hand in the middle of my back, pushes me through the door, and locks it with the key. I turn around and slap her with a bang. Huge sound.

-Are you normal, Peter?

That's unexpected, he doesn't say a word, but to avoid being hit again or stopping me to go on, he grabs my hands and pushes me down onto a couch. Does he have a sofa? I don't have time to react or look around. He puts his weight on me and kisses me. Wildly, like an animal. His stubble is piercing, his scent excites me, and I start to get worked up as he looks at me. His eyes are shining. He bites my earlobe and then pulls off my clothes. His touch leaves tiny sparks on my skin.

-Peter, no, it's not aloud. We're in your office, don't seduce me. We cannot continue here. Think.

-We can. Nobody sees us, just enjoy it. I want to be inside of you, sweet, warrior Ann. I only respond with a sigh, I'm no longer fighting. He grabs my black thong and tears it apart. I'm there naked in front of him. He leans close my pussy, gives it a kiss. Then he squeezes his head close. Slowly, he stretches out his tongue and starts circling with it. It feels awfully good... He suddenly lifts his head and looks at me.

-You make me wild. I've been waiting for this for months.

## Trust Me

I lost control, I can only think of him to continue. Nothing interests me anymore.

-Continue... please.

He leans back keeps alternating between sucking and licking my clit... He sets the perfect pace. I'm pulsing, I push my pussy closer to his face. No escape, I would moan loud if I could , but I shouldn't. I feel so wet, I just want him inside me. Now he moves his tongue up and down, sometimes moaning... I can't stand it for long... He fingers me with one finger and starts moving it as if it was his penis, circling my clit with his wonderful tongue. He instinctively knows what I like. Every second I am closer, my body is flooded with hot shock waves. He feels it, he puts his hand on my mouth, starts to do it stronger and faster, doesn't even breathe... Everything disappears, I only focus on the feeling, he flies me to the stars, I cum for him ... Then he throws another kiss on my pussy, enjoying my vulnerability. Moments later, I return to the ground and realize what we have done.

-This

-Yes, Beautiful, was wonderful. I could go on all night and I will. Your taste is heavenly.

What to say to this, thank you. It's so lame.

-Listen, it was wonderful to me too, but it was a mistake. It was a mistake to lose control here.

-Nothing wrong with what we do to each other, get this. And I hope you're not so angry with me anymore.

-I am, but we'll come back to that later.

I sit up and he brings a handkerchief.

-I'm trying to fix myself.

-I'll do it.

He crouches in front of me and sucks another last one on my pussy, kisses my inner thigh and then gently wipes it.

-Hmmm. I don't wash my face, I want to taste and smell you all day long. You should feel it too. And kisses me. He makes me feel this our first kiss, sensual, in no hurry, stroking my neck meanwhile ...

-What about my panties?

-I'll put it in my drawer.

He walks back to his desk, sits on his chair, I stay on the couch. Really pulls out one of his drawers.

-You plan to show it to people?

-No, just to always remind me of those minutes when I reach into the drawer.

-As you wish. Otherwise, did you think it through that I have to be without panties all day now?

-Yes, indeed, a lot. You will think of me as the breeze touches you or you sit in your chair and your fine silk dress touches it. You will be waiting more and more to touch you again ... Only I know you're not wearing it. And this thought, hmmm...

He smiles like a bad boy, as only a man can. He's looking at me, his gaze is honest and he focuses on me with every bit of his being... I am looking around for the first time, his office is nice. Bigger than mine. Fortunately, the shutter was down. There's a big black bookshelf full of law books. A black sofa and a desk. There is order and nowhere can I see family photos on display. Just a strange picture hanging on the wall. Colored straight lines, for me it looks like chaos and in the center a black circle, or rather a patch.

-You are evil, but evil with a nice office.

-Thanks.

-What does the picture represent?

-Me.

## Trust Me

-I don't really understand this. Are you the black spot? Or one of the colored lines? Or do I need to look from a different angle and see your hidden face? Do you mean your state of mind?

-Not really, dear Picasso. I painted it.

-I didn't know you had artistic inclinations.

-I painted once, only once. That was the picture.

-And why haven't you been painting since then? Why is this portraying you?

-I tell you some time, it's not that interesting.

-Well, ok. Otherwise, I don't see family pictures out.

-I don't like living in my shopwindow. And I wouldn't like if a stranger would be coming in and looking at my pictures, my family.

-Compared to this, today, the doctor did completely the opposite.

-A unique case. I'm not like that, you get this out of me.

-That you have to let everyone know that I am yours, and like a caveman, carry me around in front of a pack? This is what I bring out of you?

-Exactly. Everyone needs to know who you belong to. And because you made me wild.

-With what?

-You know that.

-Ok, Sir Peter. Could you be a little less possessive. My husband always did this to me.

-And you didn't like it?

-Yes and no. Maybe I subconsciously attract such men. Maybe I should try different, different types of men. Even I would need to be looking around a bit. I have time, I'm young.

-Try it.

-I may do it, we don't have oath between us.

-Don't joke with me, you want me to chain you to myself?

-Let's leave this now ... Let's talk about our visit that needs to happen in an hour thanks to you. What's your plan?

-I don't have one.

-I hope, the Doctor will find something smart. So what is that law degree for?

-For legal cases, that's not it.

-What you don't say.

-What do you think? You're the PR.

-I think it's enough for the boss to just sketch out the commercials now. He can't think of putting together a whole bunch of stuff filled with real-time data, analytics and other market research. And with you? This is not your specialty. I have been working on this perfume for some time now, I am on a campaign plan, but I am not finished yet. A lot of work.

-I don't think he expect anything like that, he just wanted to scare us. It may be Monique's fault. She saw us and went to spill the beans to the boss.

-You're right, sneaky cunt. And I believed she was my girlfriend. What does she think about herself?

-Too much.

-I remind myself, I want to buy myself a new perfume. I don't like the old one anymore, I need a change.

- Can I go with you to smell it on your neck?

- No, it's a female thing. I would like to choose. And now listen. Before our lie today, I came up with the idea the advertising should be focusing on choice. So far, I have approached the question of choice as a woman, but it could incorporate your idea of kidnapping and carrying. All we have to do is mix it all

together, based on my materials. A man's point of view is also a good help. What do you think?
 -Good, Beautiful. Tell me what kind of advertising you had in mind.

## 9 Months Before Divorce

I need to take a bath, I'm tired. It's after 10:00 p.m. I had a hard day. The workplace is like a mental hospital, Ben threw tantrums all night, I could barely sleep. Gabriel is nowhere, though he could've helped me at home. He could have unloaded the dishwasher, could've tell a story to Ben or whatever. I take off my clothes and look at myself in the mirror. My mirror image looks pale and sad. I think I lost weight, my tits became smaller. Nowadays I am more lethargic. I'm not happy. Did I change? No. Gabriel changed. It seems he is avoiding me, and his family seems to be a burden. He pulls himself out of everything, doesn't play with Ben, just sits next to him, makes a phone call, or watches him play. He doesn't stroke me in the evenings, he comes to bed late. So cold and distant. The situation was better even a month ago. I'm trying to get closer, but I hit the walls. He's not communicating with me. We used to talk through many things, he's my partner, my best friend. When I try to talk to him, he doesn't pay attention. I'll tell him about my day, the kindergarten or anything that concerns me and I see he's mind is going elsewhere. I haven't been trying sex for two weeks. For what, it doesn't make any sense as I have a feeling he is not interested in me. What's the problem? I have noticed the trouble for a while that he locks himself up. I see him often moving away from me or going to another room to minimize physical contact and communication.

I notice from the mirror that the bathroom door is opening. He is—of course—who else could be. He wears one of my favorite gray suits that I bought for him, without a tie. His face is long and his eyes worried.

-Hi.

-Hi Ann.

He starts undressing and gazes at me while throwing his clothes on the floor. When he's done, he steps next to me. He kisses my neck.

-I love this perfume, your fragrance, you're beautiful.

He touches my breast, but I suddenly move away. He watches my reaction in the mirror.

-Tell me why are you moving away from me? What was that, you no longer want me?

I'm not turning to him, talking to his reflection.

-I know you're just doing it now because you want me to sleep with you.

-What's wrong with that? You are my wife, this is a bodily desire.

He also talks to my reflection.

-See, that's what I'm talking about. This is not the case for me. You only come close when you want me. Pamper me for the sake of pampering, not because you want sex. Let's talk instead. Tell me what's wrong, I'll tell you what's wrong. Don't be alone.

-Can't do it, Ann.

-Why?

He turns around, grabs the bottle of lotion and drops it into the tub with tremendous force. The top comes off and everything is covered with whatever is in the bottle. He doesn't care, walks out naked and without explanation. I'll stay there, sit in the tub, let the water run and cry. My body trembles, I

## Trust Me

feel pressure in my chest and I can barely breathe. Why is he doing this? Am I just good for that? Why doesn't he answer? Do I mean to him so little? I love him, but I don't know what to do. Why isn't everything as it used to be? Doesn't he come back to comfort me? Doesn't he hug me in the tub so I can cry on his shoulder?... I don't feel my body anymore, just the heartbeat of my heart. I want the old Gabriel.

·····

-Ann, is there a problem?
-Why?
-You suddenly became sad. Is it going to feel like watching an advertisement? That's not good news.
-No, of course not. The perfume reminded me of something. I really need to replace it.
-What was it?
-With Gabriel was having trouble back then, we were quarreling, smashed the bottle and I got a panic attack in the tub. That's it. Yes, but before that he praised my perfume and my fragrance.
-I'm sorry.
- No, it's gone.
-Will you tell me sometime how this happened between you two? Will you open up for me?
-Yeah, I think so, but you have to do the same for me, too. It's time and we don't know each other's soul yet.
-I want to know your soul, your thoughts, every part of your past, Ann. I'm curious of you. Not just your body. I'm interested in you.

This sounds too nice, he said such things more than once to me. Does he really feel that way about me? It's still incredible.

-Let's talk about these things again another time, Peter. Let's focus on the present, we have an urgent task.

- Ok, distract me go ahead. So, what should we present?

-Something that catches his attention. Let there be many beautiful women in a park, for example. The scent would fit in that environment anyway. Let these women be dressed like nymphs. The man should think he's dreaming when he needs to see them and smell them in the air to find the most beautiful woman in the crowd. Then pick her up and take her out of there. Abduct from the Garden of Eden. Then, in the next scene, have the two of them together in the flower field, kissing, then I don't know ... It's too sugary. I'd rather, call the boss to ask for more time. It's a lame idea. I haven't figured out these yet. I only did the competitor analysis and the market research. The rest is teamwork.

- Hey, relax. We'll improvise. Let's work for more time.

-Ok. That will be the best. No, not. Listen, let's go home. I don't want to go to the boss.

-But come on, we have to leave. It's time.

We're headed for the boss's office. I'm nervous, Peter is an island of tranquility. It bothers me that my panties aren't on me and here's another conversation I don't want. We arrived. Peter knocks two vigorously twice, then let me go in front of him. His office is old-fashioned. Old furniture and matching fixtures, an ancient tape recorder, and newspapers and posters are framed on the wall. Clean 70s. Even the smell of the room is as if time had stopped here. The computer alone will interfere with this retro look. I look at the

## Trust Me

boss, he is not in a better mood.

He doesn't even look up, he's typing something. We stop at his desk waiting for his signal.

-Take a seat. and points to the two blue velvet chairs next to his desk. He looks at us at last, but like a strict dad before the big argument. Not good, I don't like it. My father used to look at me like that many times.

-Thank you.

-I called you to tell you I didn't believe your explanation for the hallway interlude. I wasn't born today, but it was a nice try.

Oh no. Why did I think the boss believed it? Now that's it for us. I'm starting to fidget in the chair, I'm ashamed. I have to apologize. Or should I tell the truth? In response, I look at Peter, who is gesturing with his head.

-Boss, me.

-I don't care about the explanation, Peter. It's a workplace. Outside the office, you two do whatever you want, but there are rules. Did I get myself understood?

-Yes! We answer at once.

-Now that we've clarified this, let's move on to perfume. Please don't come up with all kinds of crap for me here. Ann, on Friday morning, come back nine o'clock to see what you put together. Now you can go!

We both stand up at the same time, but I'll hold him for a second.

- I'll be here on Friday with the stuff put together, thank you, and I'm sorry.

-I'm over it, good job guys.

-To you too. Peter responds.

We sneak out of the office like two scolded teenagers. Fortunately, no one is in the corridor, everyone is probably working diligently.

-Let's go to work now, it's a miracle we got away with it.

-You see, Ann, our dear boss is a good guy. We should rather go home, he would be ok with that too.

-No way. I got enough shit today because of you. Don't joke with this.

-A farewell kiss?

He shapes one with his mouth. I can't stand it without smiling.

-No, don't even dream about it. Bye Peter. See you tomorrow.

-Don't worry, be happy, Beautiful. Then tomorrow.

Huh. It was all a lot for me one day. Although I try to focus on my work, it doesn't work. I look at the same thing five times in a row. The best part is that the boss will pay more attention to me now, thanks to that crazy Peter. Why did I need to tease him, let him get closer.

Ringing. It's Mom.

-Hi.

-Hi Mom.

-Are you coming in the afternoon? I wonder why you disappeared for such a long time. No excuses.

-Then I'll go to you right after the kindergarten, but wait, no. I quickly step into a store before and then I'll come.

-Ok, got it. I'm waiting for you.

And she hangs up. She's offended, I was right.

## Trust Me

I'll tell her the reason, the evening talk will be good, Mom can calm down. And if Dad knew what I was doing. He would be scolding me. I see in my mind's eye that smart, manly face, the warm brown eyes. Ann, think before you act, always go two steps ahead. Ann, who knows what comes from what? Don't act from anger ... I haven't talked to him in a week. I'll call him sometime soon. I go to the net and look for some perfume ads. Very good. I get lost in the world of perfumes, I keep planning, and I look at them until the end of my work. Shut down my computer, clean up my desk a little and head for the door. I should leave the office without accidentally running into Monique. I position my phone in front of me as if I was looking at something. I purposely don't turn right or left. Three more steps. I'm completely focused on that. Success. I get into my car without any atrocity. I get in and find the music that fits the action on the couch best. I want to think back to that scene, I don't want to be angry. I turn up the volume on Beyonce's -Haunted, a hit, to maximum. How erotic, how powerful but still subtle. I was totally crazy about letting him in, but that technique... He was good. Again, I feel the excitement below, thanks to the memories and my lack of panties. You'll get this back, dear Peter. My revenge will be sweet... I dress Ben quickly in the kindergarten and head to the mall.

    -Mom, where are we going?

    -We buy me a new perfume, I hope you help me choose. After today, I deserve it, and you can get something in the toy store too.

    -That's super! You had a bad day?

    -Yes, and I missed you. You played a lot today, didn't you?

-Yes. We built a big castle out of cubes, played games, played 'catch me if you can' at the yard, and I sat on the swing.
-It must have been very good.

I park and purposefully walk into the perfume shop. The mall is full as if the whole city were shopping today, but few people want to buy a new fragrance today because there are only three of us outside the store. The salesperson kindly is asking if she can help, but I refuse. Ben is standing beside me, I check out the news.

-Mom, choose already.
-Ok, I'm trying, but I don't want to make the wrong decision.

I test another two pieces, but I don't like them because they are very similar to mine. My little prince is already impatient.

-Smell these for me, that helps.
-Good.

Minutes pass, I'm over twenty scents. My little darling picks a few off and smells it. You need something spicier, wilder, more unique, fuller. A new era, a new perfume. Enough of my soft, floral scent.
I remove a special red and orange twisted bottle from the shelf.

-Mom, it's like a unicorn horn.
-I agree.

It smells surprising. At first it's too intense. I spray it on my wrist. I smell it again, I like it very much on my skin. A bold, full, fiery scent. Fits me. I think the ingredients are caramel, some flower, some citrus, ginger and maybe apple. Whatever it is. I'd like to use this fragrance every day, that's the point. Unique, reckless, exotic.

## Trust Me

-I choose this, we can go. What would you say to the idea of buying something for Mom? Surprise her, she deserves it.

-Good.

I'm calling the sales girl for help. I am asking her the latest floral scents. She brings three pieces. Together with Ben, we choose the one that best fits my mother. She will be happy. We'll pay for our new prey. I'm happy I found the perfect scent. Can't wait to spray on myself tomorrow morning. We also stop by the toy store on the way as I promised. Ben goes straight to the plasticine, choosing a new smart plasticine for his collection. It's a check mark. With my usual ringing, I signal Mom that we have arrived. George opens the door.

-Hi.

-Hello. Come on in, your mom's waiting for you in the kitchen. And you little pirate, you come with me and we have a huge game.

-Oh, awesome grand-dad. And look, I just got a new plasticine from Mom, let's play with it too.

The two of them leave for Ben's room, I'm walking into Mom's. She is sitting by the table reading a book.

-Hi Mom. I've read this crime story already. Exciting.

-Hi baby, I like it too.

- By the way I brought you a surprise. Close your eyes.

-Ok.

I'll give her the yellow striped box.

-You can open your eyes..

-Oh, Ann. You should not have.

-I had to. Open it, I'm excited. Spay some on yourself.

She opens it with starry eyes, tries to hide it, but I know she is very happy. Immediately she sprays her neck.

-Ann, it's divine.

I lean closer to her to feel it, and she hugs me. I sit down on the chair next to her.

-It is. This scent is as special as you are.

-Thank you, I haven't bought a new one for a long time.

-I know. I also bought one today. New life, new fragrance.

-Hm. Why did not you call me? I was worried about you.

-Sorry. Just a lot of things happened, I wanted to tell you verbally.

-Tell me.

-I'm starting with Gabriel coming on Saturday. It was strange feeling to see him again. He looked at me like he used to. It upset me, it hurt.

-It takes a long time. When me and your father divorced, every time we met each other I felt the same way. Although I haven't seen him for a couple of years.

-Good prospects. So, they left with Ben, and later I met Emma. We sat down to eat and then drink in a bar. It all started well and after two glasses of cocktails her she started to share. I just wanted to know the truth, so I sat down with her. You told me to be careful with her, you were right.

-What did she do? The truth is not clear anyway?

- She said I'm naive. I couldn't understand Gabriel, but she would have been able to.

# Trust Me

## 8 Months Before Divorce

I cannot stand it. I need to talk to him. With each passing day, the distance between us becomes more and more disturbing. I try to pretend I don't care, but it bothers me. One day, I easily realize that this is just a tide and then passes. And the next day, amid a panic attack, I fall to the ground. I am weak. I'm going in circles in the living room, crawling back and forth. Am I doing good with a conversation right now? A few days ago he said he still loves me, but he doesn't. We yell at each other a lot for little things. We fight at least five times in one night. Yesterday, he was upset with me because I didn't put my key where I used to. It's a little thing, but I think he was just looking for a reason to start a fight . I'm feeling worse... I'm afraid of how he'll react if I forced a conversation again. He's my husband, not my boyfriend. In good and bad together... I'll be honest. I shouldn't keep it to myself, I need to talk to him. I take a few deep breaths and head to his study. On the way, I peek into Ben's room, luckily he sleeps peacefully. I open the door into the study quietly and see something on the machine. He notices the door open, turns to me.

-Why did you come? It's late, go to sleep.

-I know, but I want to talk.

-Can it wait till tomorrow? I'm still working.

-No. Come on, let's go out into the living room.

-If you want it  but let's not go into deep emotional details.

We are facing each other on the couch. I'm in a crossbow, he's leaning back. His posture is relaxed, yet he is watching intently, waiting for me to start.

What am I so afraid of? He's Gabriel, we'll just talk. That's it. I'm getting into it.

-We fight a lot these days almost about everything, it's really bad for me. We are tense with each other, we don't talk, you are avoiding me and you pick a fight about stupid things. You are provoking me purposely.

-Because that's what you provoke in me. You keep pestering me, you don't understand you are cornering me. Better be far from you now.

-I tried to understand you. Accept that you have a lot of work. You used react to things differently in the past. You've changed. You don't tell me what's wrong. You're not letting me help. This has been the case for weeks.

-Because you can't help me, Ann. You'd do your best leaving me alone.

-Can't do. You're my partner. Tell me please.

-Nothing to say. Don't provoke another quarrel.

-I do not want to. I just want an answer to your behavior. I didn't fall in love with this man.

-I'm not into this dragon either who you've become. Come on, find a new hobby, just don't worry about me all the time.

-But we live together. What about sex? It's not the best anymore. I feel like you're just using me. This situation hurts, it drives me crazy..

-Don't go crazy, accept it.

-But we can change it with a common understanding. What should I do differently? Tell me and I'll do it.

Ben also feels the tension between us and sometimes sees me crying. I am about to again, I clear my throat and start to feel tightness. Is he so

## Trust Me

indifferent? He takes the situation half-seriously.
-Ann, don't cry.
-You don't understand me. Don't you sense I want things to be better? To make everything like old times? To get close again? So you would love me? Do you still love me?
-Yes.
-Does not seem like it. You're not honest with me anymore. I called you here to talk to see if we can figure out something together, but you're passive.
-Understand that I don't have a problem, it's just your reactions. Your reactions trigger me to be as far away from you as possible.
-What reactions are you referring to?
-An end-of-the-world pain sits on your face, unhappiness. I can't stand watching this every night. What the hell is he talking about? Is he kidding? Does he think this is good for me? Because of him, because of so many hurts, is it not good for him to see this? I'm going to scream at him in a minute.
-You bastard! I raise my voice. Is it bad for you to watch? Instead of helping you get better, you run away. Am I worth that much? I bear a lot of things for you, you!
-What me? Look inside yourself, Ann. You owe this situation to yourself... You're a nervous wreck.
I froze. He blames me for all this. I'll ask you what he wants, he should tell me now.
-Then what do you want, Gabriel?
He doesn't even think, he answers immediately.
-Nothing.

·····

-Ann, honey! Did you think of Gabriel again?

-Yes, sorry. I was reminded that I was really naive.

-We learn from our mistakes.

-Thanks, I would have missed these lessons. I'd rather continue the story. After Emma said that, I slapped her, yelled at her and left her. I searched for a bar down the street and drank myself to the ground. I was pathetic. I went home drunk in the evening, and then Peter was waiting for my door.

-He wasn't.

-Yes. I tried to drive away, but he was stubborn and didn't let himself to be shaken off. He asked me to give him a chance, let us date. He stayed with me in the evening, and the next morning we went for a walk along the beach.

We spend some romantic time together. We came home, started making out in the doorway, and to our surprise Gabriel appeared, he showed up sooner than expected and caught us. They fought. Gabriel left, later Peter, too. After the whole fiasco, we stayed with Ben and painted the wall of his room. This morning, I also cut Monique out of my life because she turned out to be hateful and jealous of me for many years. This is what happened to me in broad strokes.

-It's better than a novel, Ann.

-Yeah, life is the greatest screenwriter. This has been proven many times.

-I know, but let's start at the beginning.

-Wait, before we start our analysis, Peter has been forcing me to go public with him in front of co-workers.

-Beautiful. How are you after all this?

## Trust Me

-I don't even know what to say. Gabriel tried to get closer after the fight, I didn't even understand. I had a vision during which I saw myself crying. Finally I told him to leave me alone... It turned out that my two girlfriends didn't like me, they used me and wished me bad. I wouldn't have thought this, especially Monique surprised me. She made up that she was with Peter. And Peter, he's the most confusing.

-Why?

-Because he says he really wants me, not only my body. He wants to know me. It doesn't matter to him that Ben is the first one in my life, that I have a lot of wounds, he also would fight for me with Gabriel. Just you know, everything is so fast with him. I just got divorced recently. I am afraid of him. What if I let him closer and he just hurts me? Anyway, everyone at work thinks I'm a bitch after today's events in the office seeing that I already have someone. What if I got to know him better and fall in love with him? What if he throws me away after I sleep with him?... Anyway, he's so sweet. Listens to me, he's funny, masculine, and a bit dominant like Gabriel. I don't know his soul so much yet, but what he has shown so far is what I like. He wants to date me, he said he is very fond of me, he wants to settle down. He wants a serious relationship, though knowing his past this is a bit unbelievable. I got rid of him so many times, but he's kept pushing. Mom, what shall I do with him? Let him get closer? Shut him out of my life?

-Oh, baby. There is no recipe for that... And what does time matter?... If he really wants you, you will see it. Get to know him, get to know him better, if he is really is what he tells you, be with him.

You deserve to be happy again. Don't assume wrong about him immediately. I remember you told me he liked you for a long time, but he didn't try anything with you. This is positive because he waited until you were alone. Do not project the many negative feelings onto your next relationship. Don't judge based on your marriage. Every person is different. Start with a clean sheet and listen to your intuitions.

-Ok, I try not to project my stuff on him. But it's hard. You know, things are messing me up. There is Gabriel whom I will still meet often in the future. To tolerate him taking Ben and I'm thinking too much about the past. And here is Peter. I also have panic attacks, I'm still broken. Yeah, and I don't know what to do with my home purchase. Gabriel also rented out a large sublease. At least I think it's sublease. I hate having to sell our beautiful house, Mom. Okay, that's why I have a hundred thousand in the bank, but I could only buy a mini apartment here. I don't want that. I want a house with a garden again... I have an idea, don't say no right away. What if you sold this apartment and put together what we had, we would move into a semi-detached house in the countryside. One half is yours, the other is mine with Ben. We would help each other out. Good air, it would be peace. We'd go out for walks and stuff.

-We'll talk about the sale later. I'm not completely rejecting your idea... I also desire my old age for a family home, a small garden to beautify, I can help you a lot. Maybe a dog could fit in my yard.

-That's good news, I'm glad... You guessed it about Monique? And I don't want to talk about Emma now. She doesn't deserve a word.

-Unfortunately yes. She always treated you

overly sweet. I felt something sleazy in it when I first saw it. Although a woman, who never had a relationship for more than half a year, tells a lot about her character. Probably unbearable in her relationships. There were signs, but you ignored them.

-I already know, but I thought she was just a funky woman. Everyone has some corky thing. But I enjoyed to have the chance to call her with my good news, complain to her, party together, she often took care of Ben. I loved her silly things, her coolness, our beautiful afternoons. I misunderstood her, very much. She lied to me a lot… Do you think I'm a bad judge of person?

-No, she's a good actress. Her hatred fueled her for so many years, giving her the power to play… your loving girlfriend. What's wrong with you is just not listening to your feelings. You try to suppress them, but you shouldn't. I like you were finally stood up for yourself.

-Yes, I'm proud of myself too. Now, my goal is to get all my bad relationships, negative people out of my life.

-Good plan, you are right, unfortunately this sometimes needs to be done in a person's life.
-What did you do to make life easier after the divorce? In the evenings, at worst, I'm lonely. Weekend family programs are also missing. If you have experienced what it is like to live in a marriage, you will want to continue … I am sure.

-You don't remember what I did? At first, I focused all my energy and attention on you. Maybe I was annoying at the time. In addition, I tried to set goals for myself every day. Think of the smallest things. For example, I sew the broken buttons in the evening, will smile at people, cook some special food. When these small daily goals were achieved, I was glad to praise myself. It was getting easier every day. And every night I thanked for three good things that happened that day.

Don't think big things again. The sun was shining, I was solving a difficult task, someone let me go in front of them in the store. Feeling grateful brings more positive things into your life as you focus on the good things. Try to get started tonight. It may be difficult at first, but believe me it is worth it. This is a slower process but will help. I promise.

-Thanks Mom. I try to integrate it into my everyday life. I hug her, we won't let each other go for minutes.

-Are you hungry, Ann?

-A little bit what did you cook?

-Traditional potatoes dish.

-I would eat it, just a small plate, you do it very delicately. Do you have garnish?

-Pickled cucumber.

-Add that, please.

She gives me a serving, heats it up, and sits back.

-While I eat, tell me a little bit about stuff. What happened to you this weekend? Did you talk to George about stepping out somewhere sometimes?

-I didn't talk to him, only touched on the problem. We were home, as always. I read, we watched a movie.

-So the usual. Mom, why are these things happening to me? Why can't time be reversed?

-You need to live through these things, and you'll find out why. I know I always answer that, but that's how it is.

## Trust Me

-Well, good. Do you think Ben is hurt by divorce? And from having to adjust to his father when he is with him? And what if Gabriel's family provoke him against me? You know how his dear Mommy hates me. Do you remember she barely wanted to come to our wedding? How many times has she criticized my parenting? She always sets herself an example against me, how super cool Mom she was. And I'm young and inexperienced. I think I told you when Ben was about two years old and I was sick, Gabriel told her to come over to help, cook a broth and play with the little one. She schooled me on how to cook a tasty soup, then pulled a cloth out of Ben's wardrobe and put it in front of me. She said I'm folding terribly, but she will teach me the right way. I couldn't wait her to leave us. I didn't even need that kind of help... Oh, I could list her kindness for hours... I'm not missing it. For so many years, we just endured each other, and avoided the clashes because of Gabriel. I bet she opened champagne when my divorce was announced from her son. From her sweet little son. She needs a daughter-in-law she can control, who drinks her every word.

-I remember you telling me that. She also competed with me sometimes. Desperate, unhappy woman, real snake. Probably her marriage makes her this way and her basic nature, which she cannot lose. I hope she can't and won't want to turn Ben against you, but we can't be sure of that. Love is missing from that family. It's weird because Gabriel isn't like that. That's why I loved him by your side... Your luck is that our little grandchild inherited his father. He doesn't let himself be influenced, he has an independent will and he loves sincerely. He has good nature, the little treasure.

-I hope you are right. Thanks for the dinner, it was delicious.

-My pleasure. And to the question of whether he got hurt or not: Yes. You've been hurt by divorce, for example, you have less confidence in men, you have a stubborn insistence on your family idyll, your marriage... But to this day, I don't regret leaving your father. He didn't make me happy and I got a second chance with George... The injury can be small or huge, or the family model will be different... You can't predict it. We see this better when Ben becomes an adult ... Your job is to minimize the damage. I tried it with you, but you were bigger. It might be easier with Ben because he's still small. The younger kids more flexibly experience divorce . Spend as much time as you can with him, and he should see a male model in front of him always. He should feel that you are on good terms with his dad that even though you separated, you still love him. In time you can do programs for the three of you again... There are no rigid rules and guidelines. You see, I am repeating myself, I have already said these. Tell me when you're bored.

-No, you always confirm things in me. Did I chose the easier way by divorcing? Was I supposed to hold on to see if it gets better? I always ask myself these questions in my worst moments. Usually I come to the right decision, but as you say, life will prove it.

## 7 Months Before Divorce

I finally am done with the vacuuming, the mopping is next. I've been cleaning for three hours, that's what my afternoon is about, but I have to spend my energy. Ben is occupying himself, playing Lego. How little time I spend with him lately? I'm

## Trust Me

a bad mother, I don't have the patience and energy. Everything is used up by Gabriel, and pretense at my work, my home. No one can see me falling apart, my marriage is a bunch of ruins... He is very clever because he senses my state of mind, has perfect radars, and doesn't bother me. Right now, I'm like an emotionless cleaning robot... Sometimes it would be nice to really turn off my emotions so that I only feel emptiness, not pain or inertia. My own emotions strangle me, I am bound and imprisoned. And the guard is Gabriel, who's hiding the key... Someone is mumbling behind me, but it can't be Ben. I look back. Gabriel is, unloading his stuff from his black bag to the counter. I didn't miss him coming home. What a weird thing, before I've been waiting for the moment when he comes home, now I wish he wouldn't do it. How some feelings turn. I don't want to argue, fight with him.

-Hi Ann.
-Hello Gabriel. How was your day?
-Good. And yours?
-Good. I'm going to buy some food tomorrow, should I bring you something extra?
-I don't need it. And tomorrow I'll pay the checks and transfer the usual things.
-Ok. Ben will have a kindergarten perfor mance in three days, don't forget we should be there by 5.
-I'll write in my memo.
-Ok. Want dinner?
-I ate, I'm going to work.
-I'll keep cleaning.

And he goes to his little nook, far from me ... I'll put the vacuum cleaner away, run fresh mop water, put some cleaning agent in it, and get started.

My current life is like that... On the surface, bright and clear, but no one can see what's under the floor... Within a month, we arrived to another negative level with Gabriel. I tried to stop this process, but I'm just terribly alone... Now, somehow, I feel like I have resigned myself to accepting this... Our communication with each other has been reduced to general issues that affect our family. What are you cooking? Which check should I deposit? What should we buy for Ben ? Take out the garbage, refuel in the car in the afternoon, etc. It's pathetic. Like two roommates. I don't tell him anything about my days at all, he avoids extended sentences when he talks to me. Neither of us is interested in the other anymore, and I feel that ... and yet I still love him... This kind of reaction and distance is a defense mechanism by me so I don't get hurt. But with him? Would it be total coldness?

·····

-I just remembered it, Mom, when we were nearing the end of our marriage. As a result of such memories, I always feel that it is better to be alone, than to be alone in a relationship. Social loneliness is a much worse feeling.

-You are over it, honey. And the bad feelings caused by memories will fade. It's just an experience.

-Do you still think about dad after all these years?

-Yes, but not too often. Sometimes I look at you, I see him in you. Here and there one of your attributes, you are so much like him. If I suddenly notice these, I can recall memories of him. I have to compare them in myself with George, or wonder what if... This is normal, I was with your dad for

## Trust Me

many years, it remains part of my past. I have a wonderful daughter and a common grandson.

-Why couldn't you keep avoiding your divorce?

-We tried to believe me. I wanted it more, but your dad tried too... Because of you, we wanted to stay together, but this forced situation completely got the best of us. You know the details, though.

I see Ben peeking into the kitchen.

-Can't believe my eyes, my little prince. Come on, sit on my lap.

George follows Ben into the kitchen, than he sits next to Mom.

- Mom, let's go home now and continue painting my wall. It wasn't finished.

-Didn't you eat here by Grandma before? She made casserole.

-No.

I look at the clock, we've been talking about the big things of life for two hours. I still have to take a bath with Ben, before he has dinner. But I don't feel like painting.

-Let's go then. George, thank you for playing with the little rascal. Mom, thanks for the emotional support.

-Anytime. they respond at once.

I love them, they really are my supports. George instinctively feels when he has to leave me and Mom alone. Let's just say he was never intrusive, he didn't want to get between us. He treats Ben amazingly, can keep him occupied, he may have an inexhaustible magical box of ideas. Surely, he wants to compensate Ben for being neglected by his other grandfathers. We say goodbye, pick up our stuff and go home. Throughout the ride, Ben talks about the colors he wants to paint on the wall... We finally we get home.

-Mom, let's go paint.

-Baby, I'm tired.

-But, pleaaaase! You promised me.

He is right, anyways he will not leave me alone until we finish our creation.

-Good, but before that I need to get comfortable. I'll put on a sweater and give Ben a home outfit.

He is excited, tries to hurry me.

-Then, I'll start with the water, you mean the little island.

-What color should that be, Mom?

-Let's say light green.

I'm moving forward slowly, coloring accurately, and he's going quick and with large brushstrokes.
-Do you like it, Mom?

Now should I tell him his coloring is not overly nice? I can't break his enthusiasm and I don't want to hurt him. It must be his creation. Why do I expect a child to be perfect?

-Yes.

We are alternating to color the smallest details. We're starting to get tired, but I persuade him to finish today rather than tomorrow. Two hours later, we finish the job with our hands covered with paint and being exhausted.

-Mom, thank you. It's beautiful.

He hugs me and kisses my face many times.

-My pleasure. It became really beautiful, and the main thing was that we were doing it, together.

-I still have walls.

-I know, but be content with that for now. Let's go eat and then bathe and sleep.

No objection, he is tired too. I make two

## Trust Me

sandwiches quickly, eat it quickly and then take him for a bath. He can barely keep his eyes open while he is in the tub. He's half asleep when I finally put him in his bed. I give him a kiss on his face.

-I love you, little son. Goodnight.

-Me too.

And within a minute he is asleep. It's time for me to get ready for sleep too. While bathing, I think about today's events. It was an eventful day. I'm not sane. I'm a crazy chick who forgot to think. But life is beautiful because of it, isn't it? Sometimes you have to be like that. I went public with Peter... Ok, he left me no choice. Maybe I didn't really want to resist ... I was just getting more trouble on my shoulder. Isn't that enough?... I'm getting into bed, trying to get comfortable... My phone signaled, a message arrived. It's Peter.

-You're just what I am thinking... Listen to Ed Sheeran's "Dive," he will say everything for me now...

I look for the song, close my eyes and focus only on the lyrics. Jesus, does he feel that for me? I can't believe it. Every line of the song touches me. "Maybe I was too pushy, maybe I waited too long" ... "I am someone who gives it all." You are mystery, I traveled the world yet never met anyone like you... Don't say you need me if you don't think so. "..." So tell me the truth before I dive into you completely."... "So don't call my dear unless you are serious. "... I listen to this beautiful song twice. Do you really want this? Do I want to tell him? My tears are falling. I don't know... Damn it. I want him but I'm afraid... He asks me to call if I think seriously. I'd rather answer him with a song, I hope he understands.

- Instead of words, Ed Sheeran, "Give me love" Hope he understands. I am awaiting his answer with a trembling stomach.

-Sweet Ann, Ellie Goulding, "Love me like you do!" Nah, good. Let's hear his answer:

"...You are the only thing I want to touch. I never thought it could mean that much. You brought me to life, so love me in your own way. Every inch of your skin is a Holy Grail to discover. Only you can set my heart on fire. I'll let you give me speed because I don't think clearly. What are you waiting for?"

You allow me to dictate the tempo. Does he want me that much? Did I bring him to life? I? What am I waiting for? I do not know. I will answer him quickly.

-Thanks!

My phone rings immediately.

- Is this your answer? Express your feelings.

-No, Peter. I already told you in the song.

-Like me. I will keep up your pace, you are important to me. With you I can succeed.

-What?

-To live through love, becoming a real companion. Your companion.

-Is this really what you want?

-Yes. Wasn't it clear? I have said it many times already. Believe me at last.

I can't speak, he is silent too. I play with the edge of my blanket, and I sit up. What can I say to this? I sigh and start walking around the room.

-Ann, what was that big sigh?

# Trust Me

-My opinion... You know, everything you say is a bit too beautiful. Of course, I want to hear that, your words stunning me, but how do I know if they are true?

-Give me a real chance. You already agreed in the morning, but I feel it just because I forced it. I really want you to. Want me...

-I

-Come to the door.

-For what?

-Because.

With my phone on my ears in my cute polka dot pajamas, I walk to the door pretty slowly. What kind of stupid thing have he come up with again?

-I came to the door.

-Then open it.

-Yeah, okay, but I just open it out of curiosity.

No answer, but my phone is still in my hands. Slightly complicated and loud to open the three locks, I hope Ben doesn't wake up to the noise. I hold down the handle and I can't even talk from the surprise. Peter stands in front of my door life-size, with shiny eyes, ruffled hair, gray tracksuits and sneakers. He puts his phone in his pocket and comes closer to me.

-Surprise, Beautiful. I couldn't be without you.

-It is, but you can't just stop by in the middle of the night to see me.

-Why not? Who says it's forbidden? Then you won't let me in?

-Yes, if you're already here, come on in, silly. Just stay silent because Ben is asleep.

I'm not closing the door, I still have to let him out. I'm heading toward the kitchen, he's following.

-Would you like something to drink? Wine? Water? Tea?

-Not wine because I'm driving, but I'd like some tea.

I pour myself a glass of wine, I crave it, I bring him a fruit tea and start boiling the water. We sit down by the table.

-Why did you come?

-I couldn't be without you and talk to you about our thing. By the way, the taste of the pussy is missing too. I told you in the office, I could go on all night, and I will.

-So that's the main reason. Do you keep your promise?

-Of course. How was it without panties? Did you think of me when your dress touched your bare little pussy? Or me eating you out again and fly you to orgasm? Many times in a row, and you will not even know what your name is? Did you long for me being in you? How do I taste?

-No.

-You're lying, Ann.

He places his hand on my knees and moves slowly down my thigh towards my pussy. I won't even move, let him do it... he reaches under the shorts and puts his palm on my pussy without hesitation, holds it a little, and then puts one finger up.

-Ah ... mmm.

-See, I told you, you were lying. You're wet for me, and your voice you just released drives me crazy. I'm crazy for you. You twisted my head ... Now I slowly pull out my finger and only continue to pamper you if you want it. You must ask me to continue.

-You didn't leave me any choice but to want it. You made me excited again, I want you... Continue... please!

# Trust Me

He frees me from my shorts and slowly pulls the top off of me.

-As you command it, mistress... Put your feet apart. That's it, lift it up like that, then put both feet on the side of the chair. Lean back a little, come closer with your hips. And with your hands, cling to the armrest... You're beautiful. Masterpiece. I see how much you want me to touch you, but believe me I want it more. No one could do this to me so far. It hurts, I want you so much. I want all your thoughts to be me. To suffer the same if you don't see me as I do. To get under your skin just as you did to me...

-Then spoil me.

I smile at him and then throw my head back feeling sexy. I fully revealed myself to him. He leans over my ears and kisses my earlobe. He kisses my neck and then gets to my chest. He takes the nipple in his mouth and I start to fidget. He pinches one with his fingers and gently sucks the other.

-Don't move. Imagine that I am putting my erected dick in your mouth. You slowly start licking from the outside and then you put it in your mouth ... You make it wet so I can put it in easily. When he says that, he puts his two fingers up.

-After that, I start moving in you, I almost impale you, fill you up and then pull it out of you. And he really takes his finger out, impossible. Just enhances my desire with what he says. I start circling with my hips, signaling him to continue. He leans over to me and kisses me. He circles with his tongue around mine, sometimes catches mine, imitates licking.

-And you'll beg me to put it back, but I won't. I'll put it into your hand to play with it. When you no longer desire anything other than fulfillment, I suddenly bend down and he starts eating me out. How good, I can't take it. His whole head is in my pussy, his stubble is a little prickly, but sexy. His tongue plays with my clit, I howl. Ah... I hold his head and push it closer to myself. With both hands, grabs my butt and massages it.

-Peter, this is...

He goes on, I put my hands on his shoulders, leaning forward. I can't stand it for a long time, just a hair. I scratch his shoulder, he starts doing it faster. And I'm done... I shiver, I claw with my fingernails and

-Ahhhh .... I'm falling into pieces. I feel his grip on my mouth.

-More quiet, beautiful!

Then he gives one last lick to my pussy. I'm dead. For two minutes, I just flinch and finally open my eyes. I see he's standing next to me, with pulled down pants and stroking his erect penis. The word of desire would be too little to describe what I see in his eyes. That's more... I get up from my chair and kneel in front of him.

-Now I'm coming, you can't do anything meanwhile. If you do, I will stop right away.

-I won't, Ann.

He leans on the desk with his hands and waits. Now he is at my mercy. With my hands, I run from his ankle to his belly, slowly stroking him, leaving his masculinity out... Now, with my mouth, I walk the same path as before, licking, kissing. It has a delicate scent, he has the perfect body. I look up at him and see him begging with his eyes to finally get in my mouth... First I just kiss the stiff toy from the outside, then hold it in my right hand and slowly lick with my tongue all over it... I enjoy it fully. I get the tip in my

## Trust Me

mouth and hold his balls in my hands. I lick it purposely slowly as the world's best tasting lollipop. I enjoy it... I massage his balls during this, and he moves with his hips. I get it in deeper and start sucking ...

-You're awesome.

I move up and down with my head, then suddenly I take it out of my mouth into my hand. I start beating... I squeeze his balls and put them in my mouth at the same time.

-Do not stop.

I catch his penis again and push it all the way down to my throat. While moaning, I look up at him and see he has lost control. Me too, and again I get wet. He grabs my head and moves it in the same rhythm with my mouth. I feel like he is coming soon, stiffening. I take him even deeper and do it to him faster... He comes with a loud moan in my mouth and I swallow every salty drop... He stands up and pulls me to him. He kisses me, doesn't care that he just came to my mouth. Filthy and exciting.

-You gave me the best blowjob in the world right now.

He grabs me and presses me against the wall next to the table. We are both panting, our hearts beating at a crazy pace, our desire knows no bounds anymore. He's ready again. I feel the heat, our bodies are burning. He stops in front of me and pulls up my left leg.

-What are you doing?

-I'll pamper you again. You're beautiful, and you're burning of desire, you're on fire or it's me. We need help.

He presses on me, I feel everything. I can just cum from the way he looks at me. My left leg is wrapped around his waist and places my hand

over my head, just like by the door the other day...
He kisses, rubs himself.
 -I want to see you cuming. I have all the desire to put it, but I won't. Not yet.
Insert two fingers, move it in while rubbing his penis at me.
 -Ah... Peter ...
I just want him to be in me. My heart is about to pop out, I can't stop moaning. He pulls out his fingers and puts one more beside them. Playing with three. I can feel my moisture dripping down on his hands, I'm trembling underneath... he presses on me more, stops for a few moments, I know he's close. My leg is taken off his hips... He leans in and takes my tit into his mouth and goes faster with his hands. He holds his penis in the other's hand and starts jerking himself, without stopping with me. He kisses me wildly, I bite his mouth, I feel like he would devour me. I start sucking his neck, I know I'll be done in no time.
 -Ann...
He comes back to my mouth, now he's biting. I cum, and he cums with me, we tremble, my scream is absorbed by his kiss, he shoots his hot sperm on my stomach. I do not feel satisfied, need more of it. It just got my appetite worked up...
 -Ann, if you look at me like this and we're not going to bathe right now, if we're not dressing right now, I can't hold back again. I'll take you on the floor here. I can't get enough of you, I just want you even more after that. You are magnetic.
 -You too, I find it hard to stop. But it's really best to take a bath.
 I realize just how lucky we are that Ben didn't wake up. It's good that he is so tired today, he is

# Trust Me

deeply asleep. And Mom can secretly see the boyfriend. Wonderful. It's a bit like it was in high school. Just don't hear us... I'll let you bathe in the bathtub. As the water slowly runs, we'll talk.

-And why did you say you wouldn't put it in yet? That you are waiting? Why didn't you do it?

-The reason, Ann, though it was one of the hardest moments in my life but I respect you. I want to take you if you really want me to, and not just the momentary overwhelming desire. If you decided, you would really be mine and you wouldn't regret it. I don't want to take advantage of you.

-Huh, thank you... I think... You're right, it's too early to sleep with you, but only because of my feelings. I'm still uncertain, but desire is no problem. You can excite me.

-I know, and I love that. I can feel you and am waiting for you. As I said in the song, you dictate the tempo. I'll follow you.

- Really, how long have you been at my door?

- Since my first message. I was hoping you would let me in and not fall asleep during our messaging.

-You were lucky.

-I know.

And he smiles with that sweet mouth. We wash each other and get dressed.

-Come on, let's sit in the living room.

We sit down on the couch, strokes my hand and keeps looking at me.

-When will we have a date, Beautiful?

- Let's say next week.

-Too far, I can't stand it. On Friday or on the weekends?

-Not good, Ben will be with me now.

-Then the three of us go somewhere.

-I think it's too early. I like the fact you want to, but I can't tell Ben anything else about you, he wouldn't understand the situation. I'm sorry.

-Of course, but I want to spend as much time with you as possible, any alternatives?

-We'll see what I can manage.

-That sounds better, Ann.

-Tell me a little about your friends, where do you party? Where are you going to relax? How do you manage daily stress?

-I have two best friends since university. We're a true triumvirate. We've done a lot of bullshit together, and dated lot of the girls in the clubs. We go to our hometown once a month to drink and relax. I'll introduce you to them if you wish. I work out for daily stress, it always helps and that's why I'm in such good shape. And you?

-I haven't been training for a while and now I don't have any girlfriends as you know. Yeah, and I don't have time. If I do, I usually read or go with Ben. Alone, it's harder to get some time for yourself. Mom is my support, I can count on her when needed, but you already know all of them. And how often do you visit your parents?

-Not too often. My parents and I don't understand each other. I told you they were doctors and they were restricting me, at that time. I didn't study what they wanted me to and I came from home to the dorm. Ever since, when I see them sometimes because I go down to visit them in the countryside, they pick a fight over everything. There is nothing good for them in what I do. They keep worrying about why I didn't make them grandparents and why don't I have a wife. I talk to my mother on the phone every month, we always run around the usual topic. Who would be interested in this?

   -I think it hurts you somewhere deep down.

   -Sure, somewhere. I never had a relaxed relationship with them. In the beginning, I wanted to prove too much to them that my profession was worth something. I worked hard to get enough money, didn't want their help. I succeeded. I put everything second behind work. I even felt sorry for going on vacation, not because of the money, but because it would have been a waste of time. Now I want something else. Enjoying my life, enjoying my money saved. Settle down. Why do you think I came to this company? It's because it's quiet. I'm not gonna die in work. I still have a couple of clients left, but I'll help them out for a different reason. A person is always changing. And the best decision in the world was to come to this boring workplace because I met you.

   -For sure. Anyway, you want to please everyone? You approach everyone by studying their situation, themselves? What do they like, etc.?

   -Why are you asking this now?

   -I remembered that you knew a lot about me, yet didn't tell them. Or are you just a good observer? Did you research me?

   -Yes and no. I've been watching you for a while, you know how long I liked you. On the other hand, I also carefully asked the colleagues and my intuition was the rest. That's it.

   -Ok. Here's a test question. What is my favorite book?

   -Marquez: One Hundred Years of Solitude, and you love Ken Follet's books.

   -You won. What is my favorite flower?

   -The orchid.

- Last question, what is my favorite food?
-You love a lot of things.

-Ok, you're starting to scare me. What do I think of now?

-That you want to kiss me and you want me to sleep here.

-You did not win. You can't sleep here, Ben can't see you in the morning. What would we tell him?

-Well we would fall asleep, I'd get up earlier in the morning and wait for you at the door to start working together. With my car we would go to work and to the kindergarten. I'd be your driver tomorrow afternoon. We'd say to Ben that your car won't start, so I am helping.

- Tempting offer, but risky to take. In many ways.

-Let me have more stolen time with you, I would love to. For now, that's what I get from you. Please!

He looks at me so nice, how could I resist him? I have more counter-arguments, but what wrong can come out of it?

-Ok, I give in. But only on the condition that you will be a good boy, you will not take advantage of your situation, you will not spill the beans in front of Ben.

-Thank you, I promise.

He hugs me so happy and kisses me. I got totally crazy to agree with this, that's for sure.

-But now, let's go to bed, anything's shall be fine tomorrow morning. It's late. We'll set the alarm for both of us for an earlier time. You will leave until we are done and come back for us. Ok?

-Of course, it's good to stay here with you.

## Hope

I look at Ben going to bed, sleeping deep. We set our watch and lay down next to each other. Peter hugs me, and I feel calm.

-Ann, it's not that our time is short, only we wasted a lot of it.

-Who said that?

-Seneca.

-Nice thought, it might be right.

-I don't want to waste a minute of what I can spend with you. I'm glad I found you.

-How cute your romantic self is. Good night, Sir Peter.

-Good night, Lady Ann.

Who would have thought this morning that this way will end this crazy day... I give thanks for three things today as Mom advised. For my wonderful little son; because the boss didn't scold me more; and, finally, because there is someone to hug me now.

·····

I wake up to the endless annoying ringing of the alarm clock. I open my eyes, peeling off Peter's warm hands. I gently stroke his body. What a handsome man...

-Wake up, Peter. We have to get up.

-Just five more minutes, give me. Come cuddle up to me, I want to feel you more.

He climbs on me, kisses my face. He starts to touch me. It feels good, but we can't go on.

-You gotta get up, don't try. We agreed on something.

-Okay, then let's get up.

We struggle to get out of bed, he rub his eyes and stretches. He picks up his clothes and hugs me again.

-I want to wake up next to you every day.
I don't answer that, of course I would, but this is unimaginable at the moment. I'm not in that position.

-You gotta go, I'm getting ready in the meantime. Just be quiet so you don't wake Ben. What would I tell him? And in half an hour, come back for us.

-I'll be there, boss.

He grabs me and pulls me to himself.

-Let go, don't kiss me. You really have to go.
I'll give him a quick kiss and he is walking out the door quietly. I go into the bathroom, brush my teeth, makeup, and put my hair into a loose bun. I choose a sexy black dress. My new perfume fits that dress, it's hot. I'm spraying it on myself. Does he notice my new scent? Incredible, but I'm getting ready as if I'm dating. I'm a little excited, I'm upbeat. I want to please him ... It's time to wake Ben up and dress him. Before he'll arrive, we have five minutes left, so I quickly fix cocoa drink for my baby. He drinks it. Ringing, Peter arrived just in time.

-Listen honey, instead of Mom's car, my colleague takes us to kindergarten and work today. And in the afternoon, he brings us home. You met him last time, he was here with us.

-Why?

-Because our car made strange noises

yesterday afternoon, and I don't dare to go with it. He is helping us.

-Ok.

I lied to my son. Another minus point for me. We open the door and Peter is waiting for us fresh, peachy, in a new outfit.

-Hi Ben, hi Ann. The chauffeur service is ready.

-Hi Peter. - greeting him with a smile.

He had a change of clothes again, he was sure I'd let him in. Am I so predictable? Or does he always have fresh clothes when he comes to me? Or is it a habit left over from the past? He must have solved the delicate situations in the past, keeping a bag in his car with all his belongings. Just in case. This thought makes me frustrated, when I have a good moment, I'll ask him about it... Ben hurries down the stairs, we go behind him. We take the child seat out of my car and reload it. I buckle up my prince and then sit down in the mother-in-law seat. What an idyllic picture. The three of us... Well, well, I have to get this idea out of my head soon. We travel in silence, we are almost at the kindergarten when Ben speaks up.

-When will you come to play with me and the dragons?

I see in Peter, that he is as surprised by the question as I am. I prefer to answer instead.

-Peter has a lot to do, baby.

-But you said Mom, we're traveling with him in the afternoon too. Can't he come and play then? What shall I say to that now? Should I say no, because then he'll be even more part of our lives, and that's another level? Or I am afraid of you start to him? That it could be another lie? Or that could Peter see more from the situation? That it's early? Ahh...

-I'll be happy to play with you in the afternoon if your Mom allows it.

-Can you, Mom?

What's wrong can come out of this? If Ben wants it so much and it only will be one game, not more.

-Ok, you can play one round in the afternoon.

-Yay, how super. Can't wait us to play with my super dragons. I'll be with the biggest, you with the little one.

We get out by the kindergarten with Ben, Peter stays in the car. I quickly put on his inside shoes and pants and give him some hugs.

-Get them tiger, I will be in a hurry to pick you up this afternoon, I love you.

-Me too, Mom.

I get back in the car, but don't say a word. I'm fuming in myself. Why did he have to say yes to Ben?

-You thought I didn't notice how fine you smell and how sexy you are today? I'd eat you here on the spot.

-I bought the new perfume yesterday and thank you for the compliment.

-What's wrong, Ann? Is it bothering that I will play with Ben?

-Yes.

-But why?

-Because it's bothering me and that's it.

-That's not enough explanation. Tell me honestly why.

-Because you can get closer to him, and what if he start to like you too? If he wants you to come again?

-It's better, so it'll be easier to accept me beside you.

-It's early, I think.

There's also Gabriel, what do you think it would be like if Ben had told him you had played with him several times?

-I don't know the answer. But that's not the main question right now. Do you trust me? Are you sure, you want to be with me?

He turns to me, grabs my hand. I look out the window, he can't see my confusion. What do I want? He always confronts me with questions like this. Why does he want to get an answer out of me? I understand that he feels bad because he doesn't feel I am sure in us. But this is too new yet. What is for sure really? Is he really is sure of me, or he just wants to be, because he is cradling himself in illusions?

-Yes.

I answer, but I'm still not looking at him.

-You had a hard time giving the answer.

-I know, and please forgive me. It's hard for me to trust someone again, to re-establish a relationship. Be patient with me.

-I believe it's hard, I'll be patient. I want to be better because of you, Beautiful. I want to be good enough for you. I want the best for you, you change me... You make me feel things that I didn't know I existed... Up until now only my dick controlled me, my desires, now it's that is not important ... I dare to be honest with you, give myself a chance, to be happy... You opened my soul, Ann...

His words penetrate my heart, I start to cry. Wonderful, he brought it out of me again. I always fall apart.

-Thank you for being honest. I don't know what to say to this.

-Nothing, just believe it and store it in yourself.

-I promise.

He keeps his hands on my hands until we arrive at work. I look into the mirror in the car, adjust my makeup. I don't look my best but let's start the day. He opens the car door for me, grabs my hand, and we walk into the building like this.

-After all, you really take me upon yourself, Beautiful. It feels good, the best I've ever felt recently.

-To me, too although it may sound surprising. People watch us until we get to the elevators. We're the new sensation. Look at that. That's it. We arrive and kiss each other in front of my office.

-Have a nice day, my Queen.

-You too.

-I'll throw up in a second.

Monique says, disgusted from behind her desk. I look at her with a smile, not affected by her malice.

-Just do it, but please swallow it too.

And this is how I enter my office. Everything is as I left it yesterday. Piles of notes waiting on the table. Hooray. I take out from my drawer some emergency white peanut chocolate, I need the calories. I didn't even have coffee in the morning and I'm still a little comatose. Never mind. I have to start working anyway, the boss doesn't care about the excuses. I'm going to look at more recent analyzes, and I'll go over my notes so far. Unfortunately, no new ideas come to mind. We need new inspiration, a different perspective. How to get the most sales? The target group will be women between the ages of 30 and 40, they make up the majority of customers for

# Hope

every fragrance anyways. Fewer scents are made for the 50-60s. Not to mention the 20s. So we need to promote our fragrance very well. I have to sit down with the colleagues in the afternoon and start brainstorming together. I also quickly organize a meeting for 2:00pm, notify my colleagues by email. It's a check mark. Next thing, I should get some coffee and some lunch, I won't have time to go out later. I grab my bag, shut my computer, and head off to the elevator. I'll write a text to Peter to see if he needs something because I'm on a shopping trip. Immediately he responds that he needs Chinese for lunch same like me. There's a long line at the cafe, but I'm not worried, I'll wait. Until then, I take out my phone and play some skill games on it. I'm very good, there's another track coming up, when incoming call interrupts. No, it's Gabriel. I don't care. He must have ringed by accident, he will stop. No, he keeps calling. I can't be so terrible not picking up, but I don't want to talk to him. Ok, let's get over it.

-Yes, please?
- Hey, it's Gabriel.
-Hi.
-You don't see my caller ID anymore?
-I do, I just didn't pay attention to who was calling because I am ordering in a coffee shop. Why did you call me?
-To ask you how you are?
-I'm fine. And you?
-It depends. Listen, what day would be good for Ben to be with me? I miss him and I have no visitation this weekend, but I'd like to take him away.
-Huh. I don't know.
-At least you could relax.

In the meantime, I step out of the line because it's my turn, and if I order now, I'll be caught. That's it for coffee.

-Ok, come for him again on Saturday.
-If I came around at 11 o'clock?
-Yes, but then really come.
-I'll be there. And Ann,
-Yes?
-I miss you.
-Yeah. Listen, I'll hang up. Bye Gabriel.

And I turn off the phone. What the hell? Is he missing me? Or was he just kidding? He wants to drive me mad? When he was supposed to say these things, he didn't say anything just fled.

## Sometime Before Divorce Around 6 Months

Whatever. My dough doesn't stick together, it always falls apart. Hooray, I can't even make ordinary pasta. In my anger, I throw it all out. I'll start again with another cookie, staying with the always successful chocolate muffin.

-Mom, can I help you?
-Of course. Come and hand me the ingredients.

He brings his little chair, stands up on it and gives me the egg. Clever little cook, loves to help. We put all the ingredients in there, it will be nice chocolaty, now the robot machine is coming.

-Let me do it.
-Good, but slowly.

He holds the gray bowl in his hand, but it slips it out of his hand before putting it into the food processor, and the entire mass falls to the ground, of course, the kitchen furniture gets some of it, too.

-I do not believe it! Why didn't you pay more attention?

# Hope

-I clean it up.
-No, go to your room.

I hear he starts to weep a little because I screamed. I'm not going after him, only after I'll fix the kitchen. It seems, there will be no cookie today, although my plan was to be at home with Ben on Friday night to watch a good story while eating a delicious cookie. It did not work. Gabriel storms through the door, greets me with yapping and moves on. I'm trying to get the sticky stuff off the ground, how unfortunate I am. I wish not to have started it. "What did you do?" Gabriel yells from the living room.

-What?
-Why did you make Ben cry? He said you screamed at him and sent him to his room.
-Yes it's true.
-You're a crap mother.
-What? I answer him, shouting already.
-You heard that. You can't behave like that, notice that you're terrible!

With this he turns around and leaves. I start to cry while the mass sticks to my hands. Why does he blame me? He knows I'm not a crap mom. I screamed, yes, not because I am angry, but because I am tense. As I am cleaning off the drops that flew there from the furniture, I kind of hear Gabriel talking to me again.

-Did you say something?

And I get up and go out to the living room. He has a black sports bag in his hand.

-Yes. I am leaving.
-Where and why?
-We go to Chuck's holiday home with friends all weekend.

-But you weren't home last weekend.

-And it was such a great decision. I can't stand your style.

-Are you running away from me?

-Yes, and it's better to be with my buddies.

I have to try to stop him. This is very bad. He can't leave like this again. What will be the end of this? I won't beg, but I try to ask if he'd stay.

-Why don't we take Ben to Mom's? Then it could be the two of us. Or let's go somewhere the three of us this weekend for a family program. Ben barely sees you.

-No. You do what you feel like, I'll do what I like.

-But

-No, Ann. That's what I want. I'm going now because they're waiting. I'll call you from there if I can. Bye.

-Bye.

That's it? Do I deserve this much? He flees. He's running away from me, from everything. From our problems, from our lives. I can't stand this anymore. Why did we have to get this far? He didn't care about my opinion. Last weekend, I still understood he was leaving, but this is different now. It doesn't bother me so much that we communicate too little, that we have sex once a month or not even that much, but now he has said it. He said what I knew so far ... He's running away and that's good for him. It hurts more when it's said out loud than I thought. If one does not tell the other, they both silent about the truth, even though you know what it is, somehow it is not as definitive as the spoken words. The power of words... I am helpless, a disgusting woman, a nothing... The pressure comes again...

## Hope

I feel asphyxiated, sweaty, sinking deeper into the darkness every second... Even before I fall apart, I crawl for my phone for the last moment and dial.
  - Mom, come over, I'm sick ...

·····

  Of course he didn't call me from there, and after this critical occasion, he spent every weekend without us, for various reasons. It's been terrible. Why does he tell me he misses me? What does he want to achieve with this? Why does he rip open the wounds over and over again? I told him last time to forget me, that he should not approach me any way. He didn't understand. I won't even tell Peter what he said on the phone, I ignore it, too ... Now I have to focus on what kind of Chinese food I want to buy for lunch. I have no idea. I walk through the door of the crowded restaurant, the characteristic scent striking my nose. However, I do not want Chinese so much after all, I rather run across to the Italian eatery. I'll buy two servings of lasagna. I walk back in a bad mood, my thoughts are all over the place when my phone is ringing again. Dad's calling. Of course, he remembered me today. Wonderful.
  -Hi Dad.
  -Hi, my dear. How are you?
  -I'm doing ok. And you?
  -I work a lot, as always, I work a lot of overtime, this is just how the profession is. We didn't talk for a long time, are you in trouble? I can hear it in your voice. Who do I need to beat up?
  -Oh, Dad. Lots of people. I had a rough day, that's why I didn't call you. I'm sorry.

-I'm not angry, but what's wrong?
-Long story.
-I have time to listen now. I'm on my break.
-I don't have one. I'm just back in the office and I'll have a meeting. Can we talk another time?
-Of course.
-What would you say if I'd invite you for dinner on Friday? I would cook something delicious, play with Ben and talk amongst us.
-I would be glad. So far, Friday looks good to me, but let's check on Thursday night.
-Ok. Kisses, Dad. We'll talk.
-Bye, my dear.

I just got away without my father giving me a lecture, only till Friday. Anyway, I'll tell him what's happening in person. I could finally grow up and not fear his reactions. I'm an adult woman... My dad is in a separate world. I've always had a closer relationship with my mom, usually playing the bad cop. A strict father who adores his daughter anyway but tries too hard to protect her from all the nasty stuff in the world. Based on his own set of rules, he tried to steer me in the right direction during my adolescence. Mostly he used to force his own opinion on me, but it's a fact that he would die for me and crush anyone because of me. He mentioned to me that before the divorce he had contacted Gabriel. Unfortunately, I don't know what happened then because he didn't want to share, but I have some ideas. This memory makes me smile... Once Dad will be in that mood, I'll ask him. He'll be shocked over Peter's story, but I won't lie to him about my current situation. He must have some good insights to help me. Instead of the elevator, I use the stairs to walk up, to drain my excess energy. Just before I reach my door in a

# Hope

moment, I notice Peter waiting in front of it. This will be the new habit? Will he always be waiting at my door? So sweet. He opens it for me and sits down on one of the chairs.
   -I've been waiting for my queen.
   -I have noticed. I brought our lunch, bought a lasagna.
   -It was a good decision. Are we eating together now?
   -Yes. I'm sitting next to you.
   I take out two forks and get started. Fine. We eat quietly as he keeps staring at me.
   -Why do you stare so much? Did I drop food on my clothes?
   -No, I just love watching you, get lost in you.
   -But don't stare that much, I'll be embarrassed. Especially not when I eat.
   -I like to embarrass you and if you knew what I was thinking.
   -I can't see into your head so you can tell me.
   -I got a lot of impish thoughts, Ann.
   His glance tells me to look down at his pants. Well, yes, there is a visible sign of excitement.
   -Are you in the mood?
   -What Ann?
   -In the mood.
   He holds my face and strokes it.
   -You draw me like a magnet. I've been thinking about you every minute for months. Don't think that it's only your body, but the fact that I am with you and that I live with you. We only lie side by side and caress you; you cuddle with me; I wake up with you in the morning; I cook you dinner and make breakfast; you do your thing in pajamas in the apartment and I just watch you and bless my fortune for having

such luck. I know I want too much, but this is my dream. To live with you, and with Ben, of course. As a family.

-You are sweet, but let's not run that far. Time will decide everything.

-I know, I know it's time.

-Listen, I'm not hungry anymore because I'm too nervous. I set a meeting for 2pm, I want to get ready. I get up and put my food in the fridge. He puts his next to it.

-I understand, I'm going. I'll wait for you by the elevator after work. Bye, my Beautiful.

-Bye, I'll see you in the afternoon.

He gives me a kiss and he's gone. I had to send him away, I am too agitated by what he said. Should we be a family? Is he serious about me? He made a confession in the car that morning, which I must confess, scared me, somehow I opened his soul… Hm… Enough of men for a while, I have to think through the details of the meeting with colleagues. I will make a brief power point compilation of the data collected so far and the questions to be discussed. Super. I'm done and it'll start in ten minutes. I grab my tablet and take it to the meeting room. I arrive before everybody else, so I have time to set up the projector and set things up. Everyone arrives on time, they're sitting around the long table. I'm worried because I don't like presenting to so many people. I can feel curious eyes on me, I stand by the projector. I speak for twenty minutes, and my mouth is completely dry. My words followed by a great debate, but finally we agree on the main requests. We are brainstorming for two more hours before we finally end the meeting. Everyone is very enthusiastic and committed. Everything is ready to go, we're going to have a great promotion, so I'll be more relaxed with the boss at the Fridaymeeting. I let the others leave the meeting room before me, I am still sitting, I need a minute. However, someone does not get up from his chair either.

-Is something wrong, you want to talk to me Matthew? That's why you are staying?
I can tell he is embarrassed, he is creasing his checkered shirt.

-Yes. Not sure you remember, but I just asked you out on a date in the kitchen.
Of course, I remember that. What does he want? Spill it out, I don't feel like talking to him right now.

-I still remember.

-It's OK then. I'd like to ask you again if you would come with me? Because I've heard rumors that you're with Peter, but I hope that's not true and we're going to dinner. I really like you.
Cute boy, he's blushing a little. I'll be nice, I don't want to provoke more anger around me. I use my cute gaze, smile a little, and start.

-Listen, thank you for the invitation, but I can't accept it. The rumor is really true, I'm with Peter. You're a cute guy, you'll find somebody soon, I'm sure of that.

-I'm sorry. If you would break up, I'll be here. And I think you need to watch out for Peter, he's bad news. There's a lot to be heard about him in the hallway and...

-Thanks for the warning. Bye Matthew, get some more good work done.

-You too! Bye Ann.
Slightly offended, he finally stands up and leaves me alone. I close my eyes and try to relax for a few minutes. I'm doing the meditation practice I learned from

my psychologist, hoping it helps. I walk up the stairs and open the green door in front of me. The sun is shining on my shore today, but the wind is blowing a little, just right. I walk down on warm white sand all the way to the sea. The waves rippling, but the sight is always wonderful. Refills me and soothes. I sit in the sand quite close to the water and draw with my fingers. I listen to the roar of the sea, looking around. Next to me, I see a pink shell and pick it up. I admire it for a few minutes, then search for new treasures. Suddenly, this peaceful image is broken by a giant lightning in the sky. I don't understand how it's possible in such weather. I have a bad feeling, I'm shaking. I get up from the sand, sweep my clothes and head back. I pick my feet faster up than I usually do. Meanwhile, I hear a voice whispering in my ear.

-Watch out, watch out, watch out.

-I'm so scared that I'm falling. Everything will be sandy, even sand in my mouth, but I don't care, I start running. I'm more and more scared. I don't even stop at the door, I almost tear the handle, I want to get out of this place so much. I see the stairs and start over. I arrive downstairs and then open my eyes to... I'm in the meeting room again, but the bad feeling didn't go away. I brought it with me. What the hell? What do I need to watch out for? What will happen to me? I don't know how long this was taking, but it's time to go back to my office. Immersed in my thoughts in the hallway, when someone grabs me from behind. She claws her sharp nails into my arm, causing me to drop my tablet to the ground. It's Monique.

-Are you normal, Monique? Let me go.

-No, now you're listening. You'll get back the humiliation you gave me. I'll take revenge on you

# Hope

when you don't expect it. You reached your goal, Peter really became yours. You're happy now, but nothing lasts forever. My time is coming.

Lightning strikes from her eyes, her face completely disfigured from all the hate that radiates from her. She pushes her nails deeper into my skin.

-I take the challenge. Now, the only reason I don't slap you because I am in the office. You know, I sincerely feel sorry for you that in your pathetic life you have time to deal with me, you have no private life and nothing that makes you happy. Leave me alone. Have your own life, deal with yourself!
I tear my hand out of her hand, pick up my tablet, luckily it didn't break, and I storm into my little nook. Do I need more today? Do I have to be careful of her? Was this a warning about What should I do to defend myself from Monique's wickedness? I didn't hurt her over the years. It is a terrible thing that someone hates me so much... I look at my wounds, unfortunately caused by her nails will be visible for a couple of days. I sit in my chair, but I don't want to work. I would not be capable now, I'm too upset. I turn my computer back on, but only as alibi, if someone comes, would see I'm working. I take my earphones out and find a song on my playlist. I chose the song "Great Big World," by Christina Aguilera. I start it, close my eyes, and just let my feelings come out...

-"Say something, I will give up on you. I'll be the only one if you want this. I would have followed you anywhere. Tell me something, I'll give up on you."

My tears started to roll, but it's good to cry.

-"And I feel so small, everything ruled over me, I don't know anything at all..."

## 4 Months Before Divorce

The water is burning, but it is fine. It starts scratching my naked body like a thousand needles ... I start to scratch myself wherever I feel until my blood is spurned ... I want to feel pain, I want to feel I'm still alive if my soul starts to die... there is no way out... Can not bear Gabriel, my marriage. I'm helpless... What do I do? Should I divorce? Should I live alone with Ben? Should we just move to live separately? No, no, no... I can't do this... It hurts so much... I lean forward and cry. I am suffocated by the still water, I want to break out, be free, save my soul before I am finally in the darkness... the power of love is miraculous...

.....

The next few lines of the song bring me back to the present. "And I'm proud of you, you're the only one I love. And I say goodbye... "I have to say goodbye to him, finally, to cut off the last faint emotional thread. He can't stir me up over again, he can't say he's missing me. He can't... Why does it still hurt so much?... I wipe my tears, get up, open the window. I put my head out and take a few deep breaths. Breath in, breath out. Ok. I'm better, I'm strong, I'm beautiful, I'm happy, I'm successful. With renewed vigor, I start to work if my tasks that remain. I only focus on the perfume. Hooray, according to the clock on my monitor, I'm headed home in two minutes. I adjust my makeup, pick up my bag, and leave my office. The first thing I see is Peter's smiling face waiting in front of the elevator. It feels good, if he can heal my heart. Maybe if I opened myself up to

# Hope

him more, I could fall in with love him. The power of love can work wonders...

-Hi, beautiful!

-Hi Peter. By the way, I like if you call me queen better!

-I'm calling you as you please. But you can be my squirrel, kitty, baby, bunny, mousy...

-Good, good, enough. I got it. Then let's just stay on, my queen. That's what I like best.

-I understand, my queen.

-Clever boy. Come let us finally get in the elevator because Ben is waiting.

In the car we discuss our day, I tell him in detail what happened at the meeting.

-Then the picture came together?

-Yes, finally. So I don't have to feel crummy in front of the boss on Friday. And imagine I invited my dad to dinner on Friday night. I spent time with him a long time ago, I'll cook something delicious for him.

-What about our date?

-That's what I wanted to tell you. Gabriel called me today and asked if he can be with Ben on Saturday. I said yes, so

-So we'll be together all Saturday and Sunday morning?

-Yeah, we can go somewhere.

-What would my queen say if we were doing something crazy on Saturday? We should get you out of our comfort zone.

-What do you mean? Should I sew a unicorn onto my ass? Jump off a cliff? Should I get a super short bling haircut? Eat a baked beetle?

- Yeah, but I didn't mean these. Just be a surprise, then I'll organize everything.

-Good.

At the kindergarten we pick up my little prince, I see he is excited about the game. We park in front of our house and start to walk to my apartment enthusiastically. How good it is someone keeps Ben busy this afternoon. That's a big help, until I can cook something delicious. I want to impress Peter with my cooking science. We put down our stuff, but in the hall, he holds back our hands.

-Just a minute. Before we go play Ben, I want to give your mom and you something.

He pulls out an expensive white wine, a big table chocolate from his bag, and hands it to me. Then he takes out another packed box and hands it to Ben.

-Can I open it, Mom?

-Of course.

He tears off the green frog wrap with great excitement.

-Mom, Mom, this is a new Lego Dragon! Black!

He starts to jump up and down and hugs Peter.

-Guys, you could go play, but only after washing your hands. And Mom's getting ready for dinner, the wine will fit perfectly. Enjoy the game. I'd give Peter a kiss now, but it's forbidden. But I kiss Ben well before he disappears into his room. How cute Peter is that he thought of the little one and surprised him with something. Good grade for him. And I got my favorite white wine, really is a mind reader. I put on a more comfortable outfit and sit on the kitchen chair hesitantly What shall I cook? I want to do something flashy but it's not so simple. What would be the most suitable for this wine? Got it. I'm making risotto. I open the fridge to see what kind of ingredients we have. Super. There are delicious mushrooms and chicken breast. I'll take out everything

# Hope

else I need. Toast, cheaper white wine, spices, onions, Parmesan cheese. I put on my white apron and get to work. Half an hour later, since I'm doing great, I allow myself a break. I peak into the little room, I'm curious. I see they are lost in the world of dragons. Ben is sitting on Peter's back, holding his new dragon, and they go around. As they notice me they both smile at me.

-Mom, I'm the biggest dragon right now, and I'm traveling around the countryside with my dragon fellow.

-Very good, but be careful not to come across an enemy dragon and notice you.

-We'll be careful they answer at the same time. I'm walking out, let them continue playing. Peter is having a good time with Ben, and he seems to be enjoying himself, it's not forced. He leveled with my little one, and now he behaves also like a happy little boy. Could he be a good father? Maybe this is the something really missing from his life? One family? Could he really hold onto me? To set a good example for Ben, to be a part of his life? I don't know. I do not dare to really think about these things yet... It would be too beautiful a gift for me to find the first person after my divorce to be my next companion for the rest of my life. Do I deserve this? I see many women around me who are better than I am in many areas of life, but have been single for years after their divorce. They jump into worse and worse relationships just not to be alone. They hope to succeed with the next man, but unfortunately lots of men just take advantage of them. They are less and less able to trust men, and I understand that. Of course, I can't generalize, but I think that as a divorced woman you have a much less chance of having a child, or at least it's harder to find a man who really takes you seriously.

Every woman, young, old, divorced, single, deserves to be really loved and happy. You shouldn't be afraid. Everyone deserves a second chance at happiness... I hope so too. I was strong, so I divorced from Gabriel, started all over again. Secretly gave me strength to see that I can stand alone. Then, if I am strong enough on my own, I put my little soul to the right spot, and later, yearning for companionship, can find my happiness on the side of a new man. Could this be Peter? Is it possible for it to come so soon? Why not? Life has a lot of surprises... Nothing comes in the way you would expect it to be... Anyway, they are laughing now, I can hear it. So good to hear my little love laughing. I'll continue to perfect the food. I taste it, very good. I think I'm ready. In the meantime, I place three plates out, not two. It's strange... I serve a portion for all three of us, grate it with fresh parmesan and pour some wine, Ben a soda. It's time to tell them they could come eat. I go in.

-Guys, come on, dinner is ready.
-Mom, not yet, later.
-Come on Ben, I'm coming too, Mom probably cooked for us something very delicious, I'm hungry.

He grabs Ben's hand and comes out of the kitchen with me. We sit at the table.

-It smells great, Queen... or Ann. What did you create?
-Chicken and mushroom risotto and the fine wine you got. Enjoy your meal.
-Enjoy your meal everyone.

I take the first bite in my mouth and I am satisfied. It is perfect, I can still be inspired if I have the motivation.

## Hope

-Ann, this is heavenly. I haven't eaten such delicious risotto before.

-Yes, Mom, very delicious.

-I am glad.

I feel warmth in my heart as I look at them, but there is also an unexplained bad feeling. If at any moment in your life too beautiful, you almost are waiting for it to deteriorate and then you realize that this is not the reality. The picture at the table is too idyllic. But not. I have to stop. Like Mom said, I should enjoy the moment, just be and not worry too much. That's what I'm going to do now. I don't think about that anymore today. I sip on wine, it will relax me.

-Wine tastes very good. Thanks.

-For your health, I'll taste it now.

And he sips. It's becoming clear now. If he drinks, he can't drive home, so he stays with me. Damn, he played me again. He'll get for this, but not in front of Ben. I look at him, and he grins that I finally got it.

-Mom, thank you. It was enough. Can I go back to my room?

-Yes.

-And Mom, Peter can come back to play with me a little bit? We didn't finish it just yet.

-I have to talk to him, until then get in your room.

-Ok.

I hear the door to the small room close, and only then do I begin to speak.

-You've played me , Peter.

-What are you talking about, Queen?

-Don't queen me now, you know what I'm talking about.

-I have no idea.

-You brought the wine purposely, drank it directly so you couldn't drive home in the evening and there should be no other option left but to sleep over again.

-It's all made up, excuse me.

-You can excuse yourself.

-Why is I so bad at what I did? I knew you wouldn't have told me to stay, even though you wanted to, so I solved it. Are you really angry now?

- Yes, but no. Of course, it's good to have you, but you stayed here yesterday and I have to lie to Ben today. We hide like teenagers.

-Then don't hide.

-You think it's all that simple?

-Yes, Ann. You're over complicating everything.

-Because my life is more complicated than yours. You don't have to account for anyone, you don't have to take care of anyone. You live alone, you are an independent man.

-Do you think this is good for me? I'm hiding with you instead of being with you without limits. I know what is I undertook, be a little more flexible.

-Hard.

-I understand you. What's the plan for tonight?

-Do you want to go back to play with the little one?

-Yes, I promised him.

-Then you'll be playing with him for, say, an hour. Then you leave, I don't know where, walk or get in your car. I'll bathe him it, put him to sleep, and write a message when you can come back. Will you accept this?

# Hope

-Of course. Can a kiss come before ?
-I expect it.

And he kisses me. Not as hot as usual, but gentle and kind. He felt it was better to approach me gently.

-Now, go play.
-Yes, my queen.

He hurries back to the little room, I'll pack up the rest of our dinner. I'll leave the wine available, maybe we'll drink later. It's incredible how he shakes my life up. Ok, there has been no order and harmony in my daily life for a while, but I have been striving for it, and I am striving now. I started to set up a system with my little prince, we were fine, the two of us, and I am willing to let a man into my life again. I was running away from another man. But humans are social beings... My little soul, after all the hurt, craves the caring, the caressing, the attention, it's good. I'm selfish... I didn't really think what I would do if I got caught in front of Ben. What would I say? Ok now I figure out what I would tell him. Oh, honey, he'll be your step daddy or something. Ah, no. Mom is with him only sometimes, so she's not alone. Bear him, but don't love him too much, who knows when he'll leave us. Mom hasn't known him for too long, but she's starting to open up to him, so you too should accept him as a new friend into your life. Your dad always stays your dad, and these two men hate each other by the way, but this is a small thing... Neither would be a good sentence. I have no idea... I'm just drifting and being careful not to get caught. I'm forced to do so. Wonderful... Or, rather, I tell him now, go away, never come back, change jobs, or move to another country. He wouldn't leave. How many times have I asked him to look for another, but be didn't...

And the truth is, I'm starting to really like him. His sentences and actions prove that if he were with me just for sex, he would have left. That's something more. He is different than Gabriel. Here, I think of him again. There is no one in my life like my ex-husband. He is my child's father, my first love. He was my teacher, my soul mate, my friend and my lover... He didn't have the cute humor like Peter. Gabriel is a far more dominant man than Peter. It clearly radiates that he is an "alpha male." Peter, I can't say. There's a male force in him, but somehow it's different. He can grab me, but not with the elemental power like my ex. Maybe because I didn't let him close enough. Yeah, that could be the problem... But I'm afraid to open up to him... If I were in love again, would I give some of my heart to him, and what if he would throw it away in a few years? I couldn't bear it again ... My heart was already broken, and he wouldn't get a big enough part of it. One half of it and my life belongs to my son, he's first. The remaining half, though, is broken. He could get that part, if he manages to patch it. Would it be possible?

## 3 Months Before Divorce

It's past midnight, but I'm just tossing around in bed, I can't sleep. This afternoon my psychologist advised me to definitely try to tell Gabriel my current feelings. What's the point? They are so locked in, we are so alienated. I'm lonely, it hurts to see him every day, to live in this situation... I don't know what to do. If I got divorced, I'd have to sell the house, share everything, Ben would see me every two weeks, and I would have to start my life all alone... Everything

## Hope

from scratch... Can I do that? Give up a solid financial backing? Let go of my husband, my marriage? Stand alone? We have sworn eternal loyalty to each other, holding on to each other, right and wrong, until death separates... I often try to think that this is just a terrible moment, but will pass and then once and for all it will be as it used to be. I've been waiting for months for the old Gabriel to return. I had tolerated so much hurt and humiliation in these months, tried a lot of different things, but hit the walls... What could it be? For nine years, we have lived in harmony and love, and everything could change from one minute to the next ... Now I'm going to be strong and give it a final try if he wants to fix it. I get my white robe, step out of the bedroom and head for the study. Open it, but he's not there. I look in the bathroom, Ben's room, in the kitchen, but he's not there. Only the garden remains. I put on my shoes and leave the house in a robe. The night is cold, but the stars are beautifully lit. Everything is relaxed... I find him sitting at the wooden table in the garden. Only the light of the moon illuminates his troubled face. He has a glass of red wine in his hand and reads something. I'll sit down next to him.

-Hi.

-Hi Ann. Go in, I want to be alone. Too late.

-I know, but I want to talk, because if I don't tell my feelings right now, I'm going crazy.

-I don't want to talk.

-What happened to you? You can't always lock yourself in. It's terrible to live next to you. But fine that if you don't want to talk then just listen.

-All right.

He finally puts the cup down and looks at me.

-You've been doing this for months. I can't stand it anymore... You know, I tried to get things better, but they didn't get better. We only live side by side like two strangers. A great chasm separates us, we have moved away from each other... Gabriel I'm helpless... Let's try to fix it if you wanted. Let's go to a couple-therapist or wherever... We can get help. Maybe it can be repaired... It's not too late... But I beg you to quit this still water because I am drowned... Sometimes I am thinking maybe it's better to get divorced, just to end the suffering. We can't do this to each other, especially after all these years. Where the respect disappeared to? Please tell me honestly what you think. Honor me with finally saying the truth. I deserve that much... What do you want? What about us? You still love me?

I look at him with tears in my eyes, I would hold his hand but I don't dare. I don't dare touch it anymore, even to look at him hurts. My stomach cramped and my limbs became ice cold. I beg you, do you also want us to stay together... Please... Just look at me for a few moments, but he doesn't say a word. The silence drives me crazy... His gaze is cold, and there is an inexplicably deep, radiating pain. It feels as if he would be a different person ... A known stranger...

-Anna, the circle closed.
-What do you mean?
- We can't give each other anything anymore.
-This is not true. I could if you wanted me to. You're my husband. Let's fix it, everything will be good! Because of Ben, we should try... Anything possible, just want it. Let's not give up like this... Let's fight together... The three of us are a family, we have promised to stick together. I can forgive you for the past few months.

# Hope

-Sweet little butterfly... I'll let you go...
-Ann, I'll go then. Ben said goodbye, waiting for you.
-Time gone by like this? I was in my thoughts.
-Sure. I look forward to your call.
-I'll call you as we agreed.

I walk him out and then go to Ben. He's sitting at his desk and drawing. How great it is that he can stay busy this way.

-What are you drawing?
-A dragon.
-It will be very nice. Are you okay?
-Yes, Mom.
-Did you have a good time with Peter?
-Very good time. He should come and play with us again.
-Indeed?
-Yes. He said he had a lot of good game ideas.
-Maybe he'll come to us anyway. You're not sleepy yet?
-A little.
-I understand, you got tired playing. What would you say if I went to bathe you and read you a story and then we slept?
-It's ok if I have to take a bath but let me finish the dragon game.

I wait till he is done. I take him for a bath and after we finish, I lie down beside him in bed and hug him.

-What do I tell you about?
-Dragons.
- There was a giant white castle in the mountains long time ago. It had more than a hundred windows and long narrow towers. The prince lived here with his mom and dad. The castle has been built on the top of the highest mountain so that the

inhabitants can enjoy the beautiful view every day for a long time. Beneath them was the whole city, the huge pine forest, but beside them the snow covered harsh mountains. They were lonely because no one had ever come to the top of the mountain. They only ventured down the dangerous mountainside once a year out of fear. Their only amusement was reading or telling stories by the fire. One day the young prince looked out of the window, dreamed that he would love to live with the others in the woods. He noticed someone knocking on the window next to him. He turned his head to the side, wondering if he had heard incorrectly but not. It was a blue bird. He walked closer to the window and opened it. I can't continue my story because my little loved one fell asleep. I stay with him to keep from waking up. He must be dreaming about big dragons. Minutes later I get out of the crib and start looking for my phone. I still have some time, I don't call Peter right away, I prefer to shower so I don't have to, later. I'll finish soon. I let my hair down and put on a black leggings with an elongated blue t-shirt. I washed off my makeup, but I'm not going to do it again for home. If he likes me, he will like this too. In the kitchen, I pour myself a glass of wine, start drinking, and write a message to him that he can come back to our secret date in a quarter of an hour... Why can't I control my dreams? Or just to dream about beautiful things as kids? Dragons, cats, dogs, flowers ... It would be good. Unfortunately, I dream too often of that particular day and I wake up crying.

# Hope

## Two Months Before Divorce
## The Day My Heart Broke

-I look like some prepared cured ham. Look how tight the red pants are on me, the fat around my waist hangs out of this top. Ah... Everyone will laugh at me. On the other hand, you.

-Stop Ann. We came to the gym just to change that. You'd rather be happy to finally step out, someone is looking after Ben, and we have the whole night after training. The party, the drinking, can come. Olé! This should add to your strength, to your one-hour workout.

-You're right, Emma. But you know how long I haven't come to train. You are lucky I have said yes now, but only because you are such a pushy woman. What if my heart stops between two breaks? Or the pants will be torn while I'm squatting?

-Yeah will see, but now come, it's starting.

The room is full. I think there are thirty people for sure. I stand in the back row, less noticeable here, and the instructor always watches the front. I hope at least. Emma of course, puts herself fourth in the first row. What beautiful female bodies are around me. I feel like I'm out of line here, I am far from looking like that. My inferiority complex got punched again, but fortunately I didn't have time to come here. I know everyone has the time they want to make time for, but... Let's start warming up. It's still going. Hurray... too fast for me, maybe I should have gone to senior training... My tongue is out, even though it's only been half an hour since warm-up. Everybody around me is doing it casually, I am constantly lagging behind with one beat and one movement. Even though it is an aerobic exercise,

exercise, more like torture for money for an hour... I don't even know about the world, I sweat everywhere, pant, I'm red when we finally get to stretch. The hour is over, this is it, I survived. I'm a hero. At a snail's pace, I go back to the dressing room, sit on the bench, rest.

-Listen, I'd rather take a shower at home and get ready for the party there than here. Is it ok? It's just more comfortable at home, I don't want to show myself here.

-OK, Ann, but let's get going, because that'll be a lot of time. I'll get ready at your place then.

-Ok.

We pick up our stuff, we don't change our clothes, let's get to the car. We parked beside each other, Emma next to my little red car, with the white beefy SUV. We get in our cars, I leave first, she comes behind me. I still need half an hour to relax until I get home, at least my body needs a break. I turn on some nice chill music on my player. When my phone rings, I switch to my handsfree.

-Girly, the plan changed. I'm going to get ready home because Chuck just called, I have to go home before the party. I don't know what's so important, but it doesn't matter.

-Well, Emma. Then what time should I go to Green?

-Nine? But put on sexy outfit, not some sour maid gown. Be sexy.

-Ok, ok. I'll be there at nine. Bye.

Do I wear maiden clothes? Not everyone can be a fashion designer. Nah it's good, now she'll see what a real sexy Ann is tonight. I'll be wild. I think I put on a red dress, red lipstick and let my hair down. That'll be fine, though I don't go for a date, still I want to

# Hope

show Emma that she's not always the most beautiful. Just one more block and I'll be home. I can finally let go out the tired steam in the evening and have a great time with Emma. I take out my gate opener and it opens. What the hell? Gabriel's car is home, but he hasn't stepped into the garage. He doesn't get home this early. Maybe he's just stopped in for something. No problem, it won't bother me anyway. I don't park inside either, I'll leave in two hours. I pick up my training bag from the mother-in-law seat, and I don't even look for my house key, since Gabriel really left the door open. I want to hurry, so I just drop my bag in the hallway. I am sweaty everywhere, my body is sticky, but before I enter the bathroom, I hear his manly laugh from somewhere. I have to find it, I don't like it. Not in the living room, the kitchen is empty, too. It can be in the study. I open it, but he's not there. I look into Ben's room, too, but who would be there. I'm starting to get nervous, I have a bad feeling. The bedroom remains. The door is open a bit, I hear female voices, I push in the door, but I immediately stop on the doorstep. I'm frozen. That's not ... That can't be true. Tossed clothes on the floor, Gabriel is lying on the bed, his blue silk blanket is strewn around him, and a slim red-haired woman is writhing while he is stroking her butt. She rolls like a snake. They are completely absorbed in each other, visibly enjoying it, the woman moaning in his ears. What? This can't be my husband ... I close my eyes, if this is just a disgusting dream. Suddenly I open it, it's not a dream ... No sound comes out of my throat ... I'm standing still, I'm just about to vomit, I have nausea. The room starts to spin around me, everything starts to get dark. I have lost my balance, but I can suddenly hold onto the door frame. She

notices me, looks at me with her big green eyes, and then starts riding my husband even faster. No, this cannot be true. This woman is Betty... I can't move, my legs don't work. I want to go there to strangle her, but this damn leg doesn't obey. Why? Why not? I want to speak, but I can't squeak. What's with me? Am I shocked? Help! Somebody help! Someone! Or rather the earth would swallow me forever now... I want to kill her to bleed on my husband's body.
I look around at what would be the most appropriate object for this. I take my white vase on top of the dresser and hold it spastically. The bitch doesn't even embarrass herself, she keeps having sex like I'm not here. Anger is taking control of my body more and more, I feel the power that is finally controlling my body. I'm on fire, the adrenaline has finally taken over. I just focus on it, walking halfway toward them, and then the coldest blue eyes in the world look at me.

-Get out of here!

Somehow, I stumble out of the house, take my foot forward, the farther I want it to be... to disappear... Sobbing, I start running towards the dark forest. I want to die, I don't want anything else ... He doesn't love me, betrayed me, it's all over... I'm over ... I'm lying under one tree, curling up... It's cold...

.....

The ringing of my phone brings me back to reality, Peter calls.

-Beautiful, I'm standing by your door, open it to me.

-Coming.

I quickly open the door for him, his eyes lights up

# Hope

when he sees me, and then he suddenly becomes sad.
 -What's wrong beautiful ?
 -Nothing. Why?
 -You cried.
I touch my face and it really is a covered with tears.
 -Huh, maybe. I didn't even realize I was crying, I just remembered something sad.
 I close the door and we sit down in the kitchen. I pour wine to him automatically, and I drink what's still in my glass. I'll take another dose. I don't want to tell him, I just keep drinking.
 -You want to get drunk again, beautiful ?
 -Maybe it feels good now.
 -Tell me what's wrong with you.
 -I don't want to burden you, I'll be better soon.
 He just watches me and waits. If I tell him all about it now, he may be disappointed or look at me differently. What should I do? I better send him away, I'd rather cry alone.
 -Peter, I think you should go home now. Surely one of your friends would come there for you. God forbid, I'm not a good company right now. I'd better be alone today. Please.
 -No way. It's enough of drinking, it won't be helping. I won't leave you here in this condition.
He grabs my glass and takes it out of my hand. He puts it away, pulls me up and leads me to the living room.
 -You sit down with me now and tell me what's wrong. Don't close yourself in, I'm here with you, Ann.
 I sit down beside him, put my feet up and put my head on my knees. I'm starting to fall apart... He better find out, and leave me now, at the beginning.

It's very hard, but if he wants to hear that much, I'll tell him. I want to get over this. Deep breathe... For a few minutes, I only watch my breathing to calm down... It's time to talk.

-You know it started a year ago. Gabriel began to work more and more. He spent little time home. He said it would be only for two months because of the new project. That's not what happened. He started to come home later and later and didn't care for me and Ben. He began to distance himself from me. Many times he picked fights, pushed me away. I tried to talk to him, but it didn't work. He didn't want to open up to me, he didn't want to tell me what was wrong. After that, he spent the weekends separate from us. We fought a lot, I cried a lot, and I had more and more panic attacks. I was helpless and I felt like I was drowning... We barely communicated with each other, and if we did it was just about day-to-day things, sex was less and less. I got a lot of thorns in my back in these months. By then, I got hurt by just looking at him, so I avoided him... In the last few months, we only lived side by side, like two strangers, but I was hoping it was just a bad period and it will be better as his old self will be back. It didn't happen... I became more tense, lonely, everything was wrong. The still water choked me, I didn't know what to do... Three months before the divorce, I sat down to talk to him. I told him what I was feeling and asked him to be honest because I am going crazy. I would have given everything for us to be real partners again. His reply was that he's letting me go. This was worse than saying he no longer loves me or wants a divorce. You know, I was even more confused by this... Weeks passed again and I was still waiting for a miracle. I was thinking

# Hope

a lot about what was best for me and my baby. You know, every day I lost myself more and more. My soul was dying... I was a nervous wreck... So one night Emma convinced me to finally get out of the house.

-Beautiful, do you want to take a break? You start to lose your voice, you're shaking.

-No, I'd rather finish. So Emma dragged me to work out. We agreed that we would go to a party afterwards. We would have been preparing for it, but on the way home Emma called that she needs to go home to Chuck and we would meet at the nightclub. I hurried home... Gabriel's car was home, it was strange. I walked into the house and heard his laugh. I started searching, found him in the bedroom. He was making love to Betty.

-Who is Betty?

I can't answer because his phone is ringing. He doesn't take it and puts it on the table face down. I'd just continue, but they call again. He is not taking it.

-Betty?

The ringing resumes, can't be true.

-Beautiful, let me pick it up it, then I'm yours again.

-Ok, at least I can gather some strength.

He walks out, I see him walking between the kitchen and the hall, he gets upset. He speaks softly, I only hear a few words of what he says.

-I will go to you...

He says it to someone? To whom? He must be some guy.

-Do not worry, everything will be as we discussed.

He puts down the phone. He's coming back to me.

-You heard it. He rode my husband there, not embarrassed when she saw me... First I got shocked, then the adrenaline started to kick in and I wanted to kill her. I grabbed a vase and walked towards them, and then Gabriel looked at me, with such cold eyes that it hurt more than anything. He told me to get lost ... I threw the vase to them, I don't know whom and where got hit because I ran out of the bedroom. I didn't want to stay there and beat them or scream or question them, I just wanted to run away as quickly and as far away from them as possible...
I was a coward... Today I would do something else ... I ran out to the garden and threw up. Than my feet took me toward the dark forest, I kept sobbing... The next thing I remember pretty much lying on the cold ground , shaking and wanting to die. My heart broke ... I don't know how much later a car stopped next to me. It was George. Somehow I was able to dial my mom, I don't know when or what did I say to her, but she sent him for me, she felt I'm in a lot of trouble ... Since then we did not talk about this, I did not ask her about the details.

-Jesus!... And the last time you met Emma, you put together the picture.

-Exactly. How well you see the situation right away. I couldn't . I sensed it, but I didn't want to believe it. Up to the restaurant I hoped Emma didn't know everything. Well, yes, I'm really naive. That's how she and her sister plotted against me. And Gabriel...

-Ann, please don't cry. It's over.
I start sobbing again, he takes my hand and pulls me to him. He is stroking my back, soothing...

-Shh...

Minutes later, I turn towards him, unfold my

## Hope

self from his arms, want to tell him my whole story. How I got here. To finally release it from myself... I'll continue slowly.

    -You know, the next day with Ben we moved in with Mom and then here into this sublet, that was two months before the divorce. In the meantime, I filed for divorce but the administration was time consuming. He didn't even see the little one until the divorce. I lived my day as a zombie after that. I blamed myself for everything... I slept, ate sometimes, but I didn't care about anything. I became depressed for a while, Mom helped me a lot with Ben, she was with him a lot. We also sold the house, Gabriel arranged everything about the sale. I lost everything I had in my life. All that mattered to me ... I was just afraid there would be a problem with child placement, whether he wanted to take it away from me, but Gabriel accepted all the conditions I asked for... I still don't know all the answers to a lot of questions and I blame myself. Why did this happen? Why did he humiliate me so much? Why in our own bed? Why wasn't he honest? How long has he been in a relationship? How long hasn't he loved me? Why didn't I notice? Why did I wait so far? Was it my fault? Haven't I struggled enough? I wasn't enough for him? Am I not good enough? Am I really worth this little?... I would be interested in all these things... And now I'm here with you. In big strokes and skipping a lot of details, this is what happened to me. I wipe my eyes and bow my head. I dare not look at him. Here I just revealed myself. I'm empty... hurts... Too vulnerable... He lifts my head and puts it in his hands.

    -Oh, dear Ann. Thank you for opening up to me. I can't change your past, but I want to change

... your future.

-Indeed?

-Indeed. Ann, me!

Now he bows his head. He takes his hand out of my hand, gets up and starts walking around in front of me. Embarrassed.

-Yes, Peter?

-I think... I fell in love with you.

-This?

-Listen to me. I didn't want it that way, but it did. Now I had to say something I had never dared to confess to myself. Don't be scared, I'm not expecting anything in return... It's a new feeling for me, too. I've never been really in love, as I said, you opened my soul. I don't know how to love you well, but I want to learn... With you. I'm crying again. I'll go over to him, kiss him.

-Thank you, Peter.

He hugs me tightly, drying up all my tears on my face with precious kisses. Warmth passes through my body, his closeness gives me security. I feel like I'm in a good place again... For a few minutes, we just hug each other, we want to show each other that we are here for each other, this is me. Stripped down like that... See my soul?

-Do you still need me like this anyway?

-I just told you something I've never told anyone before that I love you... Ann, the way you are. And that's good to say. I love your soul, your body, your mind, your son, everything. I am completely in love with you... You are a sweet poison... You pass through everything, you crawl under my skin, you flood it, you flow with my blood, you poison... I never feel getting enough of you, I feel that I am alive again. It's incredible... Wonderful, but... Does he

# Hope

really love me? Me? Like this ? So much? Do I deserve this? Don't you go away because I'm a disaster? Because I'm unstable? Because I let my marriage fail? Because I'm weak? Because I have too many wounds that have not healed yet? Because I'm just me?

-Thanks... and... You know, I'm sorry, but I still can't believe that's how really is. I'm sorry... Give me time to arrive to you too.

-You have my time and my heart.

We sit back on the couch facing each other and get lost sight in each other. All I see now is his soul... I feel him... I like what I see... He strokes my hair and twists my hair between his fingers. Like two teenagers, we smile. I like his smile, the way he pays attention to me with all his senses, he makes a map on me, his love oozes in me.

-After we moved, I had to look strong all the time for Ben, only to fall when he didn't see it. At first it was terribly difficult, I felt I had no strength to start again, and I was feeling depressed. Then I started to reverse the situation. I changed my vision. This helped.

-What did you do?

-I started thinking instead of all the negative things, immersing myself in self-pity, how much better I am without Gabriel. How much better not to get stuck in a broken marriage, not to break down completely, but to get a second chance at life.

-If he hadn't cheated, you would have quit?

-I've been thinking about that a lot. I don't think so, but a couple of weeks later–I'm sure I would have. By cheating, he put an early end to our marriage because I was too weak then. He did the most dishonest thing possible against me, and he did it in our own bed. He humiliated me in every way, also dragged my femininity into the mud. I will never be able to forgive him... I'm back stronger than I thought. I was afraid that I would be lost forever alone, because I wouldn't have support. Recently, I'm just starting to come to the conclusion, I shouldn't make myself dependent on a man... I don't have to wait for a man to make me happy... Life has got me into a situation where I have to learn to love myself again and be alone..., then I'll be full again.

-And I've just ruined the picture.

-Something like that, but life is just that. Unpredictable. I've told you a couple of times that nothing comes the way and when you want it. God wants the best for us, we have to trust him, he knows the answer to why.

-You are right, Beautiful, I am grateful to him for our acquaintance.

-Let's talk about you. Tell me why you painted that picture? I am interested in.

-I have always loved painting. My favorite painter is Monet. When I was a kid we went to galleries and exhibitions with my grandparents. I imagined I would become a famous painter someday. I liked to draw, it relaxed me. That was one of my hobbies. I was in high school when my grandparents got the canvas you see on my wall. I started painting in the small wooden house. They always encouraged me. It reflects on my feelings at the time. When I was done with it, I was happy to take it home to show my parents. They told me how terrible I was as a painter. For them, there was only one way. I wanted to answer them. So, my wings were broken and I let them do it... I haven't painted since.

-I'm sorry. And what does the picture represent to you?

# Hope

-The black spot is me, it's sadness. Lines of color represent happiness, hope, light that can find you as they surround you.

-What a nice thought. Hope you still will paint. We must not give up our dreams.

-Should I be a poor painter instead of a wealthy lawyer? Should I?

-Oh, you're crazy, of course. Be a wealthy lawyer who paints again as his hobby in his spare time.

We both smile.

-You didn't give up your biggest dreams, Beautiful?

-No, but I often change my dreams in my life. I'm lucky because the biggest ones have come true over the years. I think our dreams inspire us and we should never give up. You have to dare to dream big, do it, and get along.

-Tell me one.

-After Mom and Dad got divorced, it was very difficult for Mom. She cried a lot, but she tried to be strong because of me. It was difficult to recover. Then I vowed if I had a child, I would do my best to raise him in a loving family... His father would always be with him. I imagined how my husband be, our future home, would look like. I dreamed every detail, the colors, the furniture. And the house of my dreams came together, I arranged everything as I had imagined years ago... I had a perfect marriage, we lived in unity. This is what I wanted, I wanted to... And here it is... I'm sorry I'm talking about this again, this is the first thing that came to my mind.

-It's ok, Ann.

-But I also imagined in high school how good it would be for my graduation ceremony to hold my diploma in front of my parents, who were crying from joy. When I was tired of learning, this image always floated in front of my eyes. This gave me power, and it happened. Now I've only told you about my biggest dreams, but there are many little things that came true. I wouldn't bore you now. And you?

-I was sitting in my room many times during high school and wanted to be free. I wanted my independent life away from my parents. Own apartment, such.

-How bad was it with them?

Many times, yes. I've always felt like an outsider in the family. They're too cold. Their immeasurable expectations were difficult to meet. For them, only the perfect is accepted. They hate that I became a lawyer, and I got more distant from them over the years, but I've told you about it.

-Is it possible they're just not be able to show their love to you?

-Possible . They worked a lot, I hardly remember a program together with them, of course, I had it all, but as an adult I really wish they had spent more time with me as a kid. I often missed them.

-It must have been bad.

-It's the past, Beautiful. Let's just look ahead.

-Yeah, that is right , I think too much about my past.

-Now close your eyes, Ann.

I close my eyes as he asked. What does he want? Does he want to kiss me?

-Now, just relax. Forget all the bad feelings, focus on your breathing... That's it.

He grabs my hand but does nothing else.

-Imagine yourself in the future.

# Hope

meditating lately.

    -Ann, all I want to do now is to make you look into the future instead of the past, to dream again. Dream something nice, now for me.

    -I will try, but only for your sake.

I don't see the green door right now. Immediately I find myself in a field. Large pines and gentle hills surround my sight. I'm in a small valley in the middle of the forest. Beautiful. I have a long white dress, my hair falls on my shoulder. I'm alone, I sit down. I watch the scenery while enjoying the warm rays of the sun blazing in my face. I recharge with the help of nature. Peter is approaching me, so I stand up and walk toward him. He's in white, too. He smiles, opens his arms inviting me to run to him. I start running, I feel the love between the two of us, I just want him to hug me at last, but suddenly someone catches me from behind. He starts tearing up my clothes, spinning. Just spins and spins. I don't look at him, I know who it is.

    -Why did you open your eyes so fast?

    -I was scared of something.

    -What was it? What did you see?

    -I was in a field with you, we ran towards each other, then Gabriel suddenly caught me.

    -Oh, Ann.

    -I didn't want to see this, believe me. My subconscious can be blamed. This cannot be my future. My desperation shows, he hugs me and lays me down. He's coddles up to me, we're forming a real little croissant-big croissant pose. He is just caressing and holding me tight, this means more than anything to me now.

    -Just feel me now... Don't think, please... I'm here for you.

# Butterfly

-Mom, Mom, Mom, wake up!
Suddenly, I open my eyes, Ben stands in front of me in pajamas, and looks at me questioningly. I turn to the side and see Peter waking up beside me. Oh no. We did not set the alarm. We fell asleep, we got caught. Jesus! Thank goodness at least we fell asleep in clothes. What do I do now? What should I tell him? I'm sweating, nothing comes to my mind. That's it. I can't even move, I'm frozen. Peter, on the other hand, suddenly sits up and grabs Ben's right hand.

-Good morning, little buddy. Can you pull me up, please? I can hardly stand up. Imagine I came back last night because I fell down the stairs and your mom helped take care of my wound and then we fell asleep.

He won't believe it, nor could he have found a more crippled explanation. We're finished.

-I help.

My little sweetheart pulls him up from beside me, and I continue to sit ruined.

-What happened?

-I went down the stairs in the dark, then saw a giant black dragon at the bottom of the stairs. His big red eyes lit up. He was waiting for me. I wanted to jump on it, but I missed. I fell by the wayside. Somehow it happened, AAAA.

He grabs Ben's arm and he wrestles him onto the carpet. He starts tickling him.

-The great dragon laughed at me like you do now.

-And then?

-Then I pulled my sword out, but the dragon spun away.

Now he spins Ben on the carpet.

-After that?

-He started running away from me so I couldn't stab him.

Ben rolls up, gets up and looks at Peter in anticipation.

-Run!

He starts running toward his room, Peter after him. They are laughing at something now, one of them probably has fallen. Ok. I must admit it was a nice defense. I can't believe we got away so easily. I get up from the couch, I have to search for my phone to see what time it is. The rest will come later. I find it on the kitchen table. It's 10 o'clock. Oh no. I should have been working already. I also have 5 missed calls. The boss called. Even better. He'll probably fire me. I have to call him back and make up a lie. If I went in now, it would be worse. I'd rather stay home. Oh, I don't know what's best. Maybe I'll come up with an illness. Let's say diarrhea stomach virus. Yes, it will be credible. Ben or I could have caught that in kindergarten. I go to the toilet and at the right moment I'll flush it. I close the door on myself, dial the boss— I can't waste time.

-Yes?

-I'm Ann, good morning.

-It's not morning.

-I know I'm sorry, but I haven't been able to get up from the toilet since morning because I got the stomach virus. That's why I'm not in yet. I'd like to

# Butterfly

ask for a day off today, I'll get better by tomorrow.
 -I hope so.
I flush the toilet for the sake of appearance.
 -Thank you, and once again sorry, boss.
 -Ann
 -Yes?
 -You're a terrible liar. See you tomorrow.

I sit down next to the toilet. Great. Not only did I lie to my son this morning, but also to my boss. At least Ben believed the story. Why did I get into this situation? This is not me. I've ruined everything again. They don't leave me ponder about my misfortune because someone knocks on the door.
 -Yes?
 -It's me Beautiful.

And he's already opening the door, I didn't say he could come in. He looks at me with those beautiful brown eyes.
 -"Hakuna Matata,"

What? Are you serious? It makes me so angry with this silly sentence in this situation that I throw a whole roll of toilet paper at him.
 -You're not funny, Peter. –I meanwhile am smiling.
 -I'll give myself up my lady, don't stone me to death with toilet papers. Please.
I throw another roll out of the holder and take two more in my hand.
 -Run away, Sir Peter, otherwise you're done.

He starts playfully dancing with me towards the living room, yelling at Ben.
 -Little buddy, come on, help me because your mom attacked me.
In a second, my baby is out of his room, and he can't miss the fun of the morning. Peter pulls out my guns

from my hand, throws them away, and wrestles me down on the couch. Ben chuckles and looks forward to his role in the game.

-Come on, my loyal gun-bearer, Sir Ben. I caught our dragon, torture it.

He doesn't need more encouragement, he throws himself in and starts tickling me. I can't keep my role anymore, I start laughing out loud. I missed that so much. Honest laughter feels good. I look at them and for the first time I can believe that I would be a good partner with Peter.

-Enough, I surrender, you won.

They let me go, Ben leans on me, leans his head on my chest. Peter goes out to the kitchen.

-Mom, can we stay home today?

-Yes, this day is only ours.

-And can Peter stay? Let's go somewhere, please...

It's a nice turn. Ben is asking Peter to stay. Of course, because they play well together, it's enough for the kids to suddenly accept someone. I'm not going to work anyways, why shouldn't we spend the day the three of us today, if that's the case. Or is it too early for a joint program? How do I do it better? Ok, I'll be spontaneous, I am just drifting.

-Yes he can stay, too. Go out to the kitchen, call him and we'll discuss it with him.

He runs into the kitchen.

-Mom and I thought you could stay here and we can go somewhere together.

-It's a great idea, I'll be happy, but I'll figure out where we're going.

-Good! Shouts Ben.

-Baby, first you go brush your teeth and wait in your room to get dressed. When we're done, Mom

## Butterfly

is ready, we have breakfast and we can go.
-I'm going.
Peter comes closer and gives me a kiss.
-Have you rested Beautiful?
-Somewhat, except I lied to Ben and my boss in the morning.
-But I saved us nicely, didn't I?
-You were brilliant, you quickly realized what you had to say to my baby. I would have been saying silly things if I would have managed to speak at all. We were irresponsible, this can't happen again. Do you agree? By the way, what did you lie to the boss?
-When you were closed in the toilet to apologize, I instead wrote him a message saying I was going on leave for a week because of a family problem. He wrote back that he was ok with that. Well done, I have a couple of days to rest and I can handle a few things.
-Do you think this isn't suspicious after our scene last time?
-Perhaps he figured it out now, but I don't care too much.
-And if he fires me?
-Oh, Ann. No way. You need to make a bigger mistake than a little lie and a request for leave.
-You may be right.
-But, let's enjoy this stolen day together, don't waste any more time. In the meantime, I make coffee, you go to Ben. Meanwhile you're with him, I'll go take a shower, then your turn. While you're getting ready, I'll make breakfast with the big boy.
-Did you plan everything in my place?
-Yes.
I head out for Ben, a little puffing in myself.
-Wonderful.

-What are you grumbling under your nose, Beautiful?

-Nothing, I said nothing.

What a good ear. Of course, I mumble in myself because he's treating me like a kid right now. It's cute and all that he plans everything for me, but it also makes me a little nervous. Could he have planned out this whole day in advance? Maybe he forgot to set the alarm on purpose? Anyway, I'll ask him. But he can't hope for more sleepovers ... But he loves... Me... Yesterday's confession today is even more incredible to me. Ben likes him, too, what else do I need? I started talking myself out of things again... Maybe I got crazy... Too nice to be true... Or am I just afraid of experiencing the good that came suddenly and therefore doubting it again because of the previous bad experiences? He said he was in love with me... But if we are going somewhere today together, it is the next step. What should I say to Ben? What if Gabriel finds out? Everything is confusing again... I'm dressing Ben, he goes to Peter in the kitchen, I enter the bathroom. I get ready fast, I look pretty ok. I look in the mirror. My eyes shining a little, it's incredible. They haven't shined like that in a long time, have they? No, it can't be. I can't feel more toward him... Enough of being brainy... I'll tell myself my usual mantra. I'm beautiful, I'm strong, I'm smart, everything will be fine.

-Mom, come on, we're ready for breakfast. We made sandwiches.

-Coming. It will be very good, though we could call it lunch, soon, it's so late.

I sit down and sip my tasty coffee. I really like Peter in my kitchen, I could get used to breakfasts like this. He's wearing a loose white shirt with jeans.

# Butterfly

How cute we dressed to each other, though my jeans are much narrower than his, and my white top has cleavage. I'm not really hungry, I just bite into my sandwich as an alibi. After the morning show I'm nervous, not nervous, more like excited. My stomach has butterflies in a good way because of the time we spent together today. We'll definitely have fun.

-Thank you guys, it was delicious.

-Mom, you didn't eat a lot, even though I put the butter on the bread.

-You know, baby, that's just enough for Mom now

-Will we leave then?

-Yes, we can go if you are done.

- I had enough. - My little prince says it immediately.

-We'll wait for Peter to eat.

-I'm ready, we can go.

We don't bother packing up any leftovers, I take my bag and Ben is bringing Mr. Grumpy. We are all excited, I can tell. I close the door and head downstairs. Peter comes closer and leans over close to my ears.

-You know what came to mind about this white top you have on, beautiful?

-What?

-The spilled red wine, the little house, your beautiful body.

Of course... I am blushing immediately as he says it, but he likes it even more. I don't even have to look at him to know the exact same images in his mind. We reach the ground floor with such flirty thoughts. It really was an unforgettable weekend. We automatically head for Peter's car. I strap my little spy into the baby seat and I sit in the mother-in-law's seat.

-Where are we going, Peter?
-The secret, for your Mom and you.
-When do we get there?
-Once for sure.
-Shall I tell you something?
-Say it.
-If I'm afraid of something in my bed at night, I imagine I'm a wizard and I will enchant the bad ones.
-With magic spells?
-Yes.
-Can you teach me magic spells, too?
-Yeah, and you know that in my room we painted that beautiful picture with Mom?
-I didn't know, but it's really nice. Do you like pirates?
-Yeah, and the dragons, the dogs, and the cars.
-Which car is your favorite?
-A Ferrari.
-I love it too, but my favorite is the Mustang.
-I have both of them in small size.

How well they talk together. Ben chats a lot along the road, which means he's feeling good. They are sweethearts, it's good to listen to them. Maybe it is this simple with all Peter … He will be quickly and unobtrusively involved in Ben's life, as in mine. I know where are going, we know this way. Would he intuitively felt this too? That cannot be possible. He's a mind reader or something.

-Sir Ben, Lady Ann, we are finally here. Let's get out.

Ben rushes taking off his belt, waiting for me

# Butterfly

to get him out of the car. When I open the door for him, he realizes where he is, he shouts in joy. He starts to pull my hand.

-Mom, this is a racing simulator place.

-Sure you have been here, little buddy.

-Yes, a friend of mine had a birthday party here, and Dad and Mom brought me one.

-Then you will lead me around.

-Good.

Ben runs almost to the entrance, and we walk a little behind.

-How did you know?

-What?

-How much does Ben love this place?

-I had a feeling.

-Don't joke- and I poke him.

-Ok. I searched the web a little bit about kid-friendly car programs to see what could be best for him. This seemed like it, but I have a couple more good ideas for the future.

-Do you want to be in such good terms with us, Sir Peter?

-I just want to make you happy, and it's not a sin if someone prepares. Or is it?

-No, really not. And I really like that you checked out ahead of time the possibilities.

-You see Beautiful, not everything is as bad as it seems at first.

-Come on, you slow snails! Let's get in! -Ben shouts to us from the door.

-We're coming! We reply at once.

Peter doesn't let me pay, he buys the entrance ticket for the three of us. This whole place, for kids and adults alike, is a great playground. It is full of simulators, but it also has billiards, table football and a snack bar. There's another special room for birthday parties, the last time we were there. To be honest, I'm not particularly fond of car simulators, but the joy of my little one is well worth the money.

-Mom, can I go play?

-Yes.

-I will go with you, sit in the simulator next to you and help set up and start the game.

-Thanks.

They're off to the simulators, and I'm heading for the buffet first. I order myself a coffee because I haven't even had breakfast. I sit down on the couch with coffee in my hand and watch them playing here. Apart from them, only two people are playing right now, no wonder, as it is early and a workday. Last night I wouldn't have thought I'd hang out here today. They are other guys, shouting at each other doing laps on the racetrack. A few minutes later Ben rushes to me.

-Is something wrong, baby?

-No mom, it's super. But you're not coming to play?

-I'm coming but only for one round .

I sit in the simulator next to them. How beautiful my loss will be.

-We play whoever wins out of the three of us can decide what we play next. Are you in Ben?

-Yes.

-Ann?

-Me too.

-Then go for it.

-Wait, one more question before. Then all three of us can go on one track?

-Yes, Mom.

Although I do not have a routine in this car

## Butterfly

rink and in such games, I am quite skilled. I'm good at driving anyway. Now, in this turn, I'll be ahead of both of them. One or two more turns and I win.

-This is it! I won!

I jump out of my chair and celebrate my unexpected victory with a funny dance move. The boys also come to me, Peter is all smiles and gives me high five.

-It was beautiful Ann. Please show me this funny move again.

-No way. This is my own victory dance and you laughed at me. You can laugh at me, but I still beat you.

-Because we let you win, Mom.

-Indeed?

-Yes, but you can choose the game now.

-Thanks guys, but I shouldn't have. I want a fair victory. Ok, so we'll play a rematch of billiard, I may have a chance.

-Mom, do I have to? I don't know how.

-Little buddy, you can go back to the car, I set everything up for you again and I'll play a round of billiard with your mom. Will that be good?

-Yes.

We take the billiard cue, take our seat at the table, and we're ready to start. Fortunately, from here, I can really see what Ben is doing, with half my eyes always on him.

-What can the winner, dear Peter, win?

-The winner may have a wish for the other. Will it be good, Beautiful?

-Perfect, but don't cheat now.

-I will not.

Peter is almost devouring me with his eyes and that feels good. I play it a bit of this now, leaning over the table more than I should. He doesn't know, but I love playing billiards, I practiced a lot during high school. There was also a table at our favorite place. We start with the tempo kick, which is how I start the game, because Peter's ball did not reach the opposite wall. Then comes the usual bullet launch and the kick start. Yay, I managed to reach my goal and hit the hole with the stripe.

-It was nice, Beautiful, then I'll be with the full.

-Thanks. I'll destroy you.

-Wait for the end.

We are completely immersed in the game, Peter has been making no mistake for quite some time, he puts one full set after the other into the hole. This is the second time I have missed mine.

-Nice, you make mistakes many times. Can I give you a lucky kiss on your beautiful mouth so you play better?

-I wish, but Ben can see us.

-Then just come closer and hug me. All I need is an innocent hug. By the way, it's a very nice sight when you bend down to the shot or when you're shaking your butt. I know you are turning me on purposely. I might have a seat at a table to be able to watch while you play. And we could try a lot of things on a table like this. Would you like that?

-Maybe.

And I look at him provocatively. We put the billiard cues down. We hug each other, but in the meantime I see Ben coming towards us, so I release Peter quickly. Hope he didn't see it.

- Mom, I'm hungry and need to pee.

- All right, then we'll go and get something delicious from the buffet.

# Butterfly

It seems our match is unfinished, no one can win. I'll take him to the bathroom and then head for the buffet. Peter is already waiting for us, with three hot sandwiches and refreshments ordered. We sit down by one of the tables.

-Thank you for being so attentive.

-It's nothing, I hope you love it. Ben do you enjoy being here?

-Yes, it's cool. Are we coming back some other time?

-We'll see, baby.

-And Mom, why did you hug Peter?

Oh no. So he saw it. Another unexpected question. What should I say? I look at Peter to say something, I hope he is smart again.

-Your mom hugged me because I was a little sad.

-Why?

-Unfortunately, I couldn't get the ball in the hole and so she won the race.

- You're awesome, Mom. Can we play together again after eating?

-Okay, little buddy.

I froze again. Wonderful. Is that always going to be like this? Peter fortunately responded well again, but I should improve myself to prevent this from happening again in crisis situations. I'm going to ask Peter for advice on whether or not he has a good idea of what to do in such situations. They finish their sandwich very quickly, I'm only at half-way.

-Mom, Ben asked.

-What did you ask my dear?

-Can we go back to play?

- Just go.

Ben runs back and Peter takes advantage of

the moment and gives me a stolen kiss.

-Your taste is delicious. Although neither of us has won, you can ask anything from me, Beautiful.

-Don't make irresponsible promises, I'll think about what I want.

What should I ask him for? Maybe a romantic dinner? A massage? Satisfaction? Each would be good, say one after the other. Chemistry works incredibly well between us, we want each other all the time, but it's more than that. He's in love and I'm starting to be. I think... I want to spend more and more time with him. I like he is not pushing for sex and waiting until I'm fully prepared. Perhaps this game will fire him up even more, though he is really at the end of his tolerance, but he deserves a compliment. Last night he was just caressing and hugging, he wouldn't have tried more, he knew he achieves more like this... What a good thing to hear Ben laugh and see that he likes Peter. They play together forever. Well yes, I really need a man every day so I really can see clearly in these type of situations. Ben loves being with me, but that's different. They race for another hour, than we are told that our time is up, we have to go. We collect our stuff and start walking to the car. Ben is still in full swing.

He asks Peter.

-What else do you want to do? We still have a lot of time.

-I do not know.

- Mom, aren't we going to the beach for ice cream?

-Let's go, we really still have a lot of time today.

We get to the shore, I sit down on a big rock, and Ben immediately starts throwing stones into the

# Butterfly

water. Peter stands beside him and starts tossing stones in the water, too. I close my eyes and only listen to the rustling of the water. I try to relax, empty my mind when a scream breaks the silence. My stomach jumps as I recognize Ben's voice. My eyes open wide and I immediately run to them to see what's wrong. Closer to them I can see that Ben is wet below his belt and Peter is squeezing the water out of his pants. Suddenly I'm very relieved.

-What happened, baby?

-I'm sorry mother, I just slipped and I was suddenly screaming because the water was very cold. Peter quickly caught me, but I got wet, do we have to go home now?

He starts to chatter, and I embrace him.

-No problem my sweet, calm down. You really have to go home now because you can't walk around here in wet clothes.

-But I don't want to, Mom.

-What would you say little buddy if we took you home for a change of clothes and then we can come back here, to the big playground. If you play skillfully, you can even get a cookie.

- Ok, hurry home.

He grabs my right hand and we try to get back to the car. Peter walks on my left, I am leaning closer to him for him to hear it. I'm angry.

-Why did you do that?

-What?

-You have decided in my place, and without asking me, what to do later. This is not the way to do it. I should have talked about what I wanted, not promising the little one playground and ice cream.

-I'm sorry, I was just trying to solve the situation so he wouldn't cry. Are you mad at me?

-A little.
-Ann, I didn't want this day to end like this, that's why I told him to come back.

What can I say to him about this? It's a really sweet thing of him. I can't be such a dragon.

-I'm trying not to be angry, but next time we need to discuss your ideas before you say them out loud.
-I promise you, but then please teach me such things. I don't have a child, I don't know much, but I want to.
-What do you want?
-A baby from you, but now just to learn things... I see you were really surprised by this, forget what I said, just tell me if I'm doing anything wrong.
-Ok, I'll tell you.
-Thanks.

Fortunately, we'll be home soon, so there's less chance of Ben catching a cold. I quickly changed my clothes, too, and Peter in the meantime playing on his phone in the hallway.

-Would you like to go to the playground my sweet?
-Very much, Mom.
-Then we go, because as I said in the morning, this is your day.
-Well, how do you like the noise of the kids?
-I didn't even notice.
-Good answer.

Ben is hanging out with another little boy around the climbing structure and we're sitting on the bench. I notice some moms like Peter. I understand. Many single moms are here to play with their babies, and they would love to sit next to my knight now. I am watching my little one as he swings when

## Butterfly

a blond-haired man about Peter's age, stops right in front of us. What does he want?

-Hi Peter. What are you doing here?

- Hi, Timothy. We came down to play.

Peter stands up and they shake hands. He grabs my hand, pulls me up, and prepares for introducing me.

-Here's my girlfriend, Ann, and her little boy, Ben. He's the cute little boy in the blue polo shirt on the climber.

-My pleasure, Ann, to finally get to know you. I've heard a lot about you. Are you bringing my friend onto the right track?

He punches on Peter's shoulder and I smile.

-We'll see.

- Tell me, Timothy, did your wife sent you down to play with Mary while she is cleaning up?

-Something like that, you know how it goes with us. I'll leave you guys, too. Peter we'll talk. Bye now.

-Bye. We say it at once.

-You never talked about him.

-I told you I have two best friends. He was one of them. We'll meet again next month to have a drink with them, you can come with me, at least they'll get to know you and you'll get to know them. You can ask about embarrassing things too.

-I like the offer better now, I'm in, and I'll work on my schedule . I couldn't introduce you to any of my girlfriends as you know.

-No problem, then there will be new ones later you can intro me to.

-I hope so.

Ben runs to us, but starts to drag Peter, not me, Peter.

-Come on with me Peter, I found a big centipede, look, let's build a mini house for him.

I see Peter at first surprised, then with a sincere joy on their face they head towards the beetle under the climber. It was weird, but it felt good. Today he's the favorite, at least he knows what it feels like to get tired by a kid. They're working hard, Peter is looking for something, Ben is digging the sand. As much as I was afraid this morning, I feel calm now. I decided to let Peter closer. There will be no trouble here. I should soon say something about it to Ben. But what? Clever little boy, he must have some ideas about this already. I go over to them and tell them I'll go to the nearby ice cream parlor to bring everyone ice cream while they build the little cottage. I get the three cones and then I start to walk back merrily. I wave to them and they come to the playground bench where I sat down.

-Thank you, Mom, it's yummy!
-Thank you, Ann.

The chocolate is divine, I make noises while eating it. Peter keeps his eyes on me, he is a little kinky. I have some ideas what is he thinking.

-I'll buy 100 servings of the same chocolate ice cream for my apartment, if you eat them the same way like now.
-Why should Mom eat them in front of you?
-Because I like to watch someone enjoying something like this.
-I love this coconut too, buy one for me.
-I'm buying you too, little buddy.
-And you see, Mom's already done, she loves it so much, and we're falling behind.
-Ben what's your favorite dish besides ice cream?

# Butterfly

-The fried chicken what Mom prepares for me every Sunday.
-You eat the same meal every Sunday?
-Yes, how do they say that Mom?
-Tradition, honey.
-That's tradition.
-I love traditions, too, Ben. Imagine, in my tradition, every Sunday night I watch a good movie on TV and eat chocolate and popcorn.
-A lot?
-Quite a lot.
-And what movie?
-I usually watch action movies.
-I can't yet watch those, only Mom. I'm used to watch fairy tales or nature movies.
-What's your favorite story?
-There are many. Mom, I ate the ice cream, I'm going back to build.
-We'll go after you, baby, I just talk to Peter for a few more words.
-What do you want to talk about Beautiful?
- We have to go home soon.
-Why?
-Ben's getting tired, just look at him.
-Well, there's something in it. Can I go up after?
-I don't think so now. Thank you so much for this wonderful day, but I would not like to explain to Ben again today.
- Can I sleep with you?
-Peter, it's not ok, I told you in the morning, see how it turned out to be.
-It turned out to be a good thing.
-I didn't mean that, what I meant is when the little one found us together in the morning.

-Did not think anything bad.

-I know, but I'd like you to sleep next time with me when I told him about the two of us. I don't want to hide like that.

-Then let's tell him now, I don't want to hide anymore either.

-You are sweet, but this is not the way to tell him.

-Than how ?

-I don't even know. I need a plan. I recently divorced his dad, but how would he feel if I announced I'm with you now, what would he feel? Not much time has passed yet. I'd shake up his little soul again. Now he's just starting to get used to that we live only the two of us and he rarely sees his dad. That would be another shock for him.

-I understand this. I don't want him anything bad.

-I'll figure it out, I promise. The perfect first step is he was with you today and he loves you.

-Thank you Ann for letting me do that. Really nice kid, I like him too. It shows you brought him up.

-He's a real treasure, but come on, let's go home.

We make our way to my apartment in silence, Ben relaxes, and the two of us delve into our thoughts.

-Well, baby, we're off.

Peter removes the child seat, puts it back in my car, and then walks us up to our door.

-Thank you for this day, I had a good time.

- I had a good time, thank you. Bye Ben, bye Ann.

-Bye, Peter. We'll meet soon.

# Butterfly

We can't kiss, so we give a kiss on the cheek. We go into the apartment, Ben rushes to his room immediately after washing his hands, and I go to the kitchen to clean up. I miss him a bit now, but the day was beautiful as it was. I am about to make a quick pastry with sour cream cheese, it will be perfect for dinner. It's ready quickly, so I call Ben for dinner.

-Baby, dinner.

-Coming, Mom.

We sit down at the table, but I see on Ben he is sad because of something.

-What's wrong? Why are you sad?

- Just because I couldn't play with Peter any longer on the playground.

-He had to come home, we played a lot together. Instead, enjoy that you did not have to go to kindergarten today and we had a relaxing day.

-I am glad.

-It's Ok then. But tomorrow kindergarten, so after you eat, we go to bathe and sleep.

He doesn't fight it, I think he's tired enough. We eat our dinner and I prepare him warm bath water. I put all his toys in the foamy water so we can play with everything. We are playing a big sea battle with the ducks and all the water monsters. By the time we finish the fight, his hands are completely soaked. We go into his room, I lay beside him, ready for the tale.

-What story should I tell you today?

-About the centipedes.

All right. Once upon a time there was a tiny village. Their little empire was hidden underneath the big oak tree, behind a giant stone. Centipedes lived in it. Each tiny cottage was made of twigs and the furniture inside was made of stone. Our story is about the tiny centipede, Long, who lives here. Long was special because he didn't live in a cottage like the others, but in an apple in the middle of the main square. A big red apple. He made a window in the apple, a door, and he had a little room full of books because he loved to read... My baby fell asleep at the beginning of the tale, no wonder after all the fun.

I kiss his face, pull the cover on him higher up and let him dream of the world of centipedes. I run the water for myself for a bath, I deserve to relax. I put in red bathing roses and light a couple of white candles for the mood. I also bring my book with me because I will be reading. I take off my clothes and indulge in the warm, scented pampering. Divine. I should do this every night. The fascinating story of my book distracts my thoughts from my life and I need it now. Immersion in another world. After half an hour I feel the water is cooling down, so I wash myself, get out of the tub and then put on my pajamas. I got relaxed, maybe a little sleepy, so I lay in the bed instead of watching TV or packing. I set my alarm so I don't fall asleep again. I am half asleep when my phone rings. Peter is calling. Looking at my watch, it shows 10 pm.

-Hi, beautiful!
-Hi.
-I miss you already, that's why I called you. What are you doing?
-I'm lying in bed. And you?
-Me too, but you should be here next to me.
-I would enjoy it, too, Peter.
-What are you wearing?
-You want to have sex on the phone now?
-Yes, so don't ruin the game, just enjoy it.
I'm wearing simple white comfortable

# Butterfly

pajamas, but I can't say that. I have to lie.

-I'm wearing a red lacy baby doll, laced at the back and see through everywhere. My nipple is showing, and my pussy line.

-Imagine I'm lying right next to you and taking a closer look at the sexy red lingerie in which you're so mouth-watering. I'm naked. You're lying on your back, looking at me with desire, I'm leaning over you. I stroke with my hand from the neck to the line of your hips and back. You'll have goose-bumps ... I'll kiss that beautiful mouth while you stroke my back. We both start to get worked up from the kiss and I lean over for your sweet little titties. Through the dress, I take your little nipple in my mouth and suck it... You touch my erected dick that only wants you and start stroking it up and down. You don't want anything else just me touching your pussy so I pull the fine lace, and now I touch myself, I know he is, too, because he got me worked up completely with as I imagined it. I gasp at the phone.

-And then?

-Then I start circling your clit with my warm tongue. I do it slowly to enjoy you and your sweet taste, which makes me crazy for you. You want more so you start doing it stronger. The sound of your panting fills the room and I lick into the hole as deep as I can. You're crazy about this, you start to move around under me, but I don't continue, instead in a single move I turn you around and put you in doggy pose...

Now I'm really panting into the phone, I can hear his desire in his voice.

-I gently pull off your underwear and for a few moments I just admire you. I will torture you by making you wait. You start begging me to put it in, but before I do, I'll lick you all around... I grab my dick and put it in a strong gesture. You give out a huge moan that makes me want you even more... I grab your round butt, grab it, pull it all over myself... I almost impale you. You feel how I fill you, I am hard for you.

-I feel it.

-We begin to move in one rhythm, with each stroke our desire grows. I release your butt and grab your two breasts as I continue to fuck you from behind... You look back at me and keep asking with your gorgeous brown eyes... Yes, this is it Ann... So good, so hot and tight... Your sweet little pussy starts to squeeze my dick and

-Ahhh...

-That's Ann... uh ... ..Yeah...

Now I'm just getting off to the ground, and we're both panting a little bit after our orgasm.

-It was wonderful my queen.

-It was fantastic, and your voice throughout drove me crazy.

-You should have heard yourself... I wish it has been real and I would have been with you really

-I know, I feel the same way. It's very difficult this way.

-It's getting harder without you every day, Ann.

-It won't always be like that.

-I hope so... Dream with me, Queen.

-You too, dear Peter.

We hang up the phone, I sit comfortably in my big bed. Although I am satisfied, but this whole game left some hole in me... It's really hard without him ... Now, it would be very good if I could sleep cuddling with him, not hugging my pillow alone, lonely. But

# Butterfly

everything is time. You can't hurry things anyway, I'm moving faster as my usual self. Of course, it would be great if we were together every night, making love, hanging out, talking, but it all comes at a price... It matters what I sacrifice and why. How long can I fight this feeling? How long are my walls still standing? When will he completely break through? How long can I still be myself instead of a poor copy, driven by a man's expectation, blinded by love doing tactics? I've given up on myself once, lost everything... Second time I can't do this... And I won't...

.....

Even before the alarm rings, my eyes open wide. I feel happy and energetic, even though it is only 4:30 in the morning. What should I do with this sudden sea of time? First, I make some coffee, then I pack the washed and ironed clothes, other times I don't like that. Finally, I'm in the bathtub and I remember last night's phone call. On the phone he was very smart in sex, that's a fact. He must have practiced it a couple of times, but I have to forget about that now. I should further enhance this hot mood. What if I sent him a nude pic or sexy lingerie photo of myself now? I've never sent such a thing to anyone. Would it be too pushy? No. After all, he is my boyfriend or something like that. I step out of the shower, I do not dry myself yet on purpose. Water drops sparkle on my skin, my hair is also wet, that's good. I will stick with the nude version, but it won't show me in full. I switch the camera to selfie mode and let's go. For a few seconds I am trying to turn the phone to look the most beneficial. On all of them

I look fat and pale, the wrong angle. I try new poses, make at least 30 different versions. This is it. Finally a good pose, I stand frontal , one of the legs is slightly bent, I hold my breasts with one hand, lean forward, so my waist looks beautiful. Now all I have to do is look sexy. All right, go for it. I'm shooting three of this setting and I'm done. It's time to check them out. The first 10 pieces are terribly bad. In reality, two of the remaining twenty are usable. I pick one in which I am most beautiful and put on a beautifying filter and turn it into black and white. Wow, it seems like a better version of myself, a wilder, freer Ann in the pictures. She is hot. Without any text, I immediately send Peter this brilliant photo before I change my mind. I'm worried, will he like it? I feel mischievous from this, even though a lot of women do this every day, many of my colleagues have told me about their experiences with it. I don't have to wait a long time for his answer, My phone signals.

-Good God! You're beautiful and desirable!

Half an hour I'll get to you, don't get dressed. I achieved my goal, so the photo really did work well. But he can't come up here now, maybe I should have thought it over before I sent him. I have to stretch the time, he has to wait until Saturday seeing me and the joy will be greater. The bait was already there, and now the anticipation is coming. Anyway, he started it last night.

-I can't... I'll leave for work soon, you just have to endure till Saturday without me.

-Do you torture me then purposely?

-Who knows...

There is no answer to that, but I don't need one. Both of us will have to wait until Saturday, it's indeed a torture even though I would like to deny it.

# Butterfly

I dry my hair, I flatten it and put on a peach-colored dress. I'm done, and my little one is still sleeping deep, it's time to wake him up. Everything goes so easily and fast with him this morning, I love this. I drop him off at the kindergarten without nervousness, and I'm in the office 5 minutes before I have to start work. I also reach our floor without delay. I look at Monique's desk, thankfully empty. She may have gotten sick of being jealous or just having a conversation with colleagues in the kitchen. I take the office key out of my bag, put it in the lock, but to my great surprise it's already open. How can this be? The cleaners may have opened it. I enter and notice Monique lounging in her pink dress in my chair, as if she were at home and she's tearing something up. My entire office is covered with red rose petals, stalks, spines, papers and yellow postcards. Anger blurs my vision and I start to tremble.

-What have you done?

I yell at her. She just smiles, enjoys the situation. I have to calm down, I can't give her the pleasure of seeing how destroyed I feel.

-Oh, nothing wrong. I think one of your guys sent you these ugly flowers in the morning, but since you weren't inside, the messenger put it on my reception desk. There was also a heart-shaped card with some sugary lines. I just brought them here for you to get it the way you deserve it. The other stuff, the wind blew all over the place.

-What a petty vengeance you have, but for this little game of yours now you're done. The cup is full, Monique.

-What will you do?

-First, I yank you out of my office, then I tell the boss about your favorite fun during working hours, and tell him about where last year's report disappeared too!

   -You threatening me, Ann?

   - You see, you're smart.

   -Why don't you suck the boss' dick too, dear little Ann, like everyone else's? That way he would like you more and believe what you are going to say.

   -You already did it for me.

I see in her face confusion, anger, it becomes red like a couple of times in such a situations. I know her, just needs a little spark and she explodes. I've been standing still since the beginning of our conversation, but she stands up, she's starting to come toward me. Now I let her start to beat me, because then I can have her fired. Workplace abuse. Come here. But with one last sentence, I have to destroy her.

   -And just so you know, Peter's size is perfect. It's a hit. I will let myself beaten up, I will have to... I will be strong... She will slap me and start scratching my face with her manicured hands wherever she can. It's really hard to stop myself from doing something or touching her. She starts to lose control, starts screaming.

   -You're a fucking bitch! A slut! You deserve all the bad! Ugly and calculating! Compared to me, no one!

   -One...

She can't finish yelling because two of my male colleagues from our corridor knock on the door and get her off me. They must have heard the screaming. One guy grabs her right armpit and the other one under her left and lead her out like this. Shit, I just got her fired. She deserved it because

# Butterfly

no one can do something like this, but I have a bit of a bad conscience. Why did I continue to provoke her? But even then, a piece of shit woman has nothing to be sorry for. She started to lose her mind and what would have happened next? My car? My apartment? Kill me? She is better not be around. That was the best I could do. Ok good, it's time to take pictures of her destruction so I have proof next to the scratch marks. It must have been a beautiful bouquet of roses, a pity that it ended up like this. Who knows what she has torn apart. I start packing the petals and all the other flower parts in a bag. I collect the papers in one place for the time being. After a quarter of an hour, I'm still cleaning up the ruins, and I continue to investigate the actual damage. I'm so deep in thoughts that I can't even hear someone talking to me only when he touches my shoulder.

-Ann!

I look around and the boss is behind me. He's pretty angry, some rumpled paper in his right hand, his left hand clenched in a fist.

-Yes Boss?

-Come into my office now.

-Coming.

That's wonderful, now I drove him mad. We are in a hurry to go to his office. He doesn't offer me to sit down, so we stay standing. That says a lot. He leans against his desk, I stand in front of him. I take a few deep breaths, start sweating from all the stress. He is very angry.

-What happened? I want to hear it from you.

-I came in the morning, Monique was waiting for me in my office. A pile of flowers and my papers on the ground were scattered. I questioned her and then she attacked me, and colleagues took her off of me. They helped.

-I fired her, instantly. This is unacceptable at our company. You are a very good work force Ann, but there is a lot of tension around you lately.

-I know, I'm sorry.

I bow my head, I prefer to sink.

-What's all this about?

-Men.

Oh, with that sentence, I was just undermining myself in front of the boss, but it slipped out. I'm dead. There is no way back, what a stupid animal I am. But instead of screaming at me he smiles a little.

-We men blame women for everything. That's just the way it is. Ann, get yourself together finally.

-You don't fire me?

-No. You'll get another chance, but this will be the last. I hope your stomach feels better, too.

-Thanks.

- Keep up the good work, Ann.

-All the best.

I sneak out of his office and lay low like a fox. I see Monique picking up her stuff from her desk. Her cute little pink flower box is half full of her stuff. Not many things can be valuable except for, let's see, her makeup kit. I turn my head quickly away and she doesn't dare to speak or come closer to me after what happened. I did the right thing. I really got fired a person. Plus, she was my girlfriend for years, and it shouldn't have ended like that. But it's her fault. I close my door and crash into my chair. I look into my makeup mirror and see that she scratched my face in a few places. I have to fix it, so I apply a ton of foundation and it will cover everything. Or not. I stand up and collect the remaining pile of papers and place them on my desk. Now I have no energy

# Butterfly

left to look through them. I stuff the rest of the trash into the bin. What shall I do? I don't have the nerve to start working right now, but I have to stay inside the office. I should calm down. I'll call Peter. I need to talk about all of this, he can reassure me. On the third ring, he picks up.

-Hi Peter.

-Hi. What's wrong? Your voice is very bad.

-I got Monique fired just now.

I'm starting to cry because the tension is too much.

-What happened?

-I came in the morning and waited in my office. The flower you sent me was torn to tiny scraps and a bunch of my papers thrown all over the place. I shouted at her and she jumped me. I must add, I provoked her to do it, to get physical in order to get fired... My face was scratched and bleeding and I didn't defend myself purposely. I couldn't stand her anymore, I was a little afraid of her lately and she crossed the line... I had enough.

-Oh, sweet Ann. Really hurts?

-A little, but that's not the point.

-I know the point, but you did everything right, Beautiful. Take it easy.

-You think?

-Yes. Who knows how far she would have gone with you.

-It was a pity to send that stupid flower.

- No, it was not a waste I wanted to make you happy, but I don't think you read the card. Although...

-No. But don't distract me.

-Ann, I'll be there in an hour and I calm you down.

-Not possible. You're off work, let's not make

things worse. If the boss sees you, he will be angry! I'll calm down, I promise.

    -You sure?

    -Yes. Be good.

    - You too, beautiful!

And I'll hang up the phone. If only he were here with me and hugged me, comforted me, but he shouldn't. I have to deal with this alone. The boss also said I had only another chance. I can't crash. I turn on my computer and just stare at the monitor, I can't do anything else. That certain bad feeling is coming back again. What should I do? Distraction. Ok, I'm going to deal with the perfume promotion, as the boss is waiting for a meeting on Friday. Now I just remember, I invited Daddy for dinner that night. I call him to confirm before returning my work.

    -Hi Dad. You picked up pretty fast.

    -Hello Darling. You were lucky because I'm still home. Are you ok?

    -No.

    -What's the problem?

    -I do not want to bore you.

    -If you were boring me, I wouldn't ask. Speak up.

    -I just got my ex-girlfriend fired because she ruined my flowers and my papers.

    -Who did you get them from?

    -Dad, that's not the point.

    -From whom?

    -From my new guy.

    -How long has it been? What's his name? What's his occupation?

    -Peter, lawyer. Not long ago, but I'll tell you about it on Friday. Don't ask any more questions now, this is not an interrogation. You're coming, right?

# Butterfly

-Yes. And what else is in the background? I don't know you as one to get someone fired for nothing.

-She's been jealous of me, hated me, for years, just pretended to be my girlfriend and had done some bad things against me.

-Then she deserved it. You're a girl who thinks over everything.

-Not so much now.

-And Gabriel?

-Long. He'll take Ben on Saturday, I allow him, though he has no visitation this weekend.

-Good job. They need time together and Gabriel

-Yes? What else did you mean?

-Nothing important, except that he must be hurting.

-Dad, if it had hurt him he wouldn't have cheated on me with the 22-year-old Betty or others few months before splitting.

-Don't be so strict.

-Why are you protecting him?

-I don't protect him, but he can be understood, too. He also lost everything.

-He caused it, but don't judge based on yourself and Mom. You cannot be compared to Gabriel. You didn't cheat on Mom.

-That's true, but

-Dad, no but. Don't annoy me, please. Let's not talk about these things more!

-Good, I only see it differently than you.

-That's a problem, Dad. You have to stand by me. You know what, I don't wanna fight with you. I'll wait for you on Friday for dinner, say 6.

-I'll be there, honey.

-Bye Dad.

My own father protects Gabriel. It's ridiculous and outrageous... He can be understood, of course. No way. Should I be sorry maybe? The poor man was left alone without his wife and child in a huge apartment, cooking, washing, cleaning.

He at least can sleep with anyone he likes. He can even have sex orgies. He became a completely free man, without bounds. Let's just say, Ben remains with him forever, but that's different... He can live in his own world, just like me. But then what did he say about missing me lately? At max, his comfort is lacking what I provided for him. He'll find another stupid one soon, because he's a handsome guy and he's rich. Single women's dream, though in my opinion a new single woman will find it harder to accept that he has a baby than the other way around. I'm still luckier, I feel. That's it... I can't believe how my dad got me upset. I just got really angry. I could blow up already... I have to walk a bit, fresh air will do good. I'll go down for a cappuccino and some cookies, if I hurry, I'll be back in a quarter of an hour and nobody will notice. I almost run to the cafe and when I get there I see a long line is waiting for their daily coffee, at least 15 in front of me. Murphy's law again. I'd really like to drink coffee so I get to the end of the line. I hope nobody asks for a special coffee, which is much more time to prepare. While waiting, I am bored, I open the gallery on my phone. My pictures are organized into folders, and I open the very first folder: "Ben." Such a beautiful little chubby baby was my little darling. I scroll through the cuter-than-cute photos, and with each picture, my memories are coming back. It was a wonderful time in my life, I was at home and all my attention

# Butterfly

was his. There's now a picture coming up of the three of us. Gabriel is bathing the little one in the blue baby bathtub, they both smile at me, and I lean over to them from the right and also smile at the camera. Yeah... We were a happy family. I close the gallery on my phone, and I become quite sad. Can I ever watch them all the way without feeling like this? I hope, though, the last time the same thing happened when my photo album was opened. So the lesson is that I can't look at old family photos yet.

-Mam, You're next. The server calls grimly.
-I'm coming, I'm sorry. I'd like one cappuccino and two extra chocolate biscuits.
-Let's have three and I'll pay.

I turn around and to my greatest regret I find myself facing Chuck. I have to get out of here right now. What kind of curse I have on me?

-Thanks but no. I'll stay at two, plus coffee, and I'll pay.

I'll take out my card quickly to get out of here as soon as possible. I'll grab the coffee and put the cookies in my bag. I don't turn around, I hurry out the door. I hear he rushes after me.

-Ann wait!

I stop on the sidewalk opposite him, but only for turning him away.

-Leave me alone!
-I want to talk to you.
-Emma sent you?
-No.
-I don't have time for you, and I'm not curious about what you want to say. I also told Emma the last time I never wanted to see her and her family again.
-It's about Gabriel.

I'm not willing to stop talking to him anymore, I'm disgusted with him.

-And that's even worse... Keep licking each other's ass, forget me. I'm going now. Bye.

He wants to say something to that, but I leave so fast that he can't react. I prevent him from following me by running. Pretty cowardly and pathetic, but I really don't want to talk to him. Fuck you, too. And everyone else ... How dare you come here near my work? He has no better business to do? He must have been waiting for me in front of the building and saw me coming out here or something. Already half of the coffee's content had spilled on me from running, my hand is sticky from it. I'm starting to run out of steam, I want to stop, but I'm just around the corner. I look back, but luckily I don't see Chuck anywhere, he decided better not to follow me after my monologue. I allow myself a break to rest leaning against the wall of the building. Nausea, I'm nervous. Stupid coffee! Angrily, I throw the whole thing into the green trash bin in front of me. The brown liquid splashes everywhere and the paper cup flies away. People passing by giving me a stare. I want to scream, to rage. I'm really pathetic... I'm a little calmed down after my tossing off the stuff, so I walk the other few feet to the office, breathing deeply. I've gotten through the worst of things today, right? Yes, yes, and yes. I'm strong, I'm good, but if someone gives me a bad comment today or makes a dirty joke or just looks at me funny, they're done.

The rest of the day passes uneventfully, giving the appearance of a normal working day. No one looked at me badly, asked me about the morning events, only because I haven't met them, maybe they don't even dare to come to me. I sit in front of my

# Butterfly

computer constantly and focus on my work. I am successful, slowly completing my goal for today. Unfortunately, Monique tore up a lot of my important notes, but luckily I also saved a few on my computer. It is what it is, I can't change that anymore. I show the boss that I'm good, that motivates me... I'm ready to leave before the end of my working hours. This day is finally over. I'm taking the stairs to make sure I don't run into anyone. Hiding. I have been the subject of countless rumors lately, and today I have served up another big dose to the malicious group. They can brilliantly distort any facts, not focusing on their own stuff, and that's the biggest problem. There are such people in every workplace and community. The best tactic that works for me is to show complete indifference, I do not react and explain. Everyone thinks whatever they want, I don't live with them.

    I arrive at the kindergarten and instead of greeting the worker is telling me that Ben beat one of his groupmates. He kicked him in the stomach and then kicked him on his knees. Even here today, only problems await me. This is not typical of my little son. There must have been a compelling reason for this. They bring him out of the group room, I sit him down in front of his wardrobe cabinet and immediately start asking him questions.

    -Hi sweetie. Are you Ok?
    -Yes.
    -The teacher said you beat someone. Tell me what happened.
    -We played, but John started to laugh at me as I won with the cars.
    -What did he say that you beat him for?
    - He said my dad doesn't love me, he's gone

because I'm dumb—and that's why I'm just with mom with you. And he hates me!

-Oh, baby, that's not true!

I hug him, I kiss him. He's good that he was beating that little bad kid, but that's not the best solution. I have to handle this wisely.

-I know, Mom, but he can't tell me things like that.

-Of course not. You were right to protect yourself. Do this again, but don't fight if you don't have to. If they hurt you with words, you can't hit anyone. Maximum if he attacks you that already counts as self-defense and you should. But come on, let's go home, we'll continue talking in the car.

Before leaving, I'll go over to the kindergarten teacher and tell her I talked to Ben, he'll apologize to the little boy tomorrow and talk to him, but I stressed that I think it's a between the kids' matter. Sometimes it happens with such boys. Take care of them, of course, I despise physical violence. We get into the car, Ben is just silent, in a bad mood. I still need to calm him down.

-Baby, Mom is proud of you.

-Why?

-Because you stood up for yourself. That's how it should be. At least he learned that he can't have more fun with you.

-Indeed?

-Yes, but tomorrow, for the sake of peace, just tell him you are sorry. They expect that.

-Do I have to?

-Unfortunately. Sometimes we have to do things in life that we do not want, even though we are right.

-Ok.

## Butterfly

-And believe me, he won't tease you anymore, because today you showed him what you would do. I also have some good news to make you feel better.

-What is it, Mom?

-Daddy will come for you on Saturday and you'll be with him again this weekend.

-Yay, good.

-See, he misses you, he loves you very much.

-How many nights I have to sleep in the meantime?

-Three more.

-That's a lot.

-It'll go fast, believe me.

I can see, the news that Gabriel is coming for him, Ben got in a better mood. Let's just say it's a pleasure for me also to meet Peter again and have a whole day together. He said he would take me to a place that would move me out of my comfort zone. Where are we going? I like surprises. In essence, it does not matter, let's just be together. On the other hand, I'm afraid of meeting Gabriel, and I have stomach cramps even of the idea of seeing each other again.

-Mom, hurry up because I want to play.

-We'll be home in a minute. Just a few streets.

-Good.

We go up the stairs fast, but Ben wants to hurry even further, so he rushes forward.

-Mom, I see a lot of flowers.

-Where?

-Here at our door, they are beautiful red.

I come upstairs and see at least 100 bunches of red roses in front of our door. They're beautiful, tied with a big red silk ribbon. I open the locks, then grab the flowers and place them on the coffee table

table in the living room. I change Ben, and then I also get into more comfortable home clothes.

-Sweetie wash your hands and go play.
-Ok, Mom.

I sit down on the couch and take a white greeting card hidden in the flower. I can guess who sent it.

-I can't wait for Saturday to see you again. I love you!

How sweet, that attention feels good. He wrote that he loves me. I'll read it twice more because I really like what he wrote and it's so romantic. I can see he tried to write nicely on the card instead of his usual cat scratch. I'll call him to thank you. He was waiting for my call because he answers it on the second ring.

-Hi.
-Hi, beautiful!
-Thank you for the beautiful bouquet.
-Well, if you didn't get it in the morning. I thought I'd send you a new one that will surely reach you.
-It's very sweet.
-Are you feeling better yet?
-I think so, but I don't need any more of those days. And you?
-I was running errands all day. I'm sorry I couldn't be with you. Why didn't you let me come in?
-The boss told me when he called me that I had only one more chance. He will not kick me out of the office cause I am a good worker, but I need to pull myself together. That's why.
-I could have been hiding under your desk.
-You are so crazy!

# Butterfly

-It's so hard for me not to see you today. I miss you. Terribly.
-Me too, but now it will be the best. It's because of Ben too.
-Open your door.
-Don't do this again. I won't open it.
-Please, beautiful!

It's crazy. He can't put him in that position. I want to see him too, cuddle too, but how do I explain to Ben? Why did Mom's colleague come here again? To play? To talk? It's hard to decide what to do. My mind says something and my heart says something different.

-Ann, are you still alive?
-Of course, I was just wondering if I could open the door for you. Got it. I only open it if you give me the password.
-Is that a joke?
-Maybe, so what's the password, dear Peter?
-Abrakadabra?
-You didn't win, two more attempts.
-Sesame, open up?
-Again, wrong. Last chance. Think more about it!
-Magic pussy.

I have to laugh at. No more teasing, I open the door. He looks at me and kisses me instead of greeting. With lots of passion, you can see, he's really crazy for me! His mouth is divine, the scent of his skin is delicious. After a long kiss he lets go and looks at me questioningly.

-Can I come in, my queen?
-Come on in, but you can't stay long.
-I'll stay as long as you let me.
-Perfect answer.

As soon as I close the door, Ben rushes out of his room to see who came to see us.
-Hi Peter. Why did you come?
-Hi, little buddy. Just because.
-You wanted to see us or play?
-Both.
-What's that bag in your hand?
-Open it, I brought it for you.
-Mom, a slingshot, like in the fairy tales and tin cans, and small gray stones.
-It was mine when I was a child. My dad made it for me. I thought we could play with these.
-I don't know how to do it.
-I'll teach you.
-Slower boys. Where do you want to shoot with this? And right now in late afternoon.
-Mom, it's still light outside. On the beach, is good?
-Not really, little buddy, but a field would be a good place.
-Peter, there are no fields around here.
-I know a place where it is.
-Oh no. It is far away and by the time we get there it would be dark.
-If we start now, we'll have time before dark. Till eight is light.
-What place you were talking about?
-It's close to you. I have a little chalet there, a huge field nearby.
-Mom, I want to go. Please! Please! Please!
-Wait a minute, sweetheart, I'll talk to Peter alone first, so please go back to your room.
-I'm going.
-You put me in a position where he gets enthusiastic and you know I can't say no to that.

# Butterfly

-Ann, be spontaneous. I wanted to give him pleasure, and after this terrible day you will have a good time relaxing. Trust me. Let's go.

-You're right, let's go, but it's just because of Ben.

-Word.

I'll tell him, ready can go. Ben starts jumping with joy. I'll pack some food for ourselves, drinks, and a bag of biscuits in case we get hungry. We leave with Peter's car. There is no traffic and he drives faster than he should, so we take a normally much longer journey, in half an hour. We park around the house, get out of the car. We don't even go inside the house, we head straight to the field. Ben leaves his mouth open admiring the beautiful scenery. My little one runs around me like a puppy who finally got out of his cage. I look at Peter, and I see sincere joy in his eyes.

-Mom, this is beautiful.

-I know, baby.

The grass is green, the birds are chirping, only we are here. We camp under a tree selected by Peter. Although we don't have a blanket to put down now, I still sit in the grass. Meanwhile, the two of them put the tin cans on a high platform. How predictable I am. He knew we were coming with him, so he already prepared everything.

-Peter, come here a little bit.

-Yes, Beautiful?

-Did you put the platform here?

-Yes, in the morning.

-And if we hadn't come?

-I knew you would, so I prepared everything.

-You're sweet, but now just go back to play with Ben before it gets dark.

-Beautiful, look behind the big tree next to you.

-What will be there? Tell me it's not a rabbit cavity we're going to move to Wonderland if I fall in.

-I don't know what's waiting for you, but if you meet the white rabbit, tell him I say hello.

With a wide smile he goes back to Ben, and according to the instructions, I look behind the big tree. I can't find a rabbit cavity to my great regret, but a picnic basket is waiting for me. I open it and there's a blanket inside; a bottle of white wine, my favorite; a glass; strawberry and white chocolate. Oh no. How sweet ... I lay down the blanket, take out the wine, and pour myself a glass. I sip. I look at them, Peter is showing how to shoot. He hits all the boxes for first attempt. It's loud when the stones bounce. Clever. He also puts Ben in the right position and gives him instructions. I can't believe it, my little love shot all of them right away. True hewas closer than Peter. Talented. I'm yelling at him.

-You're incredibly smart, honey!

-Thanks Mom.

-And I? asks Peter with a smile.

-You are a pro. He is a professional seducer.

- Well, Ann. I do not understand what you mean. I am not a seducer but I am in love. That is something else.

-I do not know what to say to this.

-Mom, what does it mean to be in love?

-If a boy likes a girl and pleases her a lot.

- Like Peter does to you?

-Something like that, sweetheart, but I'd rather play now.

How smart. Ok, I am sorry I said this before him, but it slipped. But he didn't ask anything else, maybe it doesn't bother him? Could he have accepted all of this from Peter and me? Or did Peter tell him something when they were two of them? Or is he just a kid and doesn't care more about it because he focuses on the game? Or he became accustomed to Peter and the fact that he is sometimes with us? Any of these options could happen... Now I'm gonna put a nice big strawberry in my mouth. Succulent ... Peter was right, that's what I really missed today, a little relaxation on the beautiful meadow with a glass of wine and strawberries. If he goes on like this, I'll really get mad about him not listening to my mind... They are tossing the canes, Ben is very enthusiastic, yelling when he can hit them. Sometimes the shot goes to the wrong direction or the stone falls out of the slingshot prematurely, and then he picks it up angrily. Peter plays with him with full energy, teaches him constantly, and I enjoy watching them. I drank half of the wine, this is a nice achievement, the chocolate is gone too. I'm starting to get a little cold, so I get up and walk to them. Would we be ok with Peter in the long run? If the flame is gone, the love, would I have a faithful companion? I think about these things as Ben hugs me, and I can see Peter would do the same...

-It's getting dark, can we go back?
-Mom, no.
-Little buddy, let's go!
-But I still want to play.
-Now I'll bring you here next time again, will it be good?
-Yes. Are we going inside the house?
-The next time, we'll go in there, baby. Let's go home now. Tomorrow is kindergarten, and mom has to work.

-But, pretty please.
-No. Don't be insatiable.

A little grumpy, but he gets in the car. I sit down, Peter puts the picnic basket in the trunk. On the way home, it is very difficult not to touch each other. It almost hurts to be sitting next to him yet I can't touch him in front of Ben. I feel the same vibes coming from him. Anyway, I will withstand it until it is time to take our relationship public. Everything is good as it is... By the time we get to my apartment, it is completely dark and Ben has fallen asleep in the backseat. At 17 kg, I ask Peter to bring my sleeping prince upstairs. I have no heart to wake him up, he'd take a bath in the morning. Peter carefully puts him in his crib, I pull off the dirty clothes, and cover him. We go out into the living room and I know we're gonna jump on each other if I don't send him home right away.

-Thanks for this beautiful afternoon. It was a good idea to play sling-shot, I wouldn't have thought of it. The wine, the sweets and strawberries were also delicious. You surprised me.
-Anytime.

He embraces me, starts grabbing my ass. I like it, not a little, but now I'll tell him to go home before he takes away the rest of my common sense.

-You have to go.
-Where?
-Home.
-Why?
-Because we agreed on something when I let you in in the afternoon.
-What was that?
-To stay as long as I let you.
-I don't remember that.

# Butterfly

He embraces again, kisses me in the neck. A small sigh leaves my mouth.

-Be a hero and go. Please.

-I've been for a while, but only because of you.

-I know and thank you.

With difficultly, he lets me go and heads toward the door. Feeling bad, but it will be the right thing. I open the door for him.

-It was good with you.

-Beautiful, for me too.

He gives me a fine little kiss, and she's gone. Huh... I would have let him stay and we have been all over each other in the living room, but not here, not now. The sleepover, I vowed not to be an option for a while... I go to shower, brush my hair, fix my eyebrows, and finally paint my nails a burgundy color. Lying in bed I remember the terrible events of this morning... I'm starting to internalize... I shouldn't do that. I'm strong... What was so awful? I have to look at the situations from another angle. Monique was let go with my help. Is this good? Yeah, because we won't be at the same workplace, so she can't pick a fight with me. Did I meet Chuck? Indeed, but I handled this unexpected thing well. Ben got into a fight? At least he protected himself, put that little boy back in his place. Was the afternoon good, did my baby and me feel better? Yes. We went out; I received flowers; candy; wine; kindness and attentiveness. So, overall, my day was extremely positive. Grateful for that... I'll start reading the book I left on my bedside table lately. Very exciting crime story, it catches my attention. An hour later I put it down because I am sleepy. I close my eyes and I sink into the void.

·····

A message from Peter awakens from my sweet dream. I look at my phone, it's seven in the morning.

-Good morning Beauty, I am already thinking about you. Have a nice day.

-You should have a wonderful day, too. I dreamed about you...

-What did I do in it?

-You pampered me.

-It is a pity that only in your dream...

-Sure, it's a pity.

At my workplace, we continue to exchange messages I talk to him all day, but I'm not nervous about it because it feels good. We pull each other's leg, flirt, share some other little secrets. I barely work today. I'm starting to act like a teenager girl in love who's completely distracted by her boyfriend ... When I get home, I order a ham and cheese pizza for Ben and me because I don't feel like cooking anything. After eating we play a huge Lego game and play cards. After the evening routine, I lay him down and go to the living room. I want to watch a movie, but Peter calls.

-Hi, are you bored today?

-No, Beautiful. What are you doing now?

-I thought I will be watching a movie, but you called. And you?

-I listen to music and daydream about you.

-How romantic you are.

-Due to you.

-Do you enjoy your vacation time?

-So, so.. If I didn't have to do take care of some delicate things, I'd be better off.

-What are you doing?

-I have two somewhat complicated old clients, their stuff.

# Butterfly

-They won't leave you alone when you're on vacation ?
-No.
-You should turn off your phone.
-Then how would I talk to you?
-Guess you're right.

We chat for another hour and then I start watching a romantic comedy. I put a bowl of popcorn in front of me and start eating. It's a very cute movie, but too predictable. I want something else. I choose an action movie instead, I need the excitement. Apropos excitement, I will be going to the boss tomorrow and see my dad. I have to sleep to get some rest so I turn off the TV before the end of the movie. I get into my bed, but I can't sleep. I meditate, hope it helps... I find myself in front of the usual green door, I step in. It is dark, only the moonlight on the shore illuminates the narrow path to the sea. I'm not scared, I start walking on it. I enjoy the silence that surrounds me. I look up at the sky, full of stars. A stunningly beautiful sight. I come down to the water and sit in the warm white sand. I watch the never-ending dance of the waves when I notice someone swim towards me. It's Peter. The water drips from his muscular body as he comes to me. Nude. He sits down next to me. He doesn't say a word, just grabs my hand and puts it on his heart. He looks at me lovingly, kisses me softly, falls down into the sand. Pulls off my blue dress. We make love... Walking along my path together, entering the green door together... I take this as a heavenly sign...

·····

This morning I choose a white trouser suit, put up my hair, minimal makeup. My appearance becomes very determined so the boss will be satisfied. I'm nervous about what's waiting for me today. Hurrying to dress Ben, we're late and that only makes me tense. I don't take time at the kindergarten, I ask the teacher to change him. As I drive towards work, I honk at least four cars because they are moving too slowly in front of me. I finally arrive, but unfortunately with ten minutes delay. I drop my bag into my chair, turn on my desktop, and take another look at my stuff. All I have time for. I upload it to my tablet and head over to the boss. My palms are sweating, everything seems to be bothering me. I'll be good, everything will be good.

It's only the two of us. We sit down at his large table and he asks me to start my presentation. I speak for half an hour. I show him the perfume, the advertising plan, the stuff I put together with the others, the different analyzes. He never intervenes. I finally get to the last slide and I'm done. The boss is silent.

-What is your opinion?

-I don't like the name. Let there be something else instead of Eden. Think about it. I'm happy with the rest, nice work.

-Thanks.

-Then, as we agreed, you all get a month for everything. I'll find the date for the next meeting and let you know. All right.

-Keep up the good work, Ann.

-All the best to you too.

I'm almost beyond the clouds, so relieved. We succeeded. It's worth all this work. I sit back in my office cheerfully. I'll also call my dad to make sure he

comes in the evening.
-Hi Dad.
-Hello Darling.
-I'm looking for you to come tonight?
-I can't.
-Why?
-They just told me I had to work overtime again. We have an important case. I already wanted to call you.
-I'm not glad that we meet so rarely.
-We'll arrange one again.
-It would be nice to finally talk to you today, Dad.
-I agree, dear, but now I have to go for briefing. I will call you.
-Bye Dad.

The rest of my working time, I think about the name, I collect ideas, but nothing good comes to my mind. I'm in a hurry for Ben, and luckily as we're getting out of the kindergarten, now the teacher did not stop me for anything. My cheerfulness remains, although I'm sorry my Dad doesn't come for dinner.

-What would you, my sweetie say if we stopped for cookies before we go home? We can celebrate how talented Mom was at her workplace today.
-I would be glad.

He orders himself two flavors, I prefer three scoops of chocolate ice cream. We talk, I tell him what happened in the office today.

-And you, baby, did you talk to the little boy? I forgot to ask.
-Yes, I said sorry, he said so too.
-And after that?
-We were playing together.

-I'm proud of you, as always.

After we arrive home, he's playing alone in his room, and I'm about to start cleaning. I don't feel like it, but I have to. My thoughts are floating around. Tomorrow I see Gabriel, but also Peter. What should I wear? Something sexy because we're going on a date. Ben asks me to read him some story because he no longer wants to play. He sits down on the couch watching me clean up his room. I'll finish it soon, followed by my room, the kitchen, then the bathroom and toilet. I'm getting tired, but it's worth it. Finally, I reach the living room to clean up there, but I see Ben is asleep on the couch. He's so cute, embraces Mr. Grumpy and sleeps with his mouth open. I'm not taking him to his own room yet, I'd rather go for a bath. Because tomorrow I'll be dating, I'll shave myself all over to be pretty smooth. Who knows how the evening will end. I put twists on my freshly washed hair to make it pretty wavy in the morning. I go into my bedroom naked and start picking clothes for the date. None of them I really like, Peter has seen most on me. Once again, I look through all of them and my eye stops on a tight, short knee-length dress with a yellow drop shoulder. I have to try. It looks great on me, but I'll be like a canary. A sexy canary. Problem solved. I'll take Ben into his crib, and I'll put in a lot of effort to clean the living room. I'm tired so I'm going to sleep. I'll write a message to Peter.

-Good night , I will see you tomorrow.

-Finally... Let's meet at the usual place at 11:30 a.m.

-I will be there!

# Falling

**B**en wakes me up climbing into my bed. He kisses my face. It's such a fantastic feeling. He puts his cold little soles between my soles to warm him up. I hug and caress his back. He's my everything.

-Mom, let's get up because Dad's coming for me.

-I know, baby. Let's wake up.

It's nine o'clock, so we still have time to get ready. I make waffles for breakfast, it came out very tasty, we both eat two pieces of it. Ben's excited to go, and I'm nervous and have a stomach cramp. I prepare the things he is taking, put it in his bag, and dress him up. He sits down to watch a fairy tale while I get myself ready. Feeling bad because I know he's leaving. I can't get used to this... I take the curlers out of my hair and then make up my face. I make smoky eyes and choose pink lipstick. I choose from my lingerie and finally decide on a lacy black set. I pull on my yellow dress and put on the black accessories that best fit. Finally, I put on my black high heels and spray my neck and wrists with my new perfume. I look in the mirror, I look hot. Very. I pat myself on my shoulders ... Gabriel will be here soon. Now I have to start walking out with them, otherwise I'll be lateformy date. Bell is ringing. Relax, breathe deep. Hmm... Ben rushes in, he opens the door and I grab my little bag. I see Gabriel, my heart beats faster, my stomach cramps get stronger.

He's still attractive, but he lost a lot of weight, dark circles around his eyes. With his gaze he almost is undressing me. Please don't. Look at me differently. I turn my head.
-Dad!
Ben hurries over and they hug each other.
-Hi Ann.
-Hi.
I don't want to look at him again, I'd rather go back for Ben's bag and push it into his hand.
-I'm going down with you, wait, just lock the door.
-All right.
- Mom, hurry up.
-Are you going somewhere? You are very pretty.
So, I really look good. I tell him that I am going on a date, he needs to be aware, I have my life again. Although it has nothing to do with him, I still share it. Now I look at him again, trying to make an indifferent face.
-I have a date.
-With that jerk again?
-Exactly.
He no longer answers, we just start walking down the stairs. Ben runs in front and the two of us are behind. Only the sound of my shoes break the silence. I'm not going to ask about him, so I keep my silence and praying to be in my car as soon as possible. Let this awkward scene be over.
-Ann.
-Yes?
He stops on the stairs and turns to face me. There is disbelief sitting on his face, mixed with sadness.

## Falling

-I would like to talk to you.
-Gabriel, I don't have time for this now. I'm in a hurry.
-It would be important. When can I talk to you?
Never, but I can't say that because he said it was important.
-Sunday when you bring home the little one, if you really need to.
-All right.
I place Ben in the car while Gabriel puts his bag in the trunk. I thank him, I force myself.
-Bye Gabriel.
-Bye Ann. We come back Sunday afternoon.
-I love you, my life. Take care of yourself.
I'm almost crying, so I quickly kiss him and walk to my car, which fortunately is not parked far. I sit down, but in the rearview mirror I see Gabriel just standing next to his car and looking at me. Let's go, damn it. Nah, good. Then I'll go first. I start the engine and drive off stepping on the gas pedal... I feel bad and start crying. Why is it so painful to see him again? Or the fact that Ben will go with him? I cry the whole way until I get to the agreed place. I park and sit in the car for a few minutes until I collect myself. I'll be with Peter, and that's good. Very good, it's time to forget Gabriel and just focus on my date today... I step out and see Peter waiting for me on the square. He smiles, it makes my heart warm. I walk to him, he kisses me with passion, makes me forget the cause of my sadness.
-You are beautiful, my queen. Although you're a little over dressed for our current program.
-Thank you, if you told me where we are going I would have dressed to the occasion.

-Then there would have been no surprise. We walk hand in hand around on the streets, often smiling at each other.

-We've arrived.

We stop in front of a ruined building downtown. I enter through the big wooden door and find myself in a climbing room. There are three big yellow climbing walls side by side, filled with colorful handholds, with a couple of creepy climbing people on it. My palms are sweating.

-I'm not going, it's a bad idea, not a good surprise.

-Come on. Will be good.

He starts to pull my hand, but I stop.

-No. I don't have any clothes and I have agoraphobia.

-You can borrow clothes here. Cross your limits and your fears with me. We'll do it together, and you'll be proud of yourself for doing it.

-No. Anyway, I'm not going to be able to bear my own weight. I'm not in shape.

-There are simpler wall sections, you would do those. Plus, you are secured, you will be climbing with a rope, and you will receive basic training before that.

-Ok.

-Seriously?

His face brightens, I am even more nervous, but I want to prove myself in front of him.

-Yes, but it's first and last time. You're right, it's time for me to exceed my limits.

We go into the room, he takes care of everything for me. He buys me a long black pants, a black T-shirt and a simple shoe of my size. He brought clothes with him, so only I go into the dressing room. Alright, what have I undertaken... I'm done, I tie my beautiful hair

# Falling

and go out to join him.

-You've become a pretty climbing girl.

- How good for me.

The cute young instructor boy explains to me the essence of climbing and what to look for. He shows me where to start climbing and what to do if I slip. They put on the seat, the carabiner insert set. Lastly, I have to apply to my hands magnesium powder, which stops slipping. I look funny, alarmed. Meanwhile, Peter is being prepared by another guy, he seems happy. We are side by side, but I am very scared of this whole thing.

-Can we start, Beautiful?

-Let's go. How many times have you climbed anyway?

-Many times, that's why I know what a fun thing to do. Even kids do the easier stages.

-I believe it, although it may not be so much fun for someone with agoraphobia.

-Relax.

I clench my teeth and take the first step up, as the instructor said. I'm over three handrails, and the next one is coming ... It's far from the top. I look at Peter, he is so cute that he keeps pace with me, waiting for me. I'm getting further up, but I dare not look down, because then I may faint. I slowed down a bit because it was hard to pull myself up to the end. This is the starting level, but I still feel it terribly difficult.

I can't fail. I have to get to the top... I'm just concentrating on the next handrail and where to put my foot... I finally got up, I didn't die, but I still dare not look down. Now I finally look at Peter and he is up, climbing up to me. He gets beside me and we give each other a little kiss.

-Success, Peter! Did you see how brave I was?
-Yes, Beautiful, I'm proud of you.
-Thanks, but how do I get off now?
- Listen to me. I'll go ahead, you just imitate what I do.
-Ok, I'll try.

He's very skillful and is quick to descend. It will work for me too. He's down, waving to me. I gather courage and begin to descend. I'm still not looking down. I feel my feet touching the ground.

-Hooray! I did it!
-Sure Beautiful, you are the bravest woman I know.
-Don't exaggerate, but it helped a lot that you were with me and made me feel more secure.
- Can you go another round?
-Yes, but no more.

I get up much faster now and start enjoying the challenge because my fears have disappeared. I got so much into it that I ask him to go up again.

-Can another round come, Ann?
-It was enough for me three times, thank you. I got tired, but I still outperformed my capacity.
-Sure. Let's go take a shower because we are sweating.
-I don't have anything for that.
-I thought so, Beautiful.

They take back our climbing gear and we are heading to the locker room. He hands me a women's sponge bath, a clean white towel, and a white thong.

-You think of everything? You're incredible.
-I bought them for you yesterday so you don't have to worry about that.

I give a kiss on his beautiful mouth and start to walk to bathe in the women's dressing room. I really

# Falling

am sticky everywhere. Unbelievable what he can make me do... I take a shower, but I don't wash my hair in vain although it is sweaty a little because I don't see a hair dryer. I dry myself and jump into my clothes. Thank goodness I have everything in my bag that I need right now. Deodorant, perfume, makeup set. I let my hair down, do my makeup again and put on my jewelry. I blow a little more perfume on myself than I should.

-Wow, a goddess is coming to me in a yellow dress.

-You look so good in black shirts and pants too.

-Now, I'll take you to eat.

-Great idea.

As we walk towards the car, we talk about climbing.

- Let's go with my car, what do you say?

-Ok, hope mine will be ok here.

We sit down in his car and he strokes my thigh as we move towards the restaurant.

-It's very good to touch you.

-Then stroke me more.

His hand is only on my thigh , it does not move up to my panties, but it is still exciting.

-Here we are, unfortunately we have to get out, Beautiful.

He brought me to a pretty glitzy restaurant. I see he wants to spoil me. Everyone is beautifully dressed amongst the guests, quiet music, expensive setting. I haven't been here yet. Everywhere, waiters wait for the guests' wishes, circlearound the black tables. We are led to a back table by the hostess girl.

-Got your table ready.

-Thank You.

Peter pulls out the chair for me, a real knight, and he takes his seat. The waiter immediately stands next to us and pours me the pre-ordered red wine on the table. Very fine, it's a pity he can't drink with me as he drives. He puts the menu in front of us and says he'll come back when we figured out what to choose. After a long period of thinking, I order myself a grilled duck breast with pomegranate sauce, and now I don't want any appetizer or soup. Peter asks for a steak a la Rossini. Exciting. Until our main course is ready, we won't take our eyes off each other. I'll tell him how was my morning, and he tells me what he did until we met. We don't sit silent for a minute, drinking every word of each other. I see clearly that he is in love with me... They bring our orders and we begin. Heavenly, it is perfectly prepared. I add another glass of wine.

-You're a wonderful woman, Ann. You completely make me dizzy.

-With what?

He reaches over to the table and grabs my hand. His eyes are scorching, and he exudes sexuality.

-All of you. Femininity radiates from all your pores, but you are not aware of it. You know, you can just look at me, and I want you right away.

-You can't complain either. I also love the way you look at me because I can see how much you want me.

-You can't imagine how much I want you. I'd take you right here. What if we weren't eating dessert so we could just leave.

-I thought of that, too.

He pays the bill and we quickly get into his car. Before we leave, he leans over and kisses me.

- Can we go to my place? You haven't been there yet.

It's going to mean great sex. Do I want this? Yes.

# Falling

-Let's go to you.

He puts his hand on my thigh again, drives with one hand. He caresses a little, but now he is advancing his palms further up. He reaches the line of my panties, and I pull up my skirt. I spread my legs to get better access to me. I look at him flirtatiously. While he externally stimulates my pussy, I reach over to him and hold his penis through his pants. Just grasping, I'm not doing anything else with it. He pushes my panties aside and reaches in. I'm wet, his finger slips in and out easily.

-It's very good... Do it again...

-Ann, but you need to take your hand off me, because we're going to crash if you keep going.

He pulls his finger out a little later, I don't see why.

-Why did you take it out?

-I can't drive like that, Beautiful. I can't concentrate on the road, just you. We are about to arrive and you'll be done. Get ready.

He parks in a giant underground garage of a beautiful condominium. I don't care about anything anymore. He talks in a trembling voice.

-Turn off your belt and come here.

I climb over him, his body is hot. He's grabbing my butt with both hands. My moisture had already soaked my panties. I am burning.

-I want you. Here.

He starts kissing my neck while massaging my butt. I want him too, I just want him to take me in the car. I unzip him to release his beautiful standing cock.

-Sit on me. Now.

I'll drop my panties. I grab hold of the throbbing tail with one hand and insert only the tip at first, but it's so delicious that I can't stand it anymore and suddenly I sit on it. I'm starting to move slowly over it. Much better than I expected...

-Hmmm.

-God, Ann.

I grab the back of his seat while he kisses and bites at the same time. He eats me... Fits me perfectly, fills me.

-You are so fine, so perfect, so tight.

I start riding it faster, he pulls my hair back. This will make it even better. I feel every inch, I'm very close. I'd love to tear him apart. I know I'm going to cum soon, and that is how he feels.

-Let's go together, Beautiful.

He takes control, grabs my ass, and he starts moving under me faster and stronger. Doing it roughly like a wild bull. No more brakes in us anymore... I can no longer hold this intense feeling so divine... I squeeze his dick, press it harder.

-This is... Peter!

Suddenly my orgasm comes, I reach for the tops, scratch him, scream. Meanwhile, he comes while screaming my name, shakes, shoots his hot semen inside me and it is a wonderful feeling. I became his... I'm coming to him, but I'm not getting off, we're laughing at each other. She caresses my back and kisses me all over he can.

-You're fantastic, Ann... Come on, let's go up, because I'm not done with your wonderful body yet. That was the foreplay.

-I hoped so.

He opens the door, grabs me, and gently removes me and puts me on the floor. He pulls on his pants, grabs my bag.

-Can we go up?

-Yes.

# Falling

He picks me up without asking, and I find myself in his arms.
-You can't carry me this way.
- I can do it.
He carries me into the stairwell. Fortunately, there is an elevator. He pushes the seventh floor, then turns back to me and starts kissing. Kindly fondles me. I'm completely melt... We arrive upstairs, but he still doesn't put me down. He takes out his key, opens the door, but does not want to let go of me, and carries me over the door like brides do.
-Enough, put me down.
-Your request, your command.
-First, show me around.
From the foyer opens the huge living room. It has a big leather sofa, TV, bookshelf, bar and that particular female statue. The furniture is black and the floor brown. The walls are gray. Quite a manly apartment. But the view is that really catches me. There is a huge glass wall in the room and you can access the balcony through the sliding door.
-Wonderful view, from here you can see the whole city.
-We'll see it later, but let's move on.
The kitchen opens from the living room. Not too big, the furniture here is black. The bedroom is next. It has a large double bed, two bedside tables and another statue of a female body. And in the corner is a work area with a laptop and a lot of papers. The accessories and the color of the wall are also gray. We get to the bathroom. I'm not surprised that the tiles are black here too, but in combination with white furniture, there is a giant shower enclosure in the corner.

-We walked around the apartment, we arrived at the destination.

-Your apartment is very nice.

-Thanks. Now I undress, then bathe together and go back to bed.

-I don't resist.

He takes off my clothes, undoes my bra and gently pulls off my panties. I'm standing naked in front of him. Now he's next. I unbutton his black shirt, take it off, and kiss every inch of his muscular belly. He's taking off his pants, but I'm not going down on him. I hold his face, look deep into his eyes. He looks back at me in a heated manner, then French kisses me . Entirely entangled, we enter the shower. We face each other and slowly enjoy our time, bathing each other. He touches me as gently as a porcelain doll, I gently wash him too. His body is really perfect... unlike mine... Our desire is hot again, I want to be his again.

-Don't dry, juts come inside.

He grabs my hand and leads me into the bedroom. He lays me down on the bed.

-Now I kiss every single drop of water from you, my lovely Ann.

And so he does. He starts from my face and then follows my neck, chest and belly. It's such a delicious feeling... He is taking his time. He is on my thigh as I grab his head and pull it towards me. I want to see him. With my right hand, I stroke his prickly stubble, his thick mouth curve, his brown hair... we just looking at each other, everything else is gone, we are in a different world where there is only the two of us... In our bubble... Deep, sincere emotions that give me security, he enchants me...

## Falling

His gaze is foggy, his face flushed, he is breathing faster.
    -I love you, beautiful.
    -Me too!
    I finally said something that I wasn't quite sure of, but as he looked at me, he tipped over an imaginary boundary. I met and fell in love with this righteous, smart, humorous, respectful man who longs for love and love at the heart of his soul... And, here you go, the hunter has finally hunted down his innocent pray... who has been happy to be hunted down.
    -You made me the happiest man.
    I feel now my soul has started to shine again... I am shining... Because of him... He continues to spoil my body slowly, enjoying all my portions. Chasing me to madness with this... He leans on my pussy, but now he starts to lick intensely... I whine under him but he doesn't let me go, so I take his penis into my mouth. I lick the end, suck it slowly. I play with him just like he did before with me. I tease him and in a sudden motion I push his penis down to my throat and then do it again... and then I put it between my two breasts and start to pull around his hungry penis while I watch him. He moans manly, further enhancing my desire.
    -Ann, stop it because I'm coming.
    He takes it from there and lays me down again. He leans over me and gently puts his craving masculinity into my craving opening... He loves me so slowly that I feel all his folds and it's very pleasant.
    -I want to enjoy you're being mine.
    He goes on, lifts both my legs and places it around his waist. This is how the angle changed

and I feel him even deeper... I whimper in his ear, stroking him... I don't know which one is my hand and which one is his because we have become one... No matter where he touches me, every time he touches my skin sparkles... Sucking my nipple, circling my clit with his hand, accelerating at a pace. I shiver, I'm almost over and he is the same.

-Look at me while we're doing it.

I watch him and we cum all at once, going to heaven, holding each other's eyes forever...
I don't know how much later we'll get back to reality and he climbs close to me. It's good to just be by his side. He holds my hand.

-It's never been so good... I felt your beautiful soul, you finally opened up to me...

-Thank you for being here and giving it to me.

My eyes are starting to get teary from this beautiful confession and our lovemaking. He has released many things in me now... He really felt my soul, I opened up to him... It was time... He wipes my tears and caresses my face.

-I'm coming to you Peter, I don't need any more time.

-After all, my queen.

He smiles at me and that makes his whole face even more beautiful. Now he shines. He bends his head to my breasts, I caress his hair, and he grabs my hand to show that we are already together... I fell in love, who would have thought... I'm happy again ... Somewhere in the background, I hear his stupid phone ringing.

-Your phone is ringing.
-Don't deal with it and they will hang up.
-No they don't, you hear it. Irritating.
-I don't want to leave you here now.

# Falling

-But go. Turn it off, then you'll come back to me. I have two other ideas to try.
-Good, I'll go, but tell me what you want to drink, because I'll bring it plus a little surprise.
-Let's say wine and can't wait for the surprise. I wouldn't move out of here for the world.
He goes out of the room and I stand up and move my legs. I want more of it, give him more, make love to him the whole night. It was so fantastic... So different... What if I get him an erotic massage? Good idea, he'll like it. I've already given him one, but he doesn't know what I can do yet. He'll faint... He'd need some music, too, to create a more intimate atmosphere. My phone stayed in the living room, that's off. Here's his laptop on the desk, that's fine. He's not back yet, so I have some time. It just won't bother me looking for some erotic music. I sit naked in his chair and open it. Thank goodness it is not password protected so the home screen is instantly displayed. No wallpaper, luckily. Usually, men have a sexy women's image. it doesn't matter. I'm excited, and even from the thought of being his I became wet again... What I'm going to do with you soon... I'm looking for the YouTube icon. I type in his search engine erotic music. Lists are the results in turn. Which one should be? I should choose one I've heard. I'd just click on a sympathetic person when a window pops up that a message has been received. I don't care, I don't care right now, but the next one arrives. I want to get to the x to close it, but I stop at the sender's email address. I would know this out of thousands since I invented the name. White Phoenix. Gabriel's? What the hell? Why is he writing to Peter? This can only be a coincidence. My curiosity drives me further, so I quickly

click and open it. There are only a few lines in it.

-Everything goes according to plan, Peter?

-What kind of plan? I hardly can contain myself, I open the last message received, too.

-I know you're together now, pick up the phone.

-That's a joke. Would Gabriel refer to me? Impossible ... He can't know Peter closer than me. He can't... I have to find out, otherwise I'm going crazy. I am also looking for earlier messages that came from Gabriel. What? I am seeing incorrectly... His inbox is full of letters from Gabriel. God... I'll open one randomly.

-She likes white wine, sweets, strawberries. She likes to go to a restaurant.

-Let's see the next, I'm starting to get dizzy...

I keep opening emails, but I don't read them all the way. I'm going to pass out!

-She is more important to me than anything. Take good care of her.

-She loves being eaten and she enjoys if someone is pushy with her.

-Ben loves everything connected to cars.

-Be her confidante, get her trust first. Make her feel she is beautiful. Conquer her!

-Take her to nature.

-She loves coffee, she drinks it with three cubes of sugar

-Give her time!

Nausea is beginning to take over. I feel there is a lump in my throat, the letters start to blur... They know each other... Why? ... Peter got instructions about me... He controlled everything... He doesn't love me, he is not in love with me... What's all this? I see an email with a subject that I need to open.

# Falling

My will, this is for Ann in the subject. It cannot be...
 -I'm writing this because I'm mortally ill. I have half a year left. A year ago I started to plan everything... I made myself hateful to you, I wanted you to fall out of love with me...
 -You can't die! Couldn't do this to me ! Not like this... I can't read any more. I get up and start walking. My stomach feels funny, I throw up on the floor. I feel sick... My heart is about to pop out ... Jesus ... Just picture... He knew where to take me ... He knew what I like... What Ben likes... The constant phone calls... Peter's reactions... He knew what I was afraid of... He knew what myfavorite books are... He treated me the way I wanted to... He touched me the way I like it... He didn't hit back when Gabriel attacked him... And Gabriel... My dreams... No... Everything was planned and directed... I was a puppet...They played with me, with my heart and with my life...
 The room starts to feel small, the walls are spinning. I can't breathe. I open the door of the bedroom and stumble out naked. I feel dizzy. I find Peter in the kitchen making small sandwiches. He looks at me smiling. I start to walk towards him.
 -It's not fair to come out, Beautiful.
 I'm approaching the kitchen.
 -What's wrong? You look washed out.
 He runs to me, grabs my hand. He's terrified.
 -Let me go!
 I pull my hand out of his. I start to cry, my whole body is shaking. I'm going farther away.
 -What happened?
 -You lied to me and cheated on me, you bastard!

-What are you talking about?
-About Gabriel and about you! How could you do this?

I see pain is flashing in his eyes. He wants to touch me again to calm me down, but I push him with my full strength away.

-Don't you dare touch me!
-Let me explain!

He takes a step toward me.

-What? That you planned everything? I read your correspondence! Don't come closer! I can't stand being here anymore, I don't care about anything... It's all over... I go crazy, it hurts so much... eats me alive... Tears me to pieces... Kills me... With my last drop of energy I go to the bathroom and get my clothes and find my bag in the hallway. My tears are flowing, I can barely see... My chest is tight... I have to escape... Now... I would open the door when Peter grabs my hand.

-Ann, wait! I'll tell you everything, give me a chance! I love you!

I rip out my hand from his grip, step out of his apartment, and look back at him one last time, his eyes teary.

-I hate both of you!

I can't wait for the elevator to arrive, I run down the stairs. I take the steps one by one, sometimes I stumble, but I don't stop. I count the floors for myself. There are three more left. I almost can't see from a lot of tears, but I have to get rid of it. I don't look back because I know Peter won't come after me. I'm escaping again... I take the easier route, but I have no strength. Ran out... Over... Goodbye Peter, goodbye my love...

# Acknowledgments

Thank you God.

Thank you, my little girl, for always being patient when I was writing my book. Thank you for your light, smile and love. You're a real little angel that makes every day beautiful for me! Always believe in miracles!

Thank you, Mother, for always being by my side and for your direction …You are my lighthouse.

Thank you Papa for always being my support, always believing in me and helping me wherever I would go.

Thank you dear loved ones for your love, care, help, and encouragement. Without you all this wouldn't have happened!

Thank you my Husband for always giving me inspiration and thanks for everything.

Thank you my Friends for being among the first readers.

Thank you Karl for your help starting my journey, your cooperation, and the work.

Thank you Zoi for all your help and your fantastic work. You're incredibly talented—a super woman!

Thank you Sharon Lampert for your help, great job, and, for the confidence!

And finally, thank you, Known Stranger.

www.ingramcontent.com/pod-product-compliance
Lightning Source LLC
Chambersburg PA
CBHW071557080526
44588CB00010B/932